AP® COMPUTER SCIENCE A PREP

8th Edition

The Staff of The Princeton Review

PrincetonReview.com

Penguin
Random
House

The Princeton Review
110 East 42nd St, 7th Floor
New York, NY 10017

Published in the United States by Penguin Random House LLC, New York.

Terms of Service: The Princeton Review Online Companion Tools ("Student Tools") for retail books are available for only the two most recent editions of that book. Student Tools may be activated only once per eligible book purchased for a total of 24 months of access. Activation of Student Tools more than once per book is in direct violation of these Terms of Service and may result in discontinuation of access to Student Tools Services.

The material in this book is up-to-date at the time of publication. However, changes may have been instituted by the testing body in the test after this book was published.

If there are any important late-breaking developments, changes, or corrections to the materials in this book, we will post that information online in the Student Tools. Register your book and check your Student Tools to see if there are any updates posted there.

ISBN: 978-0-593-51705-5
eBook ISBN: 978-0-593-51706-2
ISSN: 2690-5345

AP is a trademark registered and owned by the College Board, which is not affiliated with, and does not endorse, this product.

The Princeton Review is not affiliated with Princeton University.

Editor: Chris Chimera
Production Editors: Ali Landreau, Sarah Litt
Production Artist: Jennifer Chapman
Content Developer: Ann Heltzel

Printed in the United States of America.

10 9 8 7 6 5 4 3 2

8th Edition

The Princeton Review Publishing Team
Rob Franek, Editor-in-Chief
David Soto, Senior Director, Data Operations
Stephen Koch, Senior Manager, Data Operations
Deborah Weber, Director of Production
Jason Ullmeyer, Production Design Manager
Jennifer Chapman, Senior Production Artist
Selena Coppock, Director of Editorial
Orion McBean, Senior Editor
Aaron Riccio, Senior Editor
Meave Shelton, Senior Editor
Chris Chimera, Editor
Patricia Murphy, Editor
Laura Rose, Editor
Isabelle Appleton, Editorial Assistant

Penguin Random House Publishing Team
Tom Russell, VP, Publisher
Alison Stoltzfus, Senior Director, Publishing
Brett Wright, Senior Editor
Emily Hoffman, Assistant Managing Editor
Ellen Reed, Production Manager
Suzanne Lee, Designer
Eugenia Lo, Publishing Assistant

For customer service, please contact **editorialsupport@review.com**, and be sure to include:

- full title of the book

- ISBN

- page number

Acknowledgments

Special thanks to Ann Heltzel for her superb content development work on the 8th edition of this book. Additionally, The Princeton Review would like to thank Jennifer Chapman, Ali Landreau, and Sarah Litt for their contributions to this title.

Contents

Get More (Free) Content
at PrincetonReview.com/prep

As easy as 1·2·3

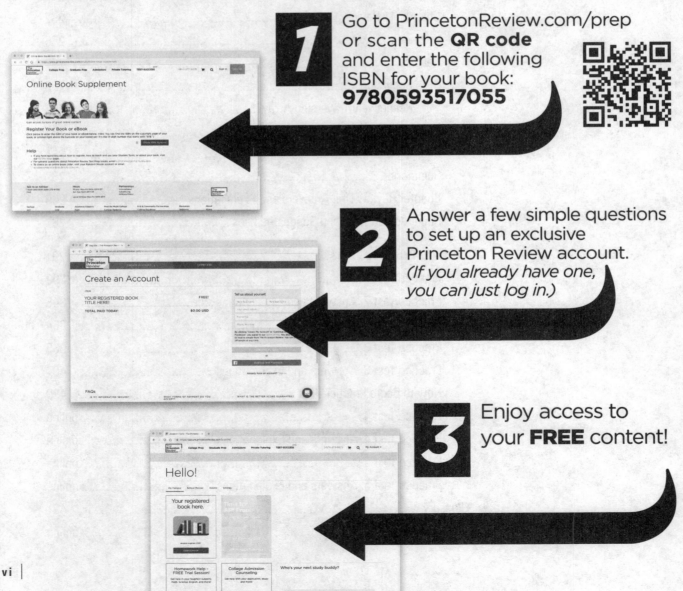

1 Go to PrincetonReview.com/prep or scan the **QR code** and enter the following ISBN for your book: **9780593517055**

2 Answer a few simple questions to set up an exclusive Princeton Review account. *(If you already have one, you can just log in.)*

3 Enjoy access to your **FREE** content!

Once you've registered, you can...

- Take a full-length practice SAT and ACT

- Access Practice Tests 4 and 5 plus detailed Answers and Explanations

- Get valuable advice about the college application process, including tips for writing a great essay and where to apply for financial aid

- If you're still choosing between colleges, use our searchable rankings of *The Best 389 Colleges* to find out more information about your dream school

- Access comprehensive study guides and a variety of printable resources including AP Score Conversion charts, Key Terms lists, and the Glossary

- Check to see if there have been any corrections or updates to this edition

- Get our take on any recent or pending updates to the AP Computer Science A Exam

Need to report a potential **content** issue?

Contact **EditorialSupport@review.com** and include:

- full title of the book
- ISBN
- page number

Need to report a **technical** issue?

Contact **TPRStudentTech@review.com** and provide:

- your full name
- email address used to register the book
- full book title and ISBN
- Operating system (Mac/PC) and browser (Chrome, Firefox, Safari, etc.)

Look For These Icons Throughout The Book

 PROVEN TECHNIQUES

 APPLIED STRATEGIES

 STUDY BREAK

 OTHER REFERENCES

 ONLINE ARTICLES

 ONLINE VIDEO TUTORIALS

Part I
Using This
Book to Improve
Your AP Score

PREVIEW: YOUR KNOWLEDGE, YOUR EXPECTATIONS

Your route to a high score on the AP Computer Science A Exam depends a lot on how you plan to use this book. Start thinking about your plan by responding to the following questions.

1. Rate your level of confidence in your knowledge of the content tested by the AP Computer Science A Exam:

   A. Very confident—I know it all.
   B. I'm pretty confident, but there are topics with which I could use help.
   C. Not confident—I need quite a bit of support.
   D. I'm not sure.

2. If you have a goal score in mind, circle it for the AP Computer Science A Exam:

   5   4   3   2   1   I'm not sure yet.

3. What do you expect to learn from this book? Circle all that apply to you.

   A. A general overview of the test and what to expect
   B. Strategies for how to approach the test
   C. The content tested by this exam
   D. I'm not sure yet.

YOUR GUIDE TO USING THIS BOOK

This book is organized to provide as much—or as little—support as you need, so you can use this book in whatever way will be most helpful to improving your score on the AP Computer Science A Exam.

- The remainder of **Part I** will provide guidance on how to use this book and help you determine your strengths and weaknesses.

- **Part II** of this book contains your first practice test, a Diagnostic Answer Key, detailed answers and explanations for each question, and a scoring guide. We recommend that you take this test before going any further in order to realistically determine:
  o your starting point right now
  o which question types you're ready for and which you might need to practice
  o which content topics you are familiar with and which you should review carefully

It's Bubble Time
Bubble sheets for the tests in this book can be found online—you can print them from your online student tools. We highly recommend that you do so before taking a practice test, as learning how to transfer your answers to a bubble sheet is an important part of preparing for the test.

Once you have nailed down your strengths and weaknesses with regard to this exam, you can focus your test preparation, build a study plan, and be efficient with your time. Our Diagnostic Answer Key will assist you with this process.

- **Part III** of this book will:
  - provide information about the structure, scoring, and content of the AP Computer Science A Exam
  - help you to make a study plan
  - point you toward additional resources

- **Part IV** of this book will explore various strategies, including:
  - how to attack multiple-choice questions
  - how to effectively answer free-response questions
  - how to manage your time to maximize the number of points available to you

- **Part V** of this book covers the content you need to know for the AP Computer Science A Exam.

- **Part VI** of this book contains Practice Tests 2 and 3, plus their answers and explanations, and a scoring guide. (Practice Tests 4 and 5 and their answers and explanations can be found online.) We recommend that you pepper in Practice Tests as you study for your exam. Don't take all the Practice Tests in a row or even in rapid succession: start with Practice Test 1 to get a sense of where you are. Then, as you complete your content review, take a Practice Test every so often to see how you are doing and whether you are improving or need to review certain topics.

You may choose to use some parts of this book over others, or you may work through the entire book. Your approach will depend on your needs and how much time you have. Now, let's look at how to make this determination.

HOW TO BEGIN

1. **Take Practice Test 1**

   Before you can decide how to use this book, you need to take a practice test. Doing so will give you insight into your strengths and weaknesses, and the test will also help you make an effective study plan. If you're feeling test-phobic, remind yourself that a practice test is a tool for diagnosing yourself—it's not how well you do that matters but how you use information gleaned from your performance to guide your preparation.

   So, before you read further, take Practice Test 1 starting on page 9 of this book. Be sure to finish it in one sitting, following the instructions that appear before the test.

Bonus Tips and Tricks...
Check us out on YouTube for test-taking tips and tricks to help you ace your next exam at www.youtube.com/ThePrincetonReview

2.   **Check Your Answers**

Using the Diagnostic Answer Key on page 52, follow our three-step process to identify your strengths and weaknesses with regard to the tested topics. This will help you determine which content review chapters to prioritize when studying this book. Don't worry about the explanations for now, and don't worry about missed questions. We'll get to that soon.

3.   **Reflect on the Test**

After you take your first test, respond to the following questions:

•   How much time did you spend on the multiple-choice questions?

•   How much time did you spend on each free-response question?

•   How many multiple-choice questions did you answer correctly and how many did you miss?

•   Do you feel you had the knowledge to address the subject matter of the free-response questions?

4.   **Read Part III of this Book and Complete the Self-Evaluation**

Part III will provide information on how the test is structured and scored. It will also set out areas of content that are tested.

As you read Part III, re-evaluate your answers to the questions above. At the end of Part III, you will revisit and refine those questions. You will then be able to make a study plan, based on your needs and available time, that will allow you to use this book most effectively.

5.   **Engage with Parts IV and V as Needed**

Notice the word *engage*. You'll get more out of this book if you use it intentionally than if you read it passively, hoping for an improved score through osmosis.

The strategy chapters will help you think about your approach to the question types on this exam. Part IV will open with a reminder to think about how you approach questions now and then close with a reflection section asking you to think about how or whether you will change your approach in the future.

The content chapters in Part V are designed to provide a review of the content tested on the AP Computer Science A Exam, including the level of detail you need to know and how the content is tested. In addition, the content chapters are broken up to exactly match the 10-unit structure of the AP Computer Science A course, as outlined by the College Board. You will have the opportunity to assess your proficiency in the content of each chapter through test-appropriate questions and a reflection section.

6.   **Take Practice Tests 2, 3, 4, and 5 and Assess Your Performance**

Once you feel you have developed the strategies you need and gained the knowledge you lacked, you should take Practice Test 2, which starts on page 293 of this book. You should do so in one sitting, following the instructions at the beginning of the test.

When you are finished, check your answers to the multiple-choice sections. See whether a teacher or friend will read your free-response answers, provide feedback, and go over them with you.

Once you have taken the test, reflect on the areas on which you still need work, and revisit the chapters in this book that address those deficiencies. Then go back and take Practice Test 3 and do the same, then Practice Test 4, then Practice Test 5. You have 5 practice tests with this book—be sure to make use of all of them! (Note that Practice Tests 4 and 5 are online PDFs found in your Student Tools. Go back a few pages for step-by-step directions on how to register your book and access all of your online resources.)

7.   **Keep Working**

As mentioned earlier, there are other resources available to you, including a wealth of information on the AP Students website (apstudent.collegeboard.org/apcourse/ap-computer-science-a). On this site, you can continue to explore areas that you could improve upon and engage in those areas right up until the day of the test. You should use a mix of web resources and book review to solidify your understanding of any question subjects that you keep getting wrong.

Need Some Guidance?
If you're looking for a way to get the most out of your studying, check out our free study guide for this exam, which you can access via your online student tools. See the "Get More (Free) Content" page for details on accessing this great resource and more.

Part II
Practice Test 1

Practice Test 1

AP® Computer Science A Exam

SECTION I: Multiple-Choice Questions

DO NOT OPEN THIS BOOKLET UNTIL YOU ARE TOLD TO DO SO.

At a Glance

Total Time
1 hour 30 minutes
Number of Questions
40
Percent of Total Score
50%
Writing Instrument
Pencil required

Instructions

Section I of this examination contains 40 multiple-choice questions. Fill in only the ovals for numbers 1 through 40 on your answer sheet.

Indicate all of your answers to the multiple-choice questions on the answer sheet. No credit will be given for anything written in this exam booklet, but you may use the booklet for notes or scratch work. After you have decided which of the suggested answers is best, completely fill in the corresponding oval on the answer sheet. Give only one answer to each question. If you change an answer, be sure that the previous mark is erased completely. Here is a sample question and answer.

Sample Question   Sample Answer

Chicago is a   Ⓐ ● Ⓒ Ⓓ Ⓔ
(A) state
(B) city
(C) country
(D) continent
(E) county

Use your time effectively, working as quickly as you can without losing accuracy. Do not spend too much time on any one question. Go on to other questions and come back to the ones you have not answered if you have time. It is not expected that everyone will know the answers to all the multiple-choice questions.

About Guessing

Many candidates wonder whether or not to guess the answers to questions about which they are not certain. Multiple-choice scores are based on the number of questions answered correctly. Points are not deducted for incorrect answers, and no points are awarded for unanswered questions. Because points are not deducted for incorrect answers, you are encouraged to answer all multiple-choice questions. On any questions you do not know the answer to, you should eliminate as many choices as you can, and then select the best answer among the remaining choices.

GO ON TO THE NEXT PAGE.

Java Quick Reference

Class Constructors and Methods	Explanation
String Class	
`String(String str)`	Constructs a new `String` object that represents the same sequence of characters as `str`
`int length()`	Returns the number of characters in a `String` object
`String substring(int from, int to)`	Returns the substring beginning at index `from` and ending at index `to - 1`
`String substring(int from)`	Returns `substring(from, length())`
`int indexOf(String str)`	Returns the index of the first occurrence of `str`; returns −1 if not found
`boolean equals(String other)`	Returns `true` if `this` is equal to `other`; returns `false` otherwise
`int compareTo(String other)`	Returns a value <0 if `this` is less than `other`; returns zero if `this` is equal to `other`; returns a value >0 if `this` is greater than `other`
Integer Class	
`Integer(int value)`	Constructs a new `Integer` object that represents the specified `int` value
`Integer.MIN_VALUE`	The minimum value represented by an `int` or `Integer`
`Integer.MAX_VALUE`	The maximum value represented by an `int` or `Integer`
`int intValue()`	Returns the value of this `Integer` as an `int`
Double Class	
`Double(double value)`	Constructs a new `Double` object that represents the specified `double` value
`double doubleValue()`	Returns the value of this `Double` as a `double`
Math Class	
`static int abs(int x)`	Returns the absolute value of an `int` value
`static double abs(double x)`	Returns the absolute value of a `double` value
`static double pow(double base, double exponent)`	Returns the value of the first parameter raised to the power of the second parameter
`static double sqrt(double x)`	Returns the positive square root of a `double` value
`static double random()`	Returns a `double` value greater than or equal to `0.0` and less than `1.0`
ArrayList Class	
`int size()`	Returns the number of elements in the list
`boolean add(E obj)`	Appends `obj` to end of list; returns `true`
`void add(int index, E obj)`	Inserts `obj` at position `index` (0 <= index <= size), moving elements at position `index` and higher to the right (adds 1 to their indices) and adds 1 to size
`E get(int index)`	Returns the element at position `index` in the list
`E set(int index, E obj)`	Replaces the element at position `index` with `obj`; returns the element formerly at position `index`
`E remove(int index)`	Removes element from position `index`, moving elements at position `index + 1` and higher to the left (subtracts 1 from their indices) and subtracts 1 from size; returns the element formerly at position `index`
Object Class	
`boolean equals(Object other)`	
`String toString()`	

GO ON TO THE NEXT PAGE.

COMPUTER SCIENCE A

SECTION I

Time—1 hour and 30 minutes

Number of Questions—40

Percent of total exam grade—50%

Directions: Determine the answer to each of the following questions or incomplete statements, using the available space for any necessary scratchwork. Then decide which is the best of the choices given and fill in the corresponding oval on the answer sheet. No credit will be given for anything written in the examination booklet. Do not spend too much time on any one problem.

Notes:
- Assume that the classes listed in the Quick Reference have been imported where appropriate.
- Assume that declarations of variables and methods appear within the context of an enclosing class.
- Assume that method calls that are not prefixed with an object or class name and are not shown within a complete class definition appear within the context of an enclosing class.
- Unless otherwise noted in the question, assume that parameters in the method calls are not `null` and that methods are called only when their preconditions are satisfied.

1. Evaluate the following expression: `4 + 6 % 12 / 4`

   (A) `1`
   (B) `2`
   (C) `4`
   (D) `4.5`
   (E) `5`

2. Which of the following expressions does NOT evaluate to `0.2`?

   (A) `(1.0 * 2) / (1.0 * 10)`
   (B) `2.0 / 10`
   (C) `(double) 2 / 10`
   (D) `(double)(2 / 10)`
   (E) `Math.sqrt(4) / Math.sqrt(100)`

3. Choose the code used to print the following:

   `"Friends"`

   (A) `System.out.print(""Friends"");`
   (B) `System.out.print("//"Friends//"");`
   (C) `System.out.print("/"Friends/"");`
   (D) `System.out.print("\"Friends\"");`
   (E) `System.out.print("\\"Friends \\"");`

GO ON TO THE NEXT PAGE.

4. Determine the output of the following code.

```
String animal1 = "elephant";
String animal2 = "lion";
swap(animal1, animal2);
animal1.toUpperCase();
animal2.toLowerCase();

System.out.println(animal1 + "    " + animal2);

public static void swap(String a1, String a2) {
    String hold = a1;
    a1 = a2;
    a2 = hold;
}
```

(A) elephant   lion
(B) ELEPHANT   lion
(C) lion   elephant
(D) LION   elephant
(E) LION   ELEPHANT

Questions 5–6 refer to the `Constellation` class below.

```
public class Constellation
    private String name;
    private String month;
    private int northernLatitude;
    private int southernLatitude;

    Constellation(String n, String m)
    {
        name = n;
        month = m;
        northernLatitude = 0;
        southernLatitude = 0;
    }

    Constellation(String n, String m, int nLat, int sLat)
    {
        name = n;
        month = m;
        northernLatitude = nLat;
        southernLatitude = sLat;
    }
    public void chgMonth(String m)
    {
        String month = m;
    }
```

GO ON TO THE NEXT PAGE.

5. Using the `Constellation class`, which of the following will cause a compiler error?

(A) `Constellation c1 = new Constellation("Hercules", "July");`
(B) `Constellation c2 = new Constellation("Pisces", "Nov", 90, 65);`
(C) `Constellation c3 = new Constellation("Aquarius", "Oct", 65.0, 90.0);`
(D) `Constellation c4 = new Constellation("Leo", "4", 0, 0);`
(E) `Constellation c5 = new Constellation("Phoenix", "Nov", 32, 90);`

6. A programmer has attempted to add three mutator methods to the `Constellation` class.

```
I.  public void chgLatitude(String direction, int latitude)
    {
        if (direction.toUpperCase().equals("N"))
            northernLatitude = latitude;
        else if (direction.toUpperCase().equals("S"))
            southernLatitude = latitude;
    }

II. public void chgLatitude(int nLatitude, int sLatitude)
    {
        northernLatitude = nLatitude;
        southernLatitude = sLatitude;
    }

III. public void chgLatitude(double nLatitude, double sLatitude)
    {
        northernLatitude = (int) nLatitude;
        southernLatitude = (int) sLatitude;
    }
```

Which of the three will compile without a compiler error?

(A) I only
(B) II only
(C) III only
(D) I and II only
(E) I, II, and III

GO ON TO THE NEXT PAGE.

7. Determine the values of x and y after the following code runs.

```
int x = 10;
int y = 5;

if (x == 10)
{
    if (y <= 5)
        y++;
    else if (y < 4)
            x = 3;
        else
            y += 6;
}
if (y > 5)
{
    if (x != 10)
    {
        x = 0;
        y = 0;
    }
    else
        x = -5;
}
```

(A) x = 0, y = 0
(B) x = -5, y = 6
(C) x = 10, y = 5
(D) x = 3, y = 5
(E) None of the above

GO ON TO THE NEXT PAGE.

8. A programmer intended to write code to print three words in ascending lexicographical order. Follow the code and determine the printed output.

```
1    String word1 = "frog";
2    String word2 = "dog";
3    String word3 = "cat";
4
5    if (word1.compareTo(word2) < 0)
6       if (word2.compareTo(word3) < 0)
7          System.out.println(word1 + " " + word2 + " " + word3);
8       else
9          System.out.println(word1 + " " + word3 + " " + word2);
10   else
11      if (word1.compareTo(word2) > 0)
12         if (word2.compareTo(word3) < 0)
13            System.out.println(word1 + " " + word2 + " " + word3);
14         else
15            System.out.println(word1 + " " + word3 + " " + word2);
16      else
17         if (word2.equals(word3))
18            System.out.println( "all the words are the same");
19         else
20            System.out.println( "word1 and word2 are duplicates");
```

(A) frog   cat   dog
(B) cat   dog   frog
(C) dog   frog   cat
(D) frog   dog   cat
(E) dog   cat   frog

9. Using the following variable declarations, determine which of the following would evaluate to `true`.

```
    int temp = 90;
    boolean cloudy = false;
```

  I. if (temp >= 90 && !cloudy)
 II. if (!(temp > 90 || cloudy))
III. if (!(temp > 90 && !cloudy))

(A) I only
(B) II only
(C) III only
(D) Two of the above will evaluate to `true`.
(E) All the above will evaluate to `true`.

GO ON TO THE NEXT PAGE.

10. Consider the following code:

```
1   String dog1 = new String("Poodle");
2   String dog2 = new String("Beagle");
3   dog1 = dog2;
4   String dog3 = new String("Beagle");
5
6   if (dog1 == dog2)
7       System.out.println("dog1 and dog2 are one and the same dog");
8   else
9       System.out.println("dog1 and dog2 are not the same dog");
10
11  if (dog1 == dog3)
12      System.out.println("dog1 and dog3 are one and the same dog");
13  else
14      System.out.println("dog1 and dog3 are not the same dog");
15
16  if (dog1.equals(dog3))
17      System.out.println("dog1 and dog3 are the same breed");
18  else
19      System.out.println("dog1 and dog3 are not the same breed");
```

Which of the following represents the output that will be produced by the code?

(A) dog1 and dog2 are one and the same dog
     dog1 and dog3 are one and the same dog
     dog1 and dog3 are the same breed

(B) dog1 and dog2 are one and the same dog
     dog1 and dog3 are one and the same dog
     dog1 and dog3 are not the same breed

(C) dog1 and dog2 are one and the same dog
     dog1 and dog3 are not the same dog
     dog1 and dog3 are the same breed

(D) dog1 and dog2 are one and the same dog
     dog1 and dog3 are not the same dog
     dog1 and dog3 are not the same breed

(E) dog1 and dog2 are not the same dog
     dog1 and dog3 are not the same dog
     dog1 and dog3 are the same breed

GO ON TO THE NEXT PAGE.

11. Choose the correct option to complete lines 3 and 4 such that `str2` will contain the letters of `str1` in reverse order.

```
1    String str1 = "banana";
2    String str2 = "";
3    // missing code
4    // missing code
5    {
6        str2 += str1.substring(i, i + 1);
7        i--;
8    }
```

(A) `int i = 0;`
    `while (i  < str1.length)`

(B) `int i = str1.length();`
    `while (i  >= 0)`

(C) `int i = str1.length() - 1;`
    `while (i  >= 0)`

(D) `int i = str1.length();`
    `while (i  > 0)`

(E) `int i = str1.length() - 1;`
    `while (i  > 0)`

12. Consider the following code excerpt :

```
9    int n = // some integer greater than zero
10   int count = 0;
11   int p = 0;
12   int q = 0;
13   for (p = 1; p < n; p++)
14       for (q = 1; q <= n; q++)
15           count ++;
```

What will be the final value of `count`?

(A) n^n

(B) $n^2 - 1$

(C) $(n - 1)^2$

(D) $n(n - 1)$

(E) n^2

13. Given the following code excerpt, determine the output.

```
1    int x = 0;
2    for (int j = 1; j < 4; j++)
3    {
4        if (x != 0 && j / x > 0)
5            System.out.print(j / x + " ");
6        else
7            System.out.print(j * x + " ");
8    }
```

(A) 0 0 0

(B) 0 0 0 0

(C) 1 2 3

(D) 1 0 2 0 3 0

(E) ArithmeticException: Divide by Zero

GO ON TO THE NEXT PAGE.

14. Consider the following code:

```
1    String space = " ";
2    String symbol = "*";
3    int num = 5;
4    for (int i = 1; i <= num; i++)
5    {
6            System.out.print(symbol);
7    }
8    System.out.print("\n");
9    for (int i = 1; i <= num; i++)
10   {
11       for (int j = num - i; j > 0; j--)
12       {
13               System.out.print(space);
14       }
15       System.out.println(symbol);
16   }
17   for (int i = 1; i <= num; i++)
18   {
19           System.out.print(symbol);
20   }
```

Which of the following represents the output?

(A) ```
*****
****
***
**
*
*****
``	(D) ```
*****
*
*
*
*
*****
``
(B) ```
*****
****
***
**
*
*****
``	(E) ```
*****
*
**
***
****
*****
``
(C) ```
*****
*
*
*
*
*****
``	

GO ON TO THE NEXT PAGE.
```

15. What will be printed as a result of the following code excerpt?

```
int sum = 0;
for (int i = 1; i < 2; i++)
  for (int j = 1; j <= 3; j++)
    for (int k = 1; k < 4; k++)
      sum += (i * j * k);

System.out.println(sum);
```

(A) 18
(B) 36
(C) 45
(D) 60
(E) 108

16. Consider the following code:

```
1    int j = 0;
2    String s = "map";
3    while ( j < s.length())
4    {
5        int k = s.length();
6        while ( k > j )
7        {
8            System.out.println(s.substring(j, k));
9            k--;
10       }
11       j++;
12   }
```

Which of the following represents the output?

(A) map	(D) m
ma	ma
m	map
ap	a
a	ap
	p
(B) map	(E) p
ma	ap
m	p
ap	map
a	ma
p	m
(C) map	
ap	
p	
ap	
p	
p	

GO ON TO THE NEXT PAGE.

17. A factorial is shown by an exclamation point(!) following a number. The factorial of 5, or 5!, is calculated by $(5)(4)(3)(2)(1) = 120$.

Assuming n is an integer greater than 1, choose the method that will return n!

I.	<pre>public static int f(int n) {
	    int factorial = 1;
	    for (int i = n; i > 0 ; i--) {
	        factorial *= n;
	    }
	    return factorial;
	}</pre>

II.	<pre>public static int f(int n) {
	    int factorial = 1;
	    int j = 1;
	    while (j <= n) {
	        factorial *= j;
	        j++;
	    }
	    return factorial;
	}</pre>

III.	<pre>public static int f(int n) {
	    if (n == 1)
	        return n;
	    return n * f(n - 1);
	}</pre>

(A) I only

(B) II only

(C) III only

(D) II and III only

(E) I, II, and III

GO ON TO THE NEXT PAGE.

Questions 18–20 refer to the code excerpt for the `Tile` class below:

```
1    public class Tile
2    {
3      private int styleNumber;
4      private String color;
5      private double width;
6      private double height;
7      private String material;
8      private double price;

9      Tile(int style, String col)
10     {
11       styleNumber = style;
12       color = col;
13     }
14     Tile(int style, String col, double w, double h, String mat, double price)
15     {
16       styleNumber = style;
17       color = col;
18       width = w;
19       height = h;
20       material = mat;
21       price = price;
22     }
23     Tile(int style, String col, String mat, double price)
24      {
25         styleNumber = style;
26         color = col;
27         material = mat;
28         price = price;
29      }
30     public void chgMaterial(String mat)
31     {
32       String material = mat;
33     }
34     public String toString()
35     {
36       return (styleNumber + " " + color + " " + width + " " + height + " " +
37               material + " " + price);
38     }
39   }
```

18. What is the output after the following client code is executed?

```
Tile t1 = new Tile(785, "grey", "ceramic", 6.95);
    t1.chgMaterial("marble");
    System.out.print(t1.toString());
```

(A) Tile@5ccd43c2
(B) 785 grey 0.0 0.0 marble 0.0
(C) 785 grey 0.0 0.0 ceramic 0.0
(D) 785 grey 0.0 0.0 ceramic 6.95
(E) 785 grey 0.0 0.0 marble 6.95

GO ON TO THE NEXT PAGE.

19. What is the output after the following client code is executed?

```
Tile t2 = new Tile(101, "blue");
System.out.print(t2);
```

(A) Tile@5ccd43c2
(B) 101 blue 0.0 0.0 null 0.0
(C) Type mismatch error
(D) NullPointerException
(E) There will be no output; the program will not compile.

20. The Tile class is going to be used for an application built for a small independent tile store. The owner wants the programmer to add a field for the number of unopened boxes of tile he has for each style of tile he has in stock and a method to change the value. What would be the proper declaration for this field?

(A) public static int inventory;
(B) private static double inventory;
(C) final int inventory;
(D) private int inventory;
(E) private int [] inventory;

21. Given the following code excerpt:

```
9   int[] nums = {11, 22, 33, 44, 55, 66};
10
11  for (int i = 0; i < nums.length; i++)
12      nums[nums[i] / 11] = nums[i];
```

Determine the final contents of nums.

(A) 1, 2, 3, 4, 5, 6
(B) 11, 11, 33, 33, 55, 55
(C) 11, 11, 22, 33, 44, 55
(D) 11, 22, 22, 33, 33, 55
(E) 11, 22, 33, 44, 55, 66

GO ON TO THE NEXT PAGE.

22. Given the following code excerpt:

```
13  int[] arr1 = {1, 2, 3, 4, 5, 6};
14  int[] arr2 = arr1;
15  int last = arr1.length - 1;
16
17  for (int i = 0; i < arr1.length; i++)
18      arr2[i] = arr1[last - i];
19
20  for (int i = 0; i < arr1.length; i++)
21      System.out.print(arr1[i] + "  ");
22
23  System.out.println(" ");
24
25  for (int i = 0; i < arr2.length; i++)
26      System.out.print(arr2[i] + "  ");
```

Determine the statement below that reflects the resulting output.

(A) 1 2 3 4 5 6
    1 2 3 4 5 6

(B) 1 2 3 4 5 6
    6 5 4 4 5 6

(C) 6 5 4 3 2 1
    6 5 4 4 5 6

(D) 6 5 4 4 5 6
    1 2 3 4 5 6

(E) 6 5 4 4 5 6
    6 5 4 4 5 6

23. Given the following code excerpt:

```
27  int[] arr3 = {1, 2, 3, 4, 5, 6};
28
29  for (int element : arr3)
30  {
31      element *= 2;
32      System.out.print(element + "  ");
33  }
34  System.out.println(" ");
35
36  for (int element : arr3)
37      System.out.print(element + "  ");
```

Determine the statement below that reflects the resulting output.

(A) 1   2   3   4   5   6
     1   2   3   4   5   6

(B) 2   4   6   8   10   12
     1   2   3   4   5   6

(C) 2   4   6   8   10   12
     2   4   6   8   10   12

(D) A compiler error will occur.

(E) A run-time exception will occur.

GO ON TO THE NEXT PAGE.

24. Given an array `numbers` containing a variety of integers and the following code excerpt:

```
38  int holdSmallest = Integer.MAX_VALUE;
39  int holdLargest = 0;
40  int a = 0;
41  int b = 0;
42  for (int i = 0; i < numbers.length; i++)
43  {
44    if (numbers[i] <= holdSmallest)
45    {
46        holdSmallest = numbers[i];
47        a = i;
48    }
49    if (numbers[i] >= holdLargest)
50    {
51        holdLargest = numbers[i];
52        b = i;
53    }
54  }
55  System.out.println(a + " " + b);
```

Determine the statement below that reflects the most successful outcome.

(A) The code will print the smallest and largest values in the `numbers` array.

(B) The code will print the locations of the smallest and largest values in the `numbers` array.

(C) The code will print the locations of the smallest and largest non-negative values in the `numbers` array.

(D) The code will print the locations of the smallest value in the `numbers` array and the largest non-negative value in the `numbers` array.

(E) The code will print the locations of the smallest non-negative value in the `numbers` array and the largest value in the `numbers` array.

GO ON TO THE NEXT PAGE.

25. Choose the missing code below that will accurately find the average of the values in the `sales` array.

```
57   int i = 0;
58   int sum = 0;
59   for (int element : sales)
60
61      //Missing code
62
63
```

(A)
```
     {
          sum += element;
     }
     double avg = (double) sum / sales.length;
```

(B)
```
     {
          sum += sales[i];
     }
     double avg = (double) sum / sales.length;
```

(C)
```
     {
          sum += sales;
     }
     double avg = (double) sum / sales.length;
```

(D)
```
     {
          sum += sales[element];
     }
     double avg = (double) sum / sales.length;
```

(E)
```
     {
          sum += element[sales];
     }
     double avg = (double) sum / sales.length;
```

GO ON TO THE NEXT PAGE.

26. A programmer has written two different methods for a client program to swap the elements of one array with those of another array.

```
11    public static void swap1(int[] a1, int[] a2)
12    {
13      for (int i = 0; i < a1.length; i++)
14      {
15       int arrhold = a1[i];
16       a1[i] = a2[i];
17       a2[i] = arrhold;
18      }
19    }
```
```
20
21  public static void swap2(int[] a1, int[] a2) {
22            int [] arrhold = a1;
23            a1 = a2;
24            a2 = arrhold;
25       }
```

Which of the following statements best reflects the outcomes of the two methods?

(A) Both methods will swap the contents of the two arrays correctly in all cases.

(B) `swap1` will swap the contents of the two arrays correctly only if both arrays have the same number of elements, whereas `swap2` will work correctly for all cases.

(C) `swap1` will swap the contents of the two arrays correctly only if both arrays have the same number of elements, whereas `swap2` will never work correctly.

(D) `swap1` will swap the contents of the two arrays correctly only if both arrays have the same number of elements or `a2` has more elements, whereas `swap2` will work correctly for all cases.

(E) Neither method will swap the contents of the two arrays correctly under any conditions.

27. Which code has declared and properly populated the given `ArrayList`?

I.	`ArrayList <String> alist1 = new ArrayList<String>();` `alist1.add("4.5");`
II.	`ArrayList <Integer> alist2 = new ArrayList<Integer>();` `alist1.add((int) 4.5);`
III.	`ArrayList <Double> alist3;` `alist3 = new ArrayList<Double>();` `alist3.add(4.5);`

(A) I only
(B) I and II
(C) I and III
(D) II and III
(E) I, II, and III

GO ON TO THE NEXT PAGE.

28. Given the following code excerpt:

```
ArrayList <Integer> alist1 = new ArrayList<Integer>();
int [] a1 = {2, 4, 6, 7, 8, 10, 11};
for (int a : a1) {
   alist1.add(a);
}
for (int i = 0; i < alist1.size(); i++) {
    if (alist1.get(i) % 2 == 0){
      alist1.remove(i);
      }
}
System.out.println(alist1);
```

Determine the output.

(A) [4, 7, 10, 11]

(B) [2, 4, 7, 10, 11]

(C) [2, 7, 10, 11]

(D) [7, 11]

(E) An `IndexOutOfBoundsException` will occur.

Questions 29–30 refer to the following code excerpt.

```
2    ArrayList <Integer> alist5 = new ArrayList<Integer>();
3    int [] a1 = {21, 6, 2, 8, 1};
4    for (int a : a1)
5    {
6        alist5.add(a);
7    }
8    for (int k = 0; k < alist5.size() - 1; k++)
9    {
10       for (int i = 0; i < alist5.size() - 2; i++)
11       {
12           if (alist5.get(i) > alist5.get(i + 1))
13           {
14               int hold = alist5.remove(i);
15               alist5.add(i + 1, hold);
16           }
17       }
18   }
19   System.out.println(alist5);
```

29. How many times will line 12 be executed?

(A) 6 times

(B) 12 times

(C) 15 times

(D) 16 times

(E) 20 times

30. What will be the final output after the code executes?

(A) [21, 8, 6, 2, 1]

(B) [6, 21, 2, 8, 1]

(C) [6, 2, 8, 21, 1]

(D) [2, 6, 8, 21, 1]

(E) [1, 2, 6, 8, 21]

GO ON TO THE NEXT PAGE.

31. Given nums—a rectangular, but not necessarily square, two-dimensional array of integers—consider the following code intended to print the array:

```
4   int [][] arr2d = {{1, 2, 3, 4}, {5, 6, 7, 8}};
5   String s = "";
6   for (int a = 0; a < arr2d[0].length; a++)
7   {
8       for (int b = 0; b < arr2d.length; b++)
9       {
10          s += arr2d [b][a] + " ";
11      }
12      s += "\n";
13  }
14  System.out.print(s);
```

Determine the resulting output.

(A) 1   2   3   4
     5   6   7   8

(B) 1   5   2   6
     3   7   4   8

(C) 1   2
     3   4
     5   6
     7   8

(D) 1   5
     2   6
     3   7
     4   8

(E) 1
     2
     3
     4
     5
     6
     7
     8

GO ON TO THE NEXT PAGE.

32. Given `nums`—a rectangular, two-dimensional array of integers—choose the code to print the entire array.

I.	```for (int r = 0; r < nums.length; r++)```
	 ```{```
	     ```for (int c = 0; c < nums[0].length; c++)```
	     ```{```
	         ```System.out.print(nums[r][c]);```
	     ```}```
	     ```System.out.print("\n");```
	 ```}```

II.	```for (int [] row : nums)```
	 ```{```
	     ```for (int col : row)```
	     ```{```
	         ```System.out.print(col + " ");```
	     ```}```
	     ```System.out.println("");```
	 ```}```

III.	```for (int r = 0; r < nums[0].length; r++)```
	 ```{```
	     ```for (int c = 0; c < nums.length; c++)```
	     ```{```
	         ```System.out.print(nums[r][c] + " ");```
	     ```}```
	     ```System.out.print("\n");```
	 ```}```

(A) I only

(B) I and II only

(C) I and III only

(D) II and III only

(E) I, II, and III

GO ON TO THE NEXT PAGE.

Questions 33–35 refer to the `Percussion` class and `Xylophone` class **below.**

```java
public class Percussion {
    private String name;
    private double weight;
    Percussion() {
    }
    Percussion(String n, double w)
    {
        name = n;
        weight = w;
    }
    public String getName()
    {
        return name;
    }
    public double getWeight()
    {
        return weight;
    }
}
public class Drums extends Percussion
{
}
public class Xylophone extends Percussion {
    private int numberOfKeys;

    Xylophone(String name, double weight, int numberOfKeys){

        <missing code>

    }
    public int getNumKeys()
    {
        return numberOfKeys;
    }
}
```

33. Which of the following is the most appropriate replacement for `<missing code>` in the `Xylophone` constructor?

    (A) `this.numberOfKeys = numberOfKeys;`
        `super(name, weight);`
    (B) `super(name, weight);`
        `this.numberOfKeys = numberOfKeys;`
    (C) `super(name, weight);`
        `numberOfKeys = this.numberOfKeys;`
    (D) `this.numberOfKeys = numberOfKeys;`
    (E) `numberOfKeys = this.numberOfKeys;`

GO ON TO THE NEXT PAGE.

34. Assuming the above classes compile correctly, which of the following will NOT compile within a client program?

(A) `Xylophone [] xylophones = new Xylophone[5];`

(B) `Percussion [] xylophones = new Xylophone[5];`

(C) `Xylophone x1 = new Xylophone ("xylophone", 65, 32);`
    `System.out.println(x1.getNumKeys());`

(D) `Xylophone x1 = new Xylophone ("xylophone", 65, 32);`
    `System.out.println(x1.numberOfKeys);`

(E) `Drums [] drums;`

35. A client program wishes to compare the two `xylophone` objects as follows:

`Xylophone x2 = new Xylophone ("xylophone", 80, 32);`
`Xylophone x3 = new Xylophone ("xylophone", 65, 32);`

The two objects should be considered "equally heavy" if and only if they have the same weight. Which of the following code excerpts accomplishes that task?

(A) `if (x2.weight == x3.weight)`
        `System.out.println("equally heavy");`
    `else`
        `System.out.println("not equally heavy");`

(B) `if (x2.weight() == x3.weight())`
        `System.out.println("equally heavy");`
    `else`
        `System.out.println("not equally heavy");`

(C) `if (x2.getWeight() == x3.getWeight())`
        `System.out.println("equally heavy");`
    `else`
        `System.out.println("not equally heavy");`

(D) `if (x2.weight.equals(x3.weight))`
        `System.out.println("equally heavy");`
    `else`
      `System.out.println("not equally heavy");`

(E) The weights of the objects cannot be compared.

GO ON TO THE NEXT PAGE.

Questions 36–37 refer to the following classes.

```java
public class Dog {
    private int height;
    private String size;
    private String color;
    Dog (int iheight, int iweight, String icolor)
    {
        height = iheight;
        color = icolor;
        if (iweight >= 65)
            size = "large";
        else
            size = "medium";
    }
    public int getheight() {return height;}
    public String getSize() {return size;}
    public String getColor() {return color;}
    public String toString() {return "    color is: " + color;}
}

public class SportingDog extends Dog {
    private String purpose;
    SportingDog(int h, int w, String c)
        {
        super(h, w, c);
        purpose = "hunting";
    }
    public String getPurpose()
    {
        return purpose;
    }
}

public class Retriever extends SportingDog{
    private String type;

    Retriever(String itype, String icolor, int iweight)
    {
        super(24, iweight, icolor);
        type = itype;
    }
        public String toString() {return "    type: " + type + super.toString();}
}
```

36. Which of the following declarations will NOT compile?

(A) Dog d1 = new SportingDog(30, 74, "Black");
(B) Dog d2 = new Retriever("Labrador", "yellow", 75);
(C) SportingDog d3 = new Retriever("Golden", "Red", 70);
(D) SportingDog d4 = new Dog(25, 80, "Red");
(E) Retriever d5 = new Retriever("Golden", "Blonde", 60);

GO ON TO THE NEXT PAGE.

37. What is the output after the execution of the following code in the client program:

```
Dog mason = new Retriever("Labrador", "chocolate", 85);
System.out.println(mason.toString());
```

(A) type: Labrador

(B) type: Labrador   color is: chocolate   purpose: hunting

(C) color is: chocolate   type: Labrador

(D) type: Labrador   purpose: hunting   color is: chocolate

(E) type: Labrador   color is: chocolate

38. The following pow method was written to return b raised to the xth power where $x > 0$, but it does not work properly. Choose the changes that should be made to the method below so that it works properly.

```
1    public double pow(double b, int x)
2    {
3    if (x == 0)
4       return 1;
5    else
6       return b + pow(b, x - 1);
7    }
```

(A) Change lines 3 and 4 to:
```
3    if (x == 1)
4       return 1;
```

(B) Change lines 3 and 4 to:
```
3    if (x == 1)
4       return b;
```

(C) Change line 6 to:
```
6    return b * pow(b, x - 1);
```

(D) Both (A) and (C)

(E) Both (B) and (C)

39. What is output given the following code excerpt?

```
System.out.println(f(8765));
public static int f(int n)
{
    if (n == 0)
        return 0;
    else
        return f(n / 10) + n % 10;
}
```

(A) 5678

(B) 8765

(C) 58

(D) 26

(E) A run-time error

GO ON TO THE NEXT PAGE.

40. Choose the best solution to complete the missing code such that the code will implement a binary search to find the variable number in `arr`.

```
int number = <some number in arr>;
System.out.println(search(arr, 0, arr.length - 1, number));

public int search(int[] a, int first, int last, int sought) {
    int mid = (first + last) / 2;

    if (<missing code>) {
        last = mid - 1;
        return search(a, first, last, sought);
    }
    else if (<missing code>)) {
        first = mid + 1;
        return search(a, first, last, sought);
    }

    return mid;

}
```

(A) a[mid] > sought   a[mid] < sought
(B) a[mid] + 1 > sought   a[mid] < sought
(C) a[mid] > sought   a[mid] - 1 < sought
(D) a[mid] + 1 > sought   a[mid] - 1 < sought
(E) a[mid] = sought   a[mid] = sought

END OF SECTION I

**IF YOU FINISH BEFORE TIME IS CALLED,
YOU MAY CHECK YOUR WORK ON THIS SECTION.**

DO NOT GO ON TO SECTION II UNTIL YOU ARE TOLD TO DO SO.

COMPUTER SCIENCE A

SECTION II

Time—1 hour and 30 minutes

Number of Questions—4

Percent of Total Grade—50%

Directions: SHOW ALL YOUR WORK. REMEMBER THAT PROGRAM SEGMENTS ARE TO BE WRITTEN IN JAVA™.

Notes:

- Assume that the classes listed in the Java Quick Reference have been imported where appropriate.

- Unless otherwise noted in the question, assume that parameters in method calls are not `null` and that methods are called only when their preconditions are satisfied.

- In writing solutions for each question, you may use any of the accessible methods that are listed in classes defined in that question. Writing significant amounts of code that can be replaced by a call to one of these methods will not receive full credit.

FREE-RESPONSE QUESTIONS

1. This question involves the implementation of a simulation of rolling two dice. A client program will specify the number of rolls of the sample size and the number of faces on each of the two dice. A method will return the percentage of times the roll results in a double. *Double* in this case means when two dice match or have the same value (not a data type).

   You will write two of the methods in this class.

```java
public class DiceSimulation {

    /** Sample size of simulation        */
    private int numSampleSize;

    /** Number of faces on each die       */
    private int numFaces;

    /** Constructs a DiceSimulation where sampleSize is the number of rolls to be simulated and
     *   faces  is the number of faces on each die (some dice have more or fewer than 6 faces)
     */
    public DiceSimulation(int numSamples, int faces) {
        numSampleSize = numSamples;
        numFaces = faces;
    }

    /** Returns an integer from 1 to the number of faces to simulate a die roll  */
    public int roll() {
                                    /* to be implemented in part (a) */
    }

    /** Simulates rolling two dice with the number of faces given, for the number of sample size
     *   rolls. Returns the percentage of matches that were rolled
     *   as an integer (eg. 0.50 would be 50).
     */
    public int runSimulation() {
                                    /* to be implemented in part (b) */


    }
}
```

GO ON TO THE NEXT PAGE.

The following table contains sample code and the expected results.

Statements and Expressions	Value Returned / Comment
`DiceSimulation s1 = new DiceSimulation(10, 6)`	(no value returned) A `DiceSimulation` `s1` is declared and instantiated.
`s1.runSimulation()`	10 rolls are simulated; only the percentage of matches is displayed. See further explanation below.

The 10 rolls might look like this (nothing is printed at this time)
```
Die1:  3      Die2:  4
Die1:  1      Die2:  5
Die1:  2      Die2:  2
Die1:  3      Die2:  4
Die1:  6      Die2:  6
Die1:  3      Die2:  4
Die1:  3      Die2:  3
Die1:  6      Die2:  4
Die1:  3      Die2:  1
Die1:  5      Die2:  5
```
The percentage the method would return is 40.

(a) Write the `roll` method to simulate the roll of one die.

```
/** Returns an integer from 1 to number of faces to simulate a die roll */
public int roll()
```

Begin your response at the top of a new page in the separate Free Response booklet and fill in the appropriate circle at the top of each page to indicate the question number. If there are multiple parts to this question, write the part letter with your response.

Class information for this question

```
public class DiceSimulation

private int numSampleSize;
private int numFaces;

public DiceSimulation (int numSamples, int faces)
public int roll()
public int runSimulation()
```

GO ON TO THE NEXT PAGE.

(b) Write the `runSimulation` method.

Begin your response at the top of a new page in the separate Free Response booklet and fill in the appropriate circle at the top of each page to indicate the question number. If there are multiple parts to this question, write the part letter with your response.

Class information for this question

```
public class DiceSimulation

private int numSampleSize;
private int numFaces;

public DiceSimulation (int numSamples, int faces)
public int roll()
public int runSimulation()
```

GO ON TO THE NEXT PAGE.

2. This question involves the implementation of a calorie counter system that is represented by the CalorieCount class. A CalorieCount object is created with 5 parameters:

- Daily calories limit—the recommended number of calories per day
- Daily calories intake—the number of calories a person has eaten in a day
- Grams of protein per day
- Grams of carbohydrate per day
- Grams of fat per day

The CalorieCount class provides a constructor and the following methods:

- addMeal—takes in calories, grams of protein, grams of carbs, and grams of fat from a meal and updates corresponding instance fields

- getProteinPercentage—returns the percent of protein in a given day (4 * grams protein / daily calorie intake)

- onTrack—returns true if the calorie intake does not exceed the daily calories limit, otherwise returns false

The following table contains sample code and the expected results.

Statements and Expressions	Value Returned (blank if no value)	Comment
`CalorieCount sunday = new CalorieCount(1500);`		Creates an instance with a 1500-calorie limit
`sunday.addMeal(716, 38, 38, 45);`		Adds 716 calories, 38 grams of protein, 38 grams of carbs, 45 grams of fat to the appropriate instance fields
`sunday.addMeal(230, 16, 8, 16);`		Adds 230 calories, 16 grams of protein, 8 grams of carbs, 16 grams of fat to the appropriate instance fields
`sunday.addMeal(568, 38, 50, 24);`		Adds 568 calories, 38 grams of protein, 50 grams of carbs, 24 grams of fat to the appropriate instance fields
`onTrack()`	false	Returns true if calorie intake does not exceed calorie limit
`getProteinPercentage()`	0.24	Multiplies grams of protein by 4 and then divides by calorie intake

GO ON TO THE NEXT PAGE.

Write the entire `CalorieCount` class. Your implementation must meet all specifications and conform to all examples.

Begin your response at the top of a new page in the separate Free Response booklet and fill in the appropriate circle at the top of each page to indicate the question number. If there are multiple parts to this question, write the part letter with your response.

GO ON TO THE NEXT PAGE.

3. This question involves the implementation of a travel planner system that is represented by the `TravelPlan` and `Tour` classes. A client will create `Tour` objects that will represent tours or activities of interest. Each `Tour` object is made up of an activity date, start time, end time, and name of the activity. The client will also create a `TravelPlan` object comprised of a destination and an `ArrayList` of `Tours`.

A partial declaration of the `Tour` class is shown below.

```
public class Tour {
      private int actDate;
      private int startTime; // times are represented in military format
      private int endTime;    // 1430  for 2:30 pm
      private String activity;

/*   Constructs a Tour
 *      All instance fields are initialized from parameters
 */
      Tour(int actDate, int startTime, int endTime, String activity)
      {
      /*   implementation not shown
      }
      public int getActDate() {  return actDate; }
      public int getStartTime() { return startTime; }
      public int getEndTime() {  return endTime; }
      public String getActivity() { return activity; }
```

A partial declaration of the `TravelPlan` class is shown below.

```
      import java.util.ArrayList;

      public class TravelPlan {
          private String destination;
          private ArrayList <Tour> plans;

/*   Constructs a TravelPlan
 *      All instance fields are initialized from parameters
 */
          TravelPlan(String destination)
          {
          /*   to be implemented in part (a)   */
          }

/*   Returns  true  if the timeframe overlaps with another Tour in plans;
 *   otherwise  false
 */
          public boolean checkForConflicts(Tour t)
          {
          /*   to be implemented in part (b)   */
          }

/*   Calls checkForConflicts, if checkForConflicts returns false
 *   (the timeframe does not overlap), adds the tour to plans, returns true
 *   otherwise returns false
 *   Must call checkForConflicts  for full credit
 */
          public boolean addTour(Tour t)
          {
          /*   to be implemented in part (c)   */
          }
```

GO ON TO THE NEXT PAGE.

The following table contains sample code and the expected results.

Statements and Expressions	Value Returned (blank if no value)	Comment
`TravelPlan p1 = new TravelPlan("Capetown");`		Creates an instance with a destination "CapeTown" and an empty `ArrayList` of type `Tour`
`Tour t1 = new Tour(1312020, 800, 1230, "Bungee jumping");`		Creates a `Tour` instance with date, start time, end time, and activity
`Tour t2 = new Tour(1312020, 900, 1430, "Body surfing");`		Creates a `Tour` instance with date, start time, end time, and activity
`p1.add(t1)`	`true`	Checks for conflicts in `plans`; since there are none, adds the `Tour` object, returns `true`
`p1.add(t2)`	`false`	Checks for conflicts in `plans`; since there is a conflict, returns `false`
`Tour t3 = new Tour(2012020, 900, 1200, "Shark cage diving");`		Creates a `Tour` instance with date, start time, end time, and activity
`p1.add(t3)`	`true`	Checks for conflicts in `plans`; since there are none, adds the `Tour` object, returns `true`

GO ON TO THE NEXT PAGE.

(a) Write the `TravelPlan` constructor. The constructor should initialize the destination and the `plans ArrayList`.

Begin your response at the top of a new page in the separate Free Response booklet and fill in the appropriate circle at the top of each page to indicate the question number. If there are multiple parts to this question, write the part letter with your response.

Class information for this question

```
public class Tour
private int actDate
private int startTime
private int endTime
private String activity

Tour(int actDate, int startTime, int endTime, String activity)
public int getActDate()
public int getStartTime()
public int getEndTime()
public String getActivity()

public class TravelPlan
private String destination;
private ArrayList <Tour> plans;

public TravelPlan(String destination)
public boolean addTour(Tour t)
public boolean checkForConflicts(Tour t)
```

GO ON TO THE NEXT PAGE.

(b) Write the `TravelPlan checkForConflicts` method.

Begin your response at the top of a new page in the separate Free Response booklet and fill in the appropriate circle at the top of each page to indicate the question number. If there are multiple parts to this question, write the part letter with your response.

Class information for this question

```
public class Tour
private int actDate
private int startTime
private int endTime
private String activity

Tour(int actDate, int startTime, int endTime, String activity)
public int getActDate()
public int getStartTime()
public int getEndTime()
public String getActivity()

public class TravelPlan
private String destination;
private ArrayList <Tour> plans;

public TravelPlan(String destination)
public boolean addTour(Tour t)
public boolean checkForConflicts(Tour t)
```

GO ON TO THE NEXT PAGE.

(c) Write the addTour method.

Begin your response at the top of a new page in the separate Free Response booklet and fill in the appropriate circle at the top of each page to indicate the question number. If there are multiple parts to this question, write the part letter with your response.

Class information for this question

```
public class Tour
private int actDate
private int startTime
private int endTime
private String activity

Tour(int actDate, int startTime, int endTime, String activity)
public int getActDate()
public int getStartTime()
public int getEndTime()
public String getActivity()

public class TravelPlan
private String destination;
private ArrayList <Tour> plans;

public TravelPlan(String destination)
public boolean addTour(Tour t)
public boolean checkForConflicts(Tour t)
```

GO ON TO THE NEXT PAGE.

4. This question involves the implementation of a class seating chart. A SeatingChart object will represent a two-dimensional string array. The number of rows and columns for the array will be sent as parameters, as well as a one-dimensional array of type Name. You may assume there will be enough rows and columns to accommodate all the entries from the array.

The declaration of the Name class is shown.

```java
public class Name
{
    private String lastName;
    private String firstName;

    Name(String lName, String fName){<implementation not shown>}
    public String getLastName() {return lastName;}
    public String getFirstName() {return firstName;}
}
```

A partial declaration of the SeatingChart class is shown below.

```java
public class SeatingChart {
    private String [][] chart;

/**    Constructs a SeatingChart having r rows and c columns. All elements contained in the
 *     names array should be placed randomly in the chart array using the format:
 *     lastName, firstName (e.g. Jolie, Angelina).
 *     Any locations not used in the chart should be
 *     initialized to the empty string.
 */
    SeatingChart(Name[] names, int rows, int cols){

            /*   to be implemented in part (a)   */

    }


/**    Returns a string containing all elements of the chart array in row-major order.
 *     The method should return a string containing all the elements in the chart array.
 *     The method padWithSpaces should be called on each
 *     element of the chart before it is added to the string to ensure each name will be
 *     printed with the same length.
 *     Each row of the chart should be separated by a line break.
 */
    public String toString() {

            /*   to be implemented in part (b)   */

    }

/**    Pads a string with spaces to ensure each string is exactly 35 characters long.   */

    private String padWithSpaces(String s) {
        String str = s;
        for (int a = s.length(); a < 35; a++) {
            str +=   " ";
        }
        return str;
    }
}
```

GO ON TO THE NEXT PAGE.

The following table contains sample code and the expected results.

Statements and Expressions	Value Returned / Comment
`SeatingChart msJones = new SeatingChart(theNames, 4, 3);`	(no value returned) A two-dimensional array is initialized with 4 rows and 3 columns. Every element in `theNames` is placed randomly in the chart in the following format: `lastname, firstname` (e.g., `Washington, George`). Empty string is placed in any unused locations.
`System.out.println(msJones.toString);`	Prints the names in the chart in row-major order. See example below:

```
Miller, Minnie        Fitzgerald, Fred        Dade, Ali
Indigo, Inde          Banner, Boris           Lane, Lois
Titon, Tim            Robilard, Robbie        Brne, Jane
Georgian, Greg
```

GO ON TO THE NEXT PAGE.

(a) Write the `SeatingChart` constructor.

Begin your response at the top of a new page in the separate Free Response booklet and fill in the appropriate circle at the top of each page to indicate the question number. If there are multiple parts to this question, write the part letter with your response.

Class information for this question

```
public class Name
    private String lastName;
    private String firstName;

    Name(String lName, String fName)
    public String getLastName() {return lastName;}
    public String getFirstName() {return firstName;}

public class SeatingChart
    private String [][] chart;

    SeatingChart(Name[] names, int rows, int cols)
    public String toString()
    private String padWithSpaces(String s)
```

GO ON TO THE NEXT PAGE.

(b) Write the `SeatingChart toString()` method.

Begin your response at the top of a new page in the separate Free Response booklet and fill in the appropriate circle at the top of each page to indicate the question number. If there are multiple parts to this question, write the part letter with your response.

Class information for this question

```
public class Name
    private String lastName;
    private String firstName;

    Name(String lName, String fName)
    public String getLastName() {return lastName;}
    public String getFirstName() {return firstName;}

public class SeatingChart
    private String [][] chart;

    SeatingChart(Name[] names, int rows, int cols)
    public String toString()
    private String padWithSpaces(String s)
```

STOP

END OF EXAM

Practice Test 1: Diagnostic Answer Key and Explanations

PRACTICE TEST 1: DIAGNOSTIC ANSWER KEY

Let's take a look at how you did on Practice Test 1. Follow the three-step process in the diagnostic answer key below and read the explanations for any questions you got wrong, or you struggled with but got correct. Once you finish working through the answer key and the explanations, go to the next chapter to make your study plan.

STEP 1 ≫ **Check your answers and mark any correct answers with a ✔ in the appropriate column.**

Section I: Multiple Choice							
Q #	Ans.	✔	Chapter #, Title	Q #	Ans.	✔	Chapter #, Title
1	E		**3**, Objects & Primitive Data	21	B		**8**, Primitives & Objects
2	D		**3**, Objects & Primitive Data **4**, The Math Class	22	E		**8**, Primitives & Objects
3	D		**4**, The String Class	23	B		**8**, Primitives & Objects
4	A		**4**, The String Class **3**, Objects & Primitive Data	24	D		**8**, Searches
5	C		**4**, The String Class	25	A		**8**, Primitives & Objects
6	E		**4**, The String Class **3**, Objects & Primitive Data	26	C		**8**, Primitives & Objects
7	B		**5**, The If Statement	27	E		**9**, Lists & ArrayLists
8	A		**5**, The If Statement **4**, The String Class	28	A		**9**, Lists & ArrayLists
9	E		**5**, The If Statement	29	B		**6**, Lists & ArrayLists
10	C		**5**, The If Statement	30	D		**9**, Lists & ArrayLists
11	C		**6**, The While Statement	31	D		**10**, 2D Arrays
12	D		**6**, The For Statement	32	B		**10**, 2D Arrays
13	A		**6**, The For Statement **5**, The If Statement	33	B		**11**, Lists & ArrayLists
14	C		**3**, Objects & Primitive Data **6**, The For Statement	34	D		**11**, Lists & ArrayLists
15	B		**6**, The For Statement	35	C		**11**, Lists & ArrayLists
16	B		**6**, The While Statement **4**, The String Class	36	D		**11**, Lists & ArrayLists
17	D		**6**, The For Statement	37	E		**11**, Lists & ArrayLists
18	C		**7**, Composition	38	E		**12**, Recursion
19	B		**7**, Composition	39	D		**12**, Recursion
20	D		**7**, Design & Structure	40	A		**12**, Recursively Traversing Arrays

Section II: Free-Response			
Q #	Ans.	✔	Chapter #, Title
1a	See Explanation		4, The Math Class
1b	See Explanation		6, The For Statement 5, The If Statement 4, The Math Class
2	See Explanation		7, Design & Structure 3, Objects & Primitive Data
3a	See Explanation		9, Lists & ArrayLists 7, Design & Structure
3b	See Explanation		9, Lists & ArrayLists 5, The If Statement 7, Methods
3c	See Explanation		9, Lists & ArrayLists 7, Methods
4a	See Explanation		10, 2D Arrays 8, Primitives & Objects 3, Objects & Primitive Data
4b	See Explanation		10, 2D Arrays

 **Tally your correct answers from Step 1 by chapter. For each chapter, write the number of correct answers in the appropriate box. Then, divide your correct answers by the number of total questions (which we've provided) to get your percent correct.**

CHAPTER 3 TEST SELF-EVALUATION

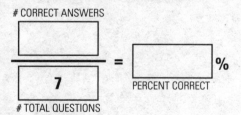

CORRECT ANSWERS

/ 7 = ___ % PERCENT CORRECT

TOTAL QUESTIONS

CHAPTER 5 TEST SELF-EVALUATION

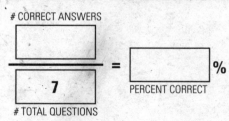

CORRECT ANSWERS

/ 7 = ___ % PERCENT CORRECT

TOTAL QUESTIONS

CHAPTER 4 TEST SELF-EVALUATION

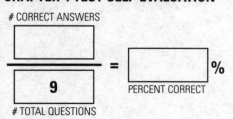

CORRECT ANSWERS

/ 9 = ___ % PERCENT CORRECT

TOTAL QUESTIONS

CHAPTER 6 TEST SELF-EVALUATION

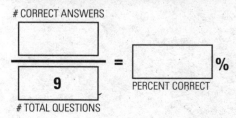

CORRECT ANSWERS

/ 9 = ___ % PERCENT CORRECT

TOTAL QUESTIONS

CHAPTER 7 TEST SELF-EVALUATION

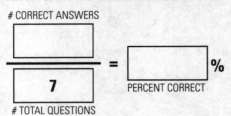

CORRECT ANSWERS

—————————— = _____ %
7   PERCENT CORRECT

TOTAL QUESTIONS

CHAPTER 8 TEST SELF-EVALUATION

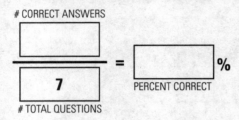

CORRECT ANSWERS

—————————— = _____ %
7   PERCENT CORRECT

TOTAL QUESTIONS

CHAPTER 9 TEST SELF-EVALUATION

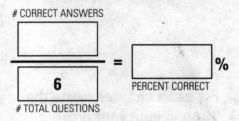

CORRECT ANSWERS

—————————— = _____ %
6   PERCENT CORRECT

TOTAL QUESTIONS

CHAPTER 10 TEST SELF-EVALUATION

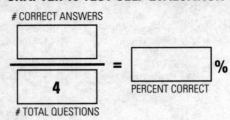

CORRECT ANSWERS

—————————— = _____ %
4   PERCENT CORRECT

TOTAL QUESTIONS

CHAPTER 11 TEST SELF-EVALUATION

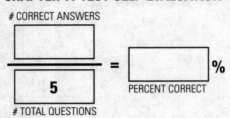

CORRECT ANSWERS

—————————— = _____ %
5   PERCENT CORRECT

TOTAL QUESTIONS

CHAPTER 12 TEST SELF-EVALUATION

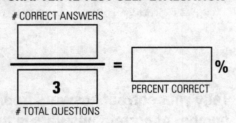

CORRECT ANSWERS

—————————— = _____ %
3   PERCENT CORRECT

TOTAL QUESTIONS

 **STEP 3** **Use the results above to customize your study plan. You may want to start with, or give more attention to, the chapters with the lowest percents correct.**

PRACTICE TEST 1 EXPLANATIONS

Section I: Multiple-Choice Questions

1. **E** Modulus division and division have the same order of precedence. Going from left to right, modulus (`%`) is first: `6 % 12` is `6`. Division (`/`) is next and will be handled as integer division, since both terms of the operation are integers: `6 / 4` is `1`. Finally, do the addition: `4 + 1 = 5`. The correct answer is (E).

2. **D** Anytime a `double` data type is used in an operation, the result will yield a `double`. In (A) `(1.0 * 2)`, (B) `(2.0)`, and (C) `((double) 2)`, the numerators are all `2.0`. Choice (E) also yields `2.0`, since the `Math.sqrt` method returns a `double`. Choice (D) attempts to cast to `double` too late. The expression inside the parentheses `(2 / 10)` yields `0` before it can be cast to a `double`.

3. **D** First off, every string literal will be enclosed in quotation marks (`""`). Next, to print a character that serves as a control character with specific meanings in Java, characters like `\`, `"`, or n to indicate a new line, each character will have to be preceded by its own `\`. Thus, to print `"Friends"`, each `"` that's printed will require its own `\`. Choices (A), (B), and (C) are missing the backslashes. Choice (E) has too many backslashes and will give a compiler error. Choice (D) is the correct answer because a backslash is used to indicate each control break.

4. **A** The `String` class is immutable. Without additional assignment statements to change the values of `animal1` and `animal2`, they will retain the values assigned in the first two lines.

5. **C** Choices (B), (D), and (E) all pass `String`, `String`, `int`, `int` as arguments to the second `Constellation` constructor. Choice (A) passes two strings to the first constructor. Choice (C) is the correct answer, as a double cannot be passed to a parameter of type `int` because there may be a loss of precision.

6. **E** Segments I and II will use an `int` parameter to update the instance field(s) of type `int`. Segment III will cast the `double` to `int` before updating the instance field of type `int`. There may be a loss of precision, but it would be a logic error, not a compiler error. The correct answer is (E), as all options will compile correctly.

7. **B**   Trace the code:

```
int x = 10;
int y = 5;

if (x == 10)              //x is 10 so follow this branch
{
    if (y <= 5)           //y is 5 so follow this branch, add 1 to y, it is now 6
        y++;
    else if (y < 4)
            x = 3;
        else
            y += 6;
}                         //the first if statement is complete
if (y > 5)                //y is 6, so follow this branch
{
    if (x != 10)          //x is 10, so skip to the else
    {
        x = 0;
        y = 0;
    }
    else                  //follow this branch, assign -5 to x
        x = -5;
}
                          //Thus, x = -5 and y = 6
```

The correct answer is (B).

8. **A**   The rules of compareTo are as follows: if string1.compareTo(string2) < 0, then the strings are in lexicographical order, whereas if string1.compareTo(string2) > 0, then the strings are in reversed order.

```
1    String word1 = "frog";
2    String word2 = "dog";
3    String word3 = "cat";
4
5    if (word1.compareTo(word2) < 0)    //frog does not come before dog, skip to the else
6        if (word2.compareTo(word3) < 0)
7          System.out.println(word1 + " " + word2 + " " + word3);
8        else
9          System.out.println(word1 + " " + word3 + " " + word2);
10   else                                    //skip to here
11       if (word1.compareTo(word2) > 0) //frog comes after dog, so follow this branch
12         if (word2.compareTo(word3) < 0)  //dog does not precede cat, skip to the else
13           System.out.println(word1 + " " + word2 + " " + word3);
14         else
15           System.out.println(word1 + " " + word3 + " " + word2);  //frog  cat  dog
16       else
17         if (word2.equals(word3))
18           System.out.println( "all the words are the same");
19         else
20           System.out.println( "word1 and word2 are duplicates");
```

The correct answer is (A).

9. **E** The following is given: `temp = 90` and `cloudy = false`. Segment I is evaluated as `true`: `temp >= 90 (true) && !cloudy(true)`. Both sides of the `&&` are true, so the entire condition is true. Option II is evaluated as `true`: De Morgan's Law can be used to simplify the `!( )`. The simplified version is `temp <= 90 && !cloudy`—which are both true, so the entire condition is true. Segment III is also evaluated as `true`. Again, De Morgan's Law can be used to simplify the `!( )`. The simplified version is `temp <= 90 || cloudy`. Since the `temp` is 90, the first condition is true. By short-circuit, the entire condition is true. The correct answer is (E).

10. **C** Line 3 assigns `dog2`'s object reference to `dog1`. These two object variables are now pointing at the same object, the contents of which is `"Beagle"`. Thus, the result of `if (dog1 == dog2)` on line 6 is `true`. Line 4 creates another object whose contents are `"Beagle"`. Thus, the result of `if (dog1 == dog3)` on line 11 is `false`. The `==` is comparing whether the variables refer to the same object, not whether the content of the objects is the same. The result of `if (dog1.equals(dog3))` on line 16 is `true`. The method `.equals` compares the contents of the two objects: they both contain `"Beagle"`. The correct answer is (C).

11. **C** Choice (A) starts at `0` and will decrement to a negative index, causing an out of bounds exception. Choices (B) and (D) start the index at `str1.length`, which is out of bounds. The last character in a string should be referenced by `length - 1`. Choice (E) correctly starts at `length - 1`; however, the loop only continues while the index is greater than 0, missing the first character of `str1`. The correct answer is (C).

12. **D** Analytical problems of this type are more easily solved by selecting a value and testing the results. In this case, substitute a small number such as 3 for `n`, and then trace the code. The outer loop executes from 1 to 2, which is 2 times. The inner loop will execute from 1 to 3, which is 3 times. The code inside the loops is simply counting by 1. The inner loop will be executed (2 times 3) 6 times, thereby adding 6 to `count`.

Now, substitute 3 for `n` in all the possible answers.

	Expression	**Result**
(A)	3^3	27
(B)	$3^2 - 1$	8
(C)	$(3 - 1)^2$	4
(D)	$3(3 - 1)$	6
(E)	3^2	9

Thus, the answer to this problem is (D), `n(n - 1)`. Analytically, you could have looked at the first loop processing from 1 to `n - 1` and the second loop processing from 1 to `n`, and made the same assessment.

13. **A** Choice (E) is eliminated with short-circuit. Line 4 looks to determine whether x != 0, but it IS 0, so logic immediately branches to the else statement on line 7. Variable x is initialized to 0, and j is initialized to 1, so line 7 multiplies j (1) times x (0) = 0 and prints the result. This eliminates (C) and (D). Both (A) and (B) are all zeroes, so the question becomes, how many 0s will be printed? Line 2 specifies j will start at 1 and end at 3, thus printing three 0s. The correct answer is (A).

14. **C** The loop located at lines 4–7 prints symbol (*) 5 times.

Line 8 is a control break to the next line.

The loop located at lines 9–16 is executed 5 times. The loop within at lines 11–14 prints 5 − j spaces, so the first time through it will print 4 spaces, next time 3 spaces, and so on. (Note: this eliminates all answers except for (C).) After the spaces are printed on each line, a single symbol (*) is printed with println (which will then move to the next line).

The loop at 17–20 is the same as the first loop, printing symbol (*) 5 times. The correct answer is (C).

15. **B** i will have only the value 1, j will range from 1 to 3, and k will range from 1 to 3. The three variables will be multiplied by each other and then added to the sum. The results will look like this:

```
i * j * k
1 * 1 * 1 = 1
1 * 1 * 2 = 2
1 * 1 * 3 = 3
1 * 2 * 1 = 2
1 * 2 * 2 = 4
1 * 2 * 3 = 6
1 * 3 * 1 = 3
1 * 3 * 2 = 6
1 * 3 * 3 = 9          The sum of which is 36.
```

The correct answer is (B).

16. **B** The substring() method has two parameters. The first specifies where to start, the second how far to go (up to but NOT including).

The outer loop at lines 3–12 is controlled by j. j starts off at 0, eventually ending at 2.

The inner loop at lines 5–10 is controlled by k. k starts off at 3 and will execute as long as it is greater than j.

The first time through the outer loop the following will be printed:

```
s.substring(0, 3)        prints map
s.substring(0, 2)        prints ma
s.substring(0, 1)        prints m
```

The second time through the outer loop the following will be printed:

```
s.substring(1, 3)        prints ap
s.substring(1, 2)        prints a
```

The final time through the outer loop the following will be printed:

```
s.substring(2, 3)        prints p
```

The correct answer is (B).

17. **D** Once again, it is helpful to choose a value for n to analyze the code. Choosing 3 for n, analyze the code.

I—Each time through the loop, factorial will be multiplied by 3. This does not follow the definition of a factorial. Eliminate (A) and (E), which include I.

II—The loop is controlled by j, which will range from 1 to n, in this case 3. Each time through the loop, factorial is multiplied by j, thereby producing a result of 1 × 2 × 3, which is correct. Eliminate (C).

III—A recursive solution that sends n (3) to the function

    First pass is   `f(3) -> 3 * f(2)`

    Second pass is `f(2) -> 2 * f(1)`

    Final pass is   `f(1) -> 1`   3 × 2 × 1 will yield 6 as expected. Eliminate (B).

The correct answer is (D), as only II and III will work.

18. **C** When a local variable is created, it is used instead of the instance variable. When the constructor is invoked, line 28 does not update the instance variable price. Without specifying `this.price = price,` the local parameter is assigned the same value it already holds. Thus, (D) and (E) are eliminated. Choice (A) is eliminated because the `toString` method has been defined in the `Tile` class to print the instance variables (not the object reference). The `chgMaterial(mat)` method at line 30 also updates a local variable rather than the instance variable, eliminating (B). The correct answer is (C).

19. **B** If a print statement is passed an object, its `toString()` method will be invoked. This eliminates all answers except (B), which is the correct answer.

20. **D** A static variable would be used for something that would belong to the entire class. Since inventory needs to exist for each style, it cannot be static, but it must be an instance of the class, eliminating (A) and (B). Choice (C) is eliminated because the keyword `final` is used only for constants that do not change value, but the owner has also asked for a method to change the value. Since `styleNumber` is an instance field, it implies that a separate instance is created for each style. Thus an array is not needed, eliminating (E). The correct answer is (D).

21. **B**   The array is initialized as `{11, 22, 33, 44, 55, 66};`

First pass:
```
nums[nums[0] / 11] = nums[0];
nums[11 / 11] = nums[0];
nums[1] = nums[0];    The array is now: {11, 11, 33, 44, 55, 66};
```

Second pass:
```
nums[nums[1] / 11] = nums[1];
nums[11 / 11] = nums[1];
nums[1] = nums[1];    The array is unchanged: {11, 11, 33, 44, 55, 66};
```

Third pass:
```
nums[nums[2] / 11] = nums[2];
nums[33 / 11] = nums[2];
nums[3] = nums[2];    The array is now: {11, 11, 33, 33, 55, 66};
```

Fourth pass:
```
nums[nums[3] / 11] = nums[3];
nums[33 / 11] = nums[3];
nums[3] = nums[3];    The array is unchanged: {11, 11, 33, 33, 55, 66};
```

Fifth pass:
```
nums[nums[4] / 11] = nums[4];
nums[55 / 11] = nums[4];
nums[5] = nums[4];    The array is now: {11, 11, 33, 33, 55, 55};
```

Sixth pass:
```
nums[nums[5] / 11] = nums[5];
nums[55 / 11] = nums[5];
nums[5] = nums[5];    The array is unchanged: {11, 11, 33, 33, 55, 55};
```

The correct answer is (B).

22. **E**   Line 14 assigns the `arr1` object reference to `arr2` object reference. Thus, both variables are now pointing to the exact same array in memory.

The loop at lines 17–18 is the only code that modifies the array.

both `arr1` and `arr2`: `{1, 2, 3, 4, 5, 6};`   `last = 5`

```
                arr2[i] = arr1[last - i];
first pass:     arr2[0] = arr1[5 - 0];   {6, 2, 3, 4, 5, 6}
second pass:    arr2[1] = arr1[5 - 1];   {6, 5, 3, 4, 5, 6}
third pass:     arr2[2] = arr1[5 - 2];   {6, 5, 4, 4, 5, 6}
fourth pass:    arr2[3] = arr1[5 - 3];   {6, 5, 4, 4, 5, 6}
fifth pass:     arr2[4] = arr1[5 - 4];   {6, 5, 4, 4, 5, 6}
last pass:      arr2[5] = arr1[5 - 5];   {6, 5, 4, 4, 5, 6}
```

The correct answer is (E).

23. **B**   The `for` loop on line 29 creates a local variable named `element` which will hold each value of `arr3` without having to use an index. Modifying this local variable does not modify the individual contents within the array. The loop multiplies each element by 2, printing it as it does so.

`2, 4, 6, 8, 10, 12`

The loop at line 36 prints the contents of the array, which remain unchanged:

`1, 2, 3, 4, 5, 6`

The correct answer is (B).

24.   **D**   Since index i is assigned to variables a and b, it is locations that are being printed. This eliminates (A). Scan the remaining answers and make a chart to help you understand the possibilities.

	Location of:	**Location of:**
(B)	Smallest integer	Largest integer
(C)	Smallest non-negative integer	Largest non-negative integer
(D)	Smallest integer	Largest non-negative integer
(E)	Smallest non-negative integer	Largest integer

The variable `holdSmallest` is initialized with `Integer.MAX_VALUE`, which is the largest integer an `int` field may hold. Thus, the code will work to find the smallest number in the array even if it is a negative number. This eliminates (C) and (E). The variable `holdLargest` is initialized to `0`, so when looking for a larger integer, it will only be replaced if it is larger than `0`, or in other words, a non-negative integer. This eliminates (B). The correct answer is (D).

25.   **A**   Choice (B) is eliminated because there is no increment to variable i. Choice (C) is eliminated because without an index, it implies the entire array (not each element) is being added to sum over and over. Choice (D) cannot use `element`, because it will contain the contents of a location within the array, rather than a location. Choice (E) uses the variable name of the array as the index. Choice (A) is correct because it uses the temporary variable `element`, which will actually hold the contents of each location within the array.

26.   **C**   Examining the code of `swap1`, you can see it will work only if the arrays are the same length. There is no accommodation for one array being longer than the other. In fact, if a1 is longer, there will be an out of bounds error on the second array. This eliminates (A), (D), and (E). The code of `swap2` does not work. Array variables hold a reference to the array, not to the actual elements. This eliminates (B). The correct answer is (C).

27.   **E**   Segment I declares an `ArrayList` of type `String` and then adds "4.5", which is a `String`. It is correct. Eliminate (D), which does not include I.
Segment II declares an `ArrayList` of type `Integer` and then casts 4.5 to an `int` before adding it to the `ArrayList`, which is acceptable. It is correct. Eliminate (A) and (C).
Segment III declares an `ArrayList` variable and then completes the declaration of the `ArrayList` as type `double` on the next line. It then adds a double to the `ArrayList`, which is correct. Eliminate (B).
The correct answer is (E).

28.   **A**   The first loop loads the contents of the array into the `ArrayList`. The next loop begins to remove elements if those elements are even. The loop will continue to run until it reaches the size of the `ArrayList`. As elements of the `ArrayList` are removed, the size will decrease, so there is no risk of going out of bounds. Eliminate (E). However, the index `i` will occasionally skip elements because of the renumbering that takes place.

```
[2, 4, 6, 7, 8, 10, 11];
```

`i = 0` The 2 is even, so it is removed; the array is now

```
[4, 6, 7, 8, 10, 11];
```

`i = 1` Notice the 4 will now be skipped. The 6 is even, so it is removed; the array is now

```
[4, 7, 8, 10, 11];
```

`i = 2` The 8 is even, so it is removed; the array is now

```
[4, 7, 10, 11];
```

`i = 3` The 10 has been skipped. The 11 is odd, so the array stays the same:

```
[4, 7, 10, 11];
```

The correct answer is (A).

29.   **B**   The size of the array is 5, so `size - 1` is 4. The outer loop executes 4 times (0–3).
`size - 2` is 3. The inner loop executes 3 times (0–2).
Since line 12 is executed every time the inner loop is executed, it will be executed (4)(3) = 12 times. The correct answer is (B).

30.   **D**   The inner loop does not go far enough to process the entire array. `size` is 5, and `size - 1` is 4, so the index can only be less than 4, stopping at index 3. The last entry in the `ArrayList` will never be sorted. The sort makes 4 passes through the `ArrayList`. The passes will look as follows:

```
0    [6, 21, 2, 8, 1]
1    [6, 2, 21, 8, 1]
2    [6, 2, 8, 21, 1]
3    [2, 6, 8, 21, 1]
```

The correct answer is (D).

31. **D** The array is printed in column-major order. The outer loop runs from 0 to row length − 1 (the number of columns). The inner loop runs from 0 to the length of the array (which means the number of rows).

The original array is

```
1   2   3   4
5   6   7   8
```

The outer loop starts with column 0, prints [0] [0]: 1   [1] [0]: 5

The outer loop increments to column 1   [0] [1]: 2   [1] [1]: 6

The outer loop increments to column 2   [0] [2]: 3   [1] [2]: 7

The outer loop increments to column 3   [0] [3]: 4   [1] [3]: 8

The correct answer is (D).

32. **B** Segment III will go out of bounds. The r (rows) will iterate as many times as there are columns. If there are fewer rows than columns, the index will go out of bounds. The correct answer is (B).

33. **B** Since name and weight are instance variables in the Percussion class, values for those variables should be passed while calling super. The call to super must be the first line in a method. Thus, (A), (D), and (E) are eliminated. The assignment statement of numberOfKeys is reversed in (C). The local variable is being initialized by the instance field. The correct answer is (B).

34. **D** The variable numberOfKeys is not visible outside the Xylophone class. Choices (A) and (B) are simply creating arrays of Xylophone objects. Choice (C) creates a xylophone object and then uses the proper accessor method to print the number of keys. Choice (E) declares a variable for an array of type Drums. Choice (D) attempts to print a private instance variable without using an accessor method. It will not comply, so the correct answer is (D).

35. **C** The accessor method getWeight() will return the weight of each instance so that they can be compared. Choice (A) is incorrect because the weight field is not visible. Choice (B) is not correct because weight() is not a defined method. Choice (D) is not correct because not only is weight not visible, but .equals is not used to compare primitive types. Choice (E) is incorrect because (C) compares the fields correctly. The correct answer is (C).

36. **D** Use the IS-A relationship to check the solutions:

(A)—SportingDog is a Dog (yes)

(B)—Retriever is a Dog (yes)

(C)—Retriever is a Sporting Dog (yes)

(D)—Dog is a Sporting Dog (no, the relationship is the opposite: not all dogs are sporting dogs)

(E)—Retriever is a Retriever (yes)

The correct answer is (D).

37. **E** The `Retriever` `toString()` method is invoked first, returning type: `Labrador +` `super.toString()`.

No `toString()` method is found in `SportingDog`, but a `toString()` method is found in `Dog`, adding `color is: chocolate` to the print line.

The correct answer is (E).

38. **E** Try substituting numbers for the variables. Try finding 3^2 by making `b = 3, x = 2`. The solution is found by multiplying 3 × 3.

The base case will be 3 (when the exponent is 1). This should imply that the `if` statement at line 3 should be

`if (x == 1)  return b;`

There is another error on line 6. Line 6 is using addition, when raising to a power is multiplying the base x times. Thus, the + sign should be changed to multiplication.

After making the changes in the code, it is advisable to test it to ensure it works:

```
         b = 3, x = 2

1    public double pow(double b, int x)
2    {
3    if (x == 1)
4       return b;
5    else
6       return b * pow(b, x - 1);
7    }
```

```
      f(3, 2)
         |
    3 * pow(3, 1)
         |
         3

    3 * 3 = 9
```

The correct answer is (E).

39. **D** It is best to walk the code.

```
System.out.println(f(8765));
public static int f(int n)
{
    if (n == 0)
        return 0;
    else
        return f(n / 10) + n % 10;
}
```

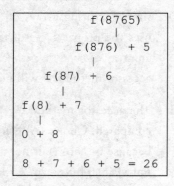

```
          f(8765)
             |
        f(876) + 5
             |
      f(87) + 6
             |
   f(8) + 7
      |
   0 + 8

   8 + 7 + 6 + 5 = 26
```

The correct answer is (D).

40. **A** If `sought` is less than the element at index `mid`, the beginning of the array should be searched. The location of the middle of the array, `mid - 1`, should be assigned to `last`. If `sought` is greater than the element at index `mid`, `mid + 1` should be assigned to `first` so that the latter half of the array can be searched. This process should be repeated until `sought` is found. The correct answer is (A).

Section II: Free-Response Questions

1.   `DiceSimulation`—Canonical Solution

(a)
```
public int roll() {

    return (int)(Math.random() * numFaces + 1);
}
```
(b)
```
public int runSimulation()
{
int die1 = 0;
int die2 = 0;
int countDouble = 0;
for (int i = 0; i < numSampleSize; i++) {
    die1 = roll();
    die2 = roll();
    if (die1 == die2) {
        countDouble++;
    }
}
return (int)((1.0 * countDouble / numSampleSize) * 100);
}
```

DiceSimulation Rubric

Part **(a)**

+3		roll **method**
	+1	`Math.random()` or the `Random` class is used
	+1	multiplied by `numFaces + 1`
	+1	result of computation is cast to `int` appropriately and returned

Part **(b)**

+6		runSimulation **method**
	+1	local variables are declared and initialized for the two dice
	+1	`roll` is used to give the dice values
	+1	a loop is used to execute sample size times (no more, no less)
	+1	the values of `die1` and `die2` are compared with `==`, doubles are counted appropriately
	+1	the percentage of doubles is calculated (avoiding integer division), multiplied by 100
	+1	percentage is returned as an `int`

2.   `CalorieCount`—Canonical Solution

```
public class CalorieCount {
    private int numCaloriesLimit;
    private int numCaloriesIntake;
    private int gramsProtein;
    private int gramsCarbohydrate;
    private int gramsFat;

    public CalorieCount (int numCal) {
        numCaloriesLimit = numCal;
        numCaloriesIntake = 0;
        gramsProtein = 0;
        gramsCarbohydrate = 0;
        gramsFat = 0;
    }
    public void addMeal(int calories, int protein, int carbs, int fat) {
        numCaloriesIntake += calories;
        gramsProtein += protein;
        gramsCarbohydrate += carbs;
        gramsFat += fat;
    }
    public double getProteinPercentage() {
        return 4.0 * gramsProtein / numCaloriesIntake;
    }
    public boolean onTrack() {
        return numCaloriesIntake <= numCaloriesLimit;
    }
}
```

`CalorieCount` Rubric

+1   Declares all appropriate `private` instance variables

+2   Constructor

    +1   declares header: `public CalorieCount (int calorieLimit)`

    +1   uses parameters and appropriate values to initialize instance variables

+2   `addMeal` method

    +1   declares header: `public void addMeal(int calories, int protein, int carbs, int fat)`

    +1   updates instance variables appropriately

+2   `getProteinPercentage` method

    +1   declares header: `public double getProteinPercentage()`

    +1   calculation and return: `return 4.0 * gramsProtein / numCaloriesIntake;`

+2   `onTrack` method

    +1   declares header: `public boolean onTrack()`

    +1   correctly returns `true` or `false`

           e.g., `return numCaloriesIntake <= numCaloriesLimit;`

3.

(a)
```
TravelPlan(String destination){
    this.destination = destination;
    plans = new ArrayList<Tour>();
}
```

(b)
```
public boolean checkForConflicts(Tour t) {
    for (int i = 0; i < plans.size(); i++)
    {
        if (t.getActDate() == plans.get(i).getActDate())
        {
            int plannedStart = plans.get(i).getStartTime();
            int plannedEnd = plans.get(i).getEndTime();
            if ((t.getStartTime() >= plannedStart && t.getStartTime() < plannedEnd) ||
                (t.getEndTime() > plannedStart && t.getEndTime() < plannedEnd))
                return true;
            if (t.getStartTime() <= plannedStart && t.getEndTime() >= plannedEnd)
                return true;
        }
    }
    return false;
}
```

(c)
```
public boolean String addTour(Tour t) {
    if (checkForConflicts(t)) {
        return false;
    }
    plans.add(t);
    return true;
}
```

TravelPlan Rubric

Part **(a)**

+3	Constructor	
	+1	constructor uses class name `TravelPlan`
	+1	updates `destination` instance field appropriately (uses `this.`)
	+1	creates `ArrayList` appropriately

Part **(b)**

+4	`checkForConflicts` method	
	+1	uses a loop to traverse every item in the `ArrayList` (no bounds errors)
	+1	uses `.get(index)` to access the object in the `ArrayList`
	+1	uses `getStartTime()` and `getEndTime()` to access the private fields in the `Tour` object
	+1	uses appropriate logic to determine whether there is a time conflict on the same day; returns `true` if there is a conflict, `false` otherwise

Part **(c)**

+2	`addTour` method	
	+1	calls `checkForConflict` method to determine whether there is a conflict (loses this point if it instead writes the logic to determine whether there is a conflict in this method), adds tour if there is no conflict
	+1	returns `true` if tour is added, or `false` if tour is not added

4.   `SeatingChart`—Canonical Solution

(a)
```java
SeatingChart(Name[] names, int r, int c)
{
  chart = new String[r][c];
  for (int i = 0; i < chart.length; i++)
  {
     for (int j = 0; j < chart[0].length; j++)
     {
          chart[i][j] = "";
     }
  }
  int count = 0;
  int i = (int) (Math.random() * names.length);
  int row = i / c;
  int col = i % c;
  while (count < names.length) {
     while (!chart[row][col].equals(""))
     {
          i = (int) (Math.random() * names.length);
          row = i / c;
          col = i % c;
     }
     chart[row][col]= names[count].getLastName() + ", " +
names[count].getFirstName();
     count ++;
  }
}
```

(b)
```java
public String toString()
   {
     String str = "";
     for (int a = 0; a < chart.length; a++) {
          for (int b = 0; b < chart[a].length; b++) {
             str += padWithSpaces(chart[a][b]);
          }
          str += "\n";
     }
     return str;
   }
```

SeatingChart Rubric

Part **(a)**

+6	Constructor	
	+1	chart is initialized using rows and columns passed in parameters
	+1	random numbers are generated in the correct range
	+1	a unique random number is used each time to place the name in the 2D array (duplicate names are avoided) and all names are placed (none are skipped)
	+1	row and column in the seating chart are derived properly from the random number
	+1	the name is stored in `chart` as a string (last name, (comma), first name), e.g., `Washington, George`
	+1	any unused spaces left in the array should be initialized to the empty string (not `null`)

Part **(b)**

+3	`toString` method	
	+1	builds a single string with all names from the 2D array, calling `padWithSpaces` to make all names an equal length
	+1	`"\n"` creates a line break after each row
	+1	returns a string

HOW TO SCORE PRACTICE TEST 1

Section I: Multiple-Choice

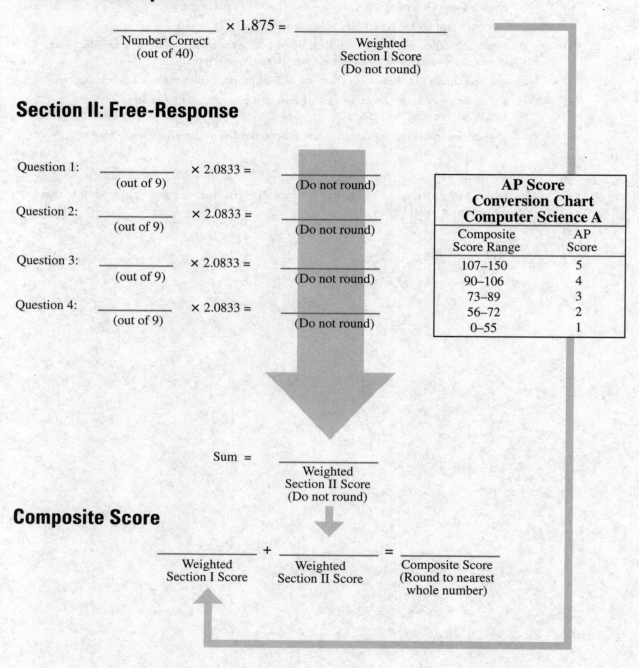

_____ × 1.875 = _____
Number Correct   Weighted
(out of 40)   Section I Score
                        (Do not round)

Section II: Free-Response

Question 1: _____ × 2.0833 = _____
            (out of 9)   (Do not round)

Question 2: _____ × 2.0833 = _____
            (out of 9)   (Do not round)

Question 3: _____ × 2.0833 = _____
            (out of 9)   (Do not round)

Question 4: _____ × 2.0833 = _____
            (out of 9)   (Do not round)

AP Score Conversion Chart Computer Science A

Composite Score Range	AP Score
107–150	5
90–106	4
73–89	3
56–72	2
0–55	1

Sum = _____
      Weighted
      Section II Score
      (Do not round)

Composite Score

_____ + _____ = _____
Weighted   Weighted   Composite Score
Section I Score Section II Score (Round to nearest
                              whole number)

Part III
About the
AP Computer
Science A Exam

THE STRUCTURE OF THE AP COMPUTER SCIENCE A EXAM

The AP Computer Science A Exam is a two-part test. The chart below illustrates the test's structure:

Section	Question Type	Number of Questions	Time Allowed	Percent of Final Grade
I	Multiple Choice	40	90 min.	50%
II	Free Response	4	90 min.	50%
	Question 1: Methods and Control Structures (9 points)			12.5%
	Question 2: Class (9 points)			12.5%
	Question 3: Array/ArrayList (9 points)			12.5%
	Question 4: 2D Array (9 points)			12.5%

The AP Computer Science A course and exam require that potential solutions of problems be written in the Java programming language. You should be able to perform the following tasks:

- design, implement, and analyze solutions to problems
- use and implement commonly used algorithms
- use standard data structures
- develop and select appropriate algorithms and data structures to solve new problems
- write solutions fluently in an object-oriented paradigm
- write, run, test, and debug solutions in the Java programming language, utilizing standard Java library classes from the AP Java subset
- read and understand programs consisting of several classes and interacting objects
- read and understand a description of the design and development process leading to such a program (examples of such solutions can be found in the AP Computer Science Labs)
- understand the ethical and social implications of computer use

The following table shows the classification categories and how they are represented in the multiple-choice section of the exam. Because questions can be classified in more than one category, the total of the percentages may be greater than 100%.

Units	Exam Weighting
Unit 1: Primitive Types	2.5–5%
Unit 2: Using Objects	5–7.5%
Unit 3: Boolean Expressions and `if` Statements	15–17.5%
Unit 4: Iteration	17.5–22.5%
Unit 5: Writing Classes	5–7.5%
Unit 6: Array	10–15%
Unit 7: `ArrayList`	2.5–7.5%
Unit 8: 2D Array	7.5–10%
Unit 9: Inheritance	5–10%
Unit 10: Recursion	5–7.5%

Have You Noticed?
You may notice that our Part V content chapters align exactly with these units. You're welcome ☺

In addition to the multiple-choice questions, there are four mandatory free-response questions. You'll have a total of 90 minutes to answer all four of them. You should spend approximately 22 minutes per question, but be aware that you must manage your own time. Additional time spent on one question will reduce the time you have left to answer the others.

The multiple-choice questions are scored by machine, while the free-response questions are scored by thousands of college faculty and expert AP teachers at the annual AP Reading. Scores on the free-response questions are weighted and combined with the weighted results of the multiple-choice questions. These composite, weighted raw scores are then converted into the reported AP Exam scores of 5, 4, 3, 2, and 1.

Score	2022 Percentage	Credit Recommendation	College Grade Equivalent
5	27.3%	Extremely Well Qualified	A
4	20.4%	Well Qualified	A–, B+, B
3	19.9%	Qualified	B–, C+, C
2	10.4%	Possibly Qualified	–
1	22.1%	No Recommendation	–

Scores from May 2022 AP Exam administration. Data taken from the College Board website.

To score your multiple-choice questions, award yourself one point for every correct answer and credit 0 points to your score for every question you got wrong.

Stay Up to Date!
For late-breaking information about test dates, exam formats, and any other changes pertaining to AP Comp Sci A, make sure to check the College Board's website at apstudents.collegeboard. org/courses/ap-computer-science-a

Free-Response Questions

Section II of the AP Computer Science A Exam is the free-response section. Free-response questions are scored from 0 to 9.

Unfortunately, we can't give you a ton of black-and-white rules about free-response question scoring—the actual scoring for each question is all based on the questions themselves. There is no one-size-fits-all way to score a Computer Science A free-response question. The College Board does map out some penalties, though, and they're in this handy list.

1-Point Penalty

- Extraneous code that causes a side effect or prevents earning points in the rubric (e.g., *information written to output*)
- Local variables used but none declared
- Destruction of persistent data (e.g., *changing value referenced by parameter*)
- Void method or constructor that returns a value

No Penalty

- Extraneous code that causes no side effect
- Extraneous code that is unreachable and would not have earned points in rubric
- Spelling/case discrepancies where there is no ambiguity
- Local variable not declared, provided that other variables are declared in some part
- `private` qualifier on local variable
- Missing `public` qualifier on class or constructor header
- Keyword used as an identifier
- Common mathematical symbols used for operators ($\times \; \bullet \; \div \; \leq \; \geq \; < \; > \; \neq$)
- [] vs. () vs. <>
- = instead of == (and vice versa)
- Array/collection element access confusion ([] vs. `set` for r-values)
- Array/collection element modification confusion ([] vs. `set` for l-values)
- Length/size confusion for array, `String`, and `ArrayList`, with or without ()
- Extraneous [] when referencing entire array
- [i, j] instead of [i][j]
- Extraneous size in array declaration, (e.g., `int[size] nums = new int[size];`)
- Missing ; provided that line breaks and indentation clearly convey intent
- Missing { } where indentation clearly conveys intent and { } are used elsewhere
- Missing ( ) on parameter-less method or constructor invocations
- Missing ( ) around `if`/`while` conditions
- Use of local variable outside declared scope (must be within same method body)
- Failure to cast object retrieved from nongeneric collection

HOW AP EXAMS ARE USED

Different colleges use AP Exams in different ways, so it is important that you visit a particular college's website in order to determine how it accepts AP Exam scores. The three items below represent the main ways in which AP Exam scores can be used.

- **College Credit.** Some colleges will give you college credit if you receive a high score on an AP Exam. These credits count toward your graduation requirements, meaning that you can take fewer courses while in college. Given the cost of college, this could be quite a benefit, indeed.

- **Satisfy Requirements.** Some colleges will allow you to "place out" of certain requirements if you do well on an AP Exam, even if they do not give you actual college credits. For example, you might not need to take an introductory-level course, or perhaps you might not need to take a class in a certain discipline at all.

- **Admissions Plus.** Even if your AP Exam will not result in college credit or even allow you to place out of certain courses, most colleges will respect your decision to push yourself by taking an AP course. In addition, if you take an AP Exam outside of an AP course, they will likely respect that drive too. A high score on an AP Exam shows proficiency in more difficult content than is typically taught in high school courses, and colleges may take that into account during the admissions process.

Some people think that AP courses are reserved for high school seniors, but that is not the case. Don't be afraid to see about being placed into an AP course during your junior or even sophomore year. A good AP Exam score looks fantastic on a college application and can set you apart from other candidates.

How Will I Know?
Your dream college's website may explain how it uses the AP Exam scores, or you can contact the school's admissions department to verify AP Exam score acceptance information.

More Great Books

The Princeton Review writes tons of books to guide you through test preparation and college admissions. If you're thinking about college, check out our wildly popular book *The Best 389 Colleges* and visit our website PrincetonReview.com for gobs of college rankings and ratings.

OTHER RESOURCES

There are many resources available to help you improve your score on the AP Computer Science A Exam, not the least of which are your teachers. If you are taking an AP course, you may be able to get extra attention from your teacher, such as feedback on your free-response answers. If you are not in an AP course, you can reach out to a teacher who teaches AP Computer Science A and ask whether that teacher will review your free-response answers or otherwise help you master the content.

Another wonderful resource is AP Students, the official website of the AP Exams (part of the College Board's website). The scope of information available on AP Central is quite broad and includes the following:

- course descriptions, which include further details on what content is covered by the exam
- sample questions from the AP Computer Science A Exam
- free-response question prompts and multiple-choice questions from previous years

The AP Students home page address is apstudents.collegeboard.org/

For up-to-date information about the AP Computer Science A Exam, please visit apstudents.collegeboard.org/courses/ap-computer-science-a

Finally, The Princeton Review offers tutoring and small group instruction. Our expert instructors can help you refine your strategic approach and enhance your content knowledge. For more information, call 1-800-2REVIEW.

HAVE YOU HEARD ABOUT AP COMPUTER SCIENCE PRINCIPLES?

In the fall of 2017, the College Board rolled out a new AP course and exam, AP Computer Science Principles. As the College Board puts it, "AP Computer Science Principles introduces students to the central ideas of computer science, instilling the ideas and practices of computational thinking and inviting students to understand how computing changes the world. Students develop innovative computational artifacts using the same creative processes artists, writers, computer scientists, and engineers use to bring ideas to life."

This course is a great on-ramp into computer science, a world that has historically been quite daunting to many people. But "comp sci," as they call it, is more bark than bite: computer science is a program in which you learn how to "speak" (code) a language, just as you might learn French or Spanish or Mandarin. And learning a language probably doesn't seem quite as intimidating as learning computer science, now does it?

You are probably enrolled in an AP Computer Science A course if you bought this book, but we wanted to tell you a bit more about AP Comp Sci Principles for your edification. It's useful to know more about this new course so that if a friend ever says to you, "I don't think that I could handle computer science," you can say, "Friend! Yes you can! Do you know how to use creative processes or think about patterns or study languages? Computer Science is for everyone!" [stares off into the sunset to let inspiring speech sink in] Well maybe not THAT, but this is just good stuff to know.

The College Board has split up their AP Computer Science Principles curriculum into 5 Big Ideas. Those are:

- Big Idea 1: Creative Development (CRD)
- Big Idea 2: Data (DAT)
- Big Idea 3: Algorithms and Programming (AAP)
- Big Idea 4: Computing Systems and Networks (CSN)
- Big Idea 5: Impact of Computing (IOC)

The College Board isn't kidding—these are some BIG ideas!

Computational Thinking Practices

The College Board drills down this course into computational thinking practices. Those items are:

PRACTICE 1: COMPUTATIONAL SOLUTION DESIGN

Design and evaluate solutions for a purpose.

Students are expected to:

- investigate the situation, context, or task
- determine and design an appropriate method or approach to achieve the purpose
- explain how collaboration affects the development of a solution
- evaluate solution options

PRACTICE 2: ALGORITHMS AND PROGRAM DEVELOPMENT

Develop and implement algorithms.

Students are expected to:

- represent algorithmic processes without using a programming language
- implement an algorithm in a program

PRACTICE 3: ABSTRACTION IN PROGRAM DEVELOPMENT
Develop programs that incorporate abstractions.

Students are expected to:

- generalize data sources through variables
- use abstraction to manage complexity in a program
- explain how abstraction manages complexity

We've Got a Book for That

We have another computer science book in our AP suite: *Computer Science Principles Prep.* Check out that book if you need a guide to the newest AP Comp Sci course on the block.

PRACTICE 4: CODE ANALYSIS
Evaluate and test algorithms and programs.

Students are expected to:

- explain how a code segment or program functions
- determine the results of code segments
- identify and correct errors in algorithms and programs, including error discovery through testing

PRACTICE 5: COMPUTING INNOVATIONS
Investigate computing innovations.

Students are expected to:

- explain how computing systems work
- explain how knowledge can be generated from data
- describe the impact of a computing innovation
- describe the impact of gathering data
- evaluate the use of computing based on legal and ethical factors

PRACTICE 6: RESPONSIBLE COMPUTING
Contribute to an inclusive, safe, collaborative, and ethical computing culture.

Students are expected to:

- collaborate in the development of solutions
- use safe and secure methods when using computing devices
- acknowledge the intellectual property of others

Your AP Computer Science Principles teacher has quite a bit of room for interpretation and choice in how to teach these things, so each course will be unique. The Exam, though, is somewhat cut and dried. The College Board maps out the Exam as this:

Section I: Multiple-Choice Questions

70 Multiple-Choice Questions | 2 Hours | 70% of Score

- Single-Select: 57 Questions, select 1 answer from 4 options
- Single-Select with Reading Passage about a Computing Innovation: 5 Questions, select 1 answer from 4 options based on reading passage
- Multi-Select: 8 Questions, select 2 answers from 4 options

Section II: Create Performance Task

1 Task | 30% of Score

- Create applications from ideas
- Develop a computer program of the students' choice

Please note that the College Board rolled out changes to AP Computer Science Principles very recently and this is the most up-to-date information. This information is correct as of March 2023, so please look at the College Board's website for any additional information. This is what was available at the time this book went to print.

For the sake of sharing information, let's do a side-by-side comparison of Comp Sci A versus Principles. Check out the differences in the chart on the next page.

	Computer Science A	Computer Science Principles
What it's about	The fundamentals of programming and problem solving using the JAVA language	The fundamentals of computing, including problem solving, working with data, understanding the Internet, cybersecurity, and programming. Teachers choose the programming language they will use.
Goals	Developing skills for future study or a career in computer science or other STEM fields	Broadening your understanding of computer science for use in a diversity of majors and careers
The Exam	One end-of-year exam: multiple choice and free response	• One end-of-year exam: multiple choice questions in single- and multi-select • One performance task administered by the teacher during the course

We've Got a Book for That!

The test prep experts at The Princeton Review wrote a book to help students prepare for AP Computer Science Principles, too! It's called, unsurprisingly, *AP Computer Science Principles Prep,* and it's a page-turner!

IN CONCLUSION

AP Computer Science Principles (APCSP) can be a great course to get comfortable in the computer science space. If you have already signed up for AP Computer Science A (APCS-A) (which you likely have, since you have purchased this book), then we assume that you are already comfortable with the Big Ideas of Comp Sci. So we'll dive into APCS-A in just a moment—first, let's quickly think about how you might wish to use your AP Exam score.

Although many schools award credit for both exams, *each exam has a different course equivalent*; for example, AP Computer Science A might replace a STEM major programming course, while AP Computer Science Principles replaces a more applied and/or general education requirement course. Consult the school's website for further clarification.

Here's an assortment of information from a number of schools to give you a sense of who accepts what (or anything!). More information can be found online at each school's website.

School	APCS-A Score Accepted	Credits Awarded	APCSP Score Accepted	Credits Awarded
Boston University	4 or 5	4	4 or 5	4 (both)
Rutgers University	4 or 5	3 for a 4; 4 for a 5	4 or 5	3
West Chester University	3 or higher	3	4 or higher	3
The Ohio State University	3 or higher	3 for a 3; 6 for a 4 or 5	3 or higher	3
University of Alabama	4 or higher	4	3 or higher	3
UCLA	3 or higher	8	3 or higher	8
Duke University	4 or 5	200-level placement	5	100-level placement
Howard University	4 or 5	3	4 or 5	3
University of Miami	4 or 5	4	4 or 5	3
Wesleyan University	4 or 5	1	4 or 5	1

Note: The colleges state on their websites that these figures are "subject to change."

As is true for everything college-related, there is no clear-cut decision that can be made here. In many cases, AP Computer Science A is the best bang-for-the-buck regarding credits; however, a 3 is accepted for AP Computer Science Principles more often than for AP Computer Science A. AP Computer Science A will often satisfy a major Comp Sci programming requirement, but the Principles course will not. Then again, if you're not embarking on a STEM journey, why not "AP out" of a general education course to bang out a requirement? Decisions, decisions, decisions!

For more information, hit up Google and search for your college name followed by "ap credits."

Part IV
Test-Taking Strategies for the AP Computer Science A Exam

PREVIEW

Review your Practice Test 1 results and then respond to the following questions:

- How many multiple-choice questions did you miss even though you knew the answer?

- On how many multiple-choice questions did you guess randomly?

- How many multiple-choice questions did you miss after eliminating some answers and guessing based on the remaining answers?

- Did you find any of the free-response questions easier or harder than others—and, if so, why?

HOW TO USE THE CHAPTERS IN THIS PART

Before reading the following strategy chapters, think about how you are approaching tests right now—tests in school, other standardized tests. Do certain sections of tests challenge you more than others? Are certain sections a breeze? As you read and engage in the directed practice, be sure to think critically about the ways you can change your approach.

Chapter 1
How to Approach Multiple-Choice Questions

THE BASICS

The directions for the multiple-choice section of the AP Computer Science A Exam are pretty simple. They read as follows:

Directions: Determine the answer to each of the following questions or incomplete statements, using the available space for any necessary scratchwork. Then decide which is the best of the choices given and fill in the corresponding oval on the answer sheet. No credit will be given for anything written in the examination booklet. Do not spend too much time on any one problem.

In short, you're being asked to do what you've done on many other multiple-choice exams: pick the best answer and then fill in the corresponding bubble on a separate sheet of paper. You will not be given credit for answers you record in your test booklet (by circling them, for example) but do not fill in on your answer sheet. The section consists of 40 questions, and you will be given 90 minutes to complete it.

The College Board also provides a breakdown of the general subject matter covered on the exam. This breakdown will not appear in your test booklet; it comes from the preparatory material that the College Board publishes. Here again is the chart we showed you in Part III:

Stay Up to Date!
For late-breaking information about test dates, exam formats, and any other changes pertaining to AP Comp Sci A, make sure to check the College Board's website at apstudents.collegeboard.org/courses/ap-computer-science-a

Units	Exam Weighting
Unit 1: Primitive Types	2.5–5%
Unit 2: Using Objects	5–7.5%
Unit 3: Boolean Expressions and `if` Statements	15–17.5%
Unit 4: Iteration	17.5–22.5%
Unit 5: Writing Classes	5–7.5%
Unit 6: Array	10–15%
Unit 7: `ArrayList`	2.5–7.5%
Unit 8: 2D Array	7.5–10%
Unit 9: Inheritance	5–10%
Unit 10: Recursion	5–7.5%

A few important notes about the AP Computer Science A Exam directly from the College Board:

- Assume that the classes listed in the Java Quick Reference have been imported where appropriate.
- Assume that declarations of variables and methods appear within the context of an enclosing class.
- Assume that method calls that are not prefixed with an object or class name and are not shown within a complete class definition appear within the context of an enclosing class.
- Unless otherwise noted in the question, assume that parameters in method calls are not `null` and that methods are called only when their preconditions are satisfied.

MULTIPLE-CHOICE STRATEGIES

Process of Elimination (POE)

As you work through the multiple-choice section, always keep in mind that you are not graded on your thinking process or scratchwork. All that ultimately matters is that you indicate the correct answer. Even if you aren't sure how to answer a question in a methodically "correct" way, see whether you can eliminate any answers based on common sense and then take a guess.

Throughout the book, we will point out areas where you can use common sense to eliminate answers.

Although we all like to be able to solve problems the "correct" way, using Process of Elimination (POE) and guessing aggressively can help earn you a few more points. It may be these points that make the difference between a 3 and a 4 or push you from a 4 to a 5.

Don't Be Afraid to Guess

If you don't know the answer, guess! There is no penalty for a wrong answer, so there is no reason to leave an answer blank. Obviously, the more incorrect answers you can eliminate, the better your odds of guessing the correct answer.

Be Strategic About Long Questions

Some multiple-choice questions require a page or two of reading to answer the question. Skip any questions that will either take a long time to read or a long time to calculate. Circle the questions and come back to them after you've completed the rest of the section.

Don't Turn a Question into a Crusade!

Most people don't run out of time on standardized tests because they work too slowly. Instead, they run out of time because they spend half of the test wrestling with two or three particular questions.

You should never spend more than about 2 minutes on a question. If you find yourself stuck on a super hard question and toying with it for 3 minutes, you're derailing yourself! Just move on and get as many points as you can. If a question doesn't involve calculation, then you either know the answer, you can take an educated guess at the answer, or you don't have any idea what the answer might be. Figure out where you stand on a question, make a decision, and move on.

Any question that requires more than two minutes' worth of calculations probably isn't worth doing. Remember, skipping a question early in the section is a good thing if it means that you'll have time to get two right later on.

Watch for Special Cases in Algorithm Descriptions

On the exam, you may know that the average runtime for finding an element in a binary search tree is $O(n \; \log \; n)$. Watch out if the question casually mentions that the data is inserted in the tree in sorted order. Now the runtime deteriorates into the worst case, $O(n)$. Such questions may pop up on the AP Computer Science A Exam, so keep a sharp eye.

Remember the Base Case in Recursive Algorithms

Recursive methods without a base case run forever. Be sure that a base case exists and is the correct base case. For example, a factorial function whose base case is

```
if (n == 1){
    return 0;
}
```

is incorrect because 1! = 1.

Watch for < vs. <= and > vs. >=

The difference between < and <= or between > and >= can be huge, especially in loops. You can bet that this discrepancy will appear in multiple-choice questions!

Know How to Use the AP Computer Science Java Subset

This chapter offers strategies that will help make you a better test taker and, hopefully, a better scorer on the AP Computer Science A exam. However, there are some things you just have to know. Although you'll have a Quick Reference for the AP Computer Science Java Subset as part of the exam, review the AP Computer Science Java Subset classes beforehand and know what methods are available, what they do, and how to use them. The Quick Reference will help, but it won't substitute for knowing the classes.

Preconditions and Postconditions

Read these carefully when given. They may provide the clue needed to answer a question. For instance, a precondition may state that the array passed to a method is in sorted order.

Parameter Passing

Remember that arguments passed to methods do not keep changes made to them inside the method. For instance, it is impossible to write a method that swaps the values of two integer primitives. Don't confuse this, however, with changing the contents (attributes) of an object that is passed to a method.

Client Program vs. Method

There is likely to be at least one question that defines a class and asks you to choose among different implementations for a method. Pay close attention to whether the method is a "client program" or a method of the class. If it's a client program, the implementation of the method may not access any private data fields or private methods of the class directly. If it's a method of the class, the implementation is free to access both private data fields and private methods.

Boolean Short-Circuiting

Conditionals in `if` statements and `while` statements "short-circuit." For example,

```
if ((a != 0) && (b / a == 5))
```

is *not* the same as

```
if ((b / a == 5) && (a != 0))
```

since Java will stop evaluating a compound boolean statement once the truth value is determined. (More on this later.)

Memorize De Morgan's Laws

There will be at least one question on the exam for which these laws will be useful.

```
!(p || q) is equivalent to !p && !q
!(p && q) is equivalent to !p || !q
```

Find Data in a Class

Watch out for answer choices that have code segments that attempt to change a data field declared final. This is illegal code.

Mixing `double` and `int` in an Expression

In operations that have both an `int` variable and a `double` variable, unless explicitly cast otherwise, the `int` is converted to a `double` and the result of the operation is a `double`.

Trial and Error

If a question asks about the result of a code segment based on the values of variables, pick simple values for the variables, and determine the results based on those values. Eliminate any choice that is inconsistent with that result. This is often easier than determining the results in more general terms.

Chapter 2
How to Approach
Free-Response
Questions

FREE-RESPONSE STRATEGIES

Write Java Code, Not Pseudocode
Only Java code is graded; pseudocode is not graded. Don't waste time writing pseudocode if you don't know how to code the solution to a problem. (On the other hand, write pseudocode as a starting point to writing your Java code if it helps you to do so.)

Don't Comment on Your Code
Unless you write some code that is extremely tricky (and see below for whether or not you should do that!), there's no need to write comments. It just takes time (that you don't have a lot of), and the comments will be largely ignored by the graders anyway (you won't get points if your comment is correct but your code is wrong). You also run the risk of misleading the grader if your code is correct but your comments are incorrect.

Write Legibly
This seems obvious, but if a grader can't read your code, you won't get any points.

Don't Erase Large Chunks of Code
If you make extensive changes to the code you're writing, it's better to put a big "X" through the bad code rather than erase it. It saves you time and makes it easier for the graders to read.

Don't Write More Than One Solution to a Problem
Graders will grade the first solution they see. If you rewrite a solution, be sure to cross out the old one.

Don't Leave any Problem Blank
You don't get any points if you don't write anything down. Even if you're unsure how to answer a particular problem (or part of a problem), analyze the problem and code the method's "infrastructure."

For instance, if the method signature indicates that it creates and returns an `ArrayList`, writing

```
ArrayList returnedList = new ArrayList( );
return returnedList;
```

is likely to get you at least partial credit—even if you don't know how to fill the `ArrayList` with the correct objects.

KISS (Keep It Simple, Student)

The free-response problems are designed to make the solutions relatively straight-forward. If your solution is getting complicated, there's probably an easier or better way to solve the problem. At the same time, don't try for seemingly elegant but unreadable code. Remember that graders must read hundreds of exams in a week—they may not have time to figure out all of the nuances of your code. KEEP IT SIMPLE!

Write Standard Solutions

Use AP-style variable, class, and method names and follow the indentation style of the AP sample code (even if you don't like their style!). Although graders always try to be fair and accurate, they are human and do make mistakes. The closer your answer adheres to the sample solution given to the graders, the easier it will be for them to grade.

Wherever possible, use clear and intuitive nomenclature. For example, use `r` and `c` or `row` and `col` for looping through the rows and columns of a two-dimensional array, don't use `x` and `y` or `a` and `b` or `jack` and `jill`. This ensures that graders can easily follow the flow of your code.

If the Pseudocode for an Algorithm Is Given, Use it!

Sometimes you will have to create your own algorithm for a method. Often, though, the pseudocode for the algorithm or method is given to you as part of the problem; all you need to do is implement the algorithm. In that case, use the pseudocode that's given to you! Don't make it harder on yourself by trying to re-create the algorithm or implement your own special version. Furthermore, you can often write the code for a method based on given pseudocode even if you don't understand the underlying algorithm.

Answer Part (c) to a Problem Even If You Can't Do Parts (a) and (b)

Many parts of free-response problems build on previous parts. For example, the question in part (c) may use the methods you wrote in parts (a) and (b). However, you do not need to have answered parts (a) and (b) correctly in order to get full credit for part (c). In fact, part (c) is sometimes easier than either part (a) or (b). If part (c) states that you should use parts (a) and (b), use them!

Don't Make Easy-to-Avoid Mistakes

Students often lose points on the free-response section because they make common errors. Here are some things you can do to avoid these mistakes.

- Unless the problem *explicitly* asks you to output something (using `System.out.print`), *never* output anything in a method you write.
- Watch method signatures. Be sure to call a method with the correct name and correct number and type of parameters. If the method is not void, be sure that the method you write returns a value with the correct type as specified in the signature.
- Use the `objectName.methodName()` syntax when calling methods of a given object; use the `ClassName.methodName()` syntax when calling static methods such as the random method of the `Math` class.
- Be sure to declare any variables you use (and give them descriptive names).
- Don't create objects when you don't need to. For instance, if a method you call returns an `ArrayList`, declare it as
  ```
  ArrayList returnedList;
  returnedList = obj.getList( );
  ```
  and
  ```
  ArrayList returnedList = new ArrayList( );
  returnedList = obj.getList( );
  ```
- Use proper indentation. Even if you use curly brackets for all of your conditionals and loops, the indentation will demonstrate your intent should you forget, for example, a closing curly brace.

Design Question

One problem in the free-response section is likely to be a design problem for which you will be given a description of a class and asked to write an interface (code) for it. You may also be asked to implement selected methods in your class. Be sure to use appropriate class, method, and private data field names. For example, "method1" is not likely to be a good name for a method that returns the total price of an object; "totalPrice" is a more appropriate name. Be sure to include all methods, private data fields, and *all* of the constructors (including the default constructor) asked for in the problem. If you are asked to implement a method, be sure to use the correct class, method, and private data field names *as you defined them* in the design part.

Arrays and ArrayLists

At least one problem (probably more) on the exam is likely to involve walking through arrays and/or ArrayLists. Know the differences between the two types of structures and how to loop through elements in an array or an ArrayList. Know how to use iterators and how to work with two-dimensional arrays.

GENERAL STRATEGIES

The following strategies apply to both the multiple-choice and free-response sections of the exam.

Write in the Test Booklet

Don't try to do the questions in your head. Write things down! Take notes on the question. In addition to making the problem easier to solve, having notes in the test booklet will make it easier to go back and check your work if you have time at the end of the test.

Underline Key Words in Questions

Words like *client program, sorted, ordered, constant, positive, never, always,* and *must* all specify conditions to a problem. On both the multiple-choice and free-response sections, underline these key words as you read each question to reinforce their importance to the problem.

Don't Do More Work Than You Need To

You are not graded for your work at all on the multiple-choice section, and you are not given extra credit for clever or well-documented answers on the free-response section. Keep it simple and strive to get the answer right rather than impress the graders.

Look Through the Exam First—Use the Two-Pass System

Keep in mind that all of the multiple-choice questions are worth the same number of points, and each free-response question is worth the same number of points as the other free-response questions. There is no need to do them in order. Instead, use a two-pass system.

Go through each section twice. The first time, do all the questions that you can get answers to immediately—that is, the questions with little or no analysis or the questions on computer science topics in which you are well-versed.

On the first round, skip the questions in the topics that make you uncomfortable. Also, you might want to skip the ones that look like number crunchers (you might still be expected to crunch a few numbers—even without a calculator). Circle the questions that you skip in your test booklet so you can find them easily during the second pass.

Once you've done all the questions that come easily to you, go back and pick out the tough ones that you have the best shot at.

That's why the two-pass system is so handy. By using it, you make sure that you get to see all the questions that you can get right, instead of running out of time because you got bogged down on questions you couldn't do earlier in the test.

A word of caution though: if you skip a multiple-choice question, be sure that you take extra care in marking your answer sheet. Always be sure that the answer you bubble in on the answer sheet is for the correct question number. In addition, don't forget to circle the skipped question in the multiple-choice booklet so that you remember to come back to it if you have time at the end of the test.

Pace Yourself and Keep Track of Time

On the multiple-choice section, you should take an average of 2 minutes per problem. This will give you 3 minutes to look over the test at the beginning and 7 minutes for a final check at the end. As a comparison, if you take 3 minutes per problem, you're going to answer only 30 questions; if you take 5 minutes per problem, you're going to answer only 18 questions. Bear in mind, however, that 2 minutes per question is an average. Some questions will not require this much time, so it's okay if a few questions take you longer than 2 minutes. After the first pass, reevaluate your pacing goal based on the number of questions and the amount of time you have remaining.

On the free-response section, you should pace yourself at a rate of 20 minutes per complete problem. This will give you roughly 2 minutes per problem to check your answer and a minute at the beginning to look over the problem.

Finally...

Don't panic. If you've prepared, the test is easier than it looks at first glance. Take your time, approach each question calmly and logically, remember the tips in this chapter, and you'll be fine.

Get Ready to Move On...

Now that you have the hints, strategies, and background information locked in, it's time to move on to the serious business at hand...the content review (Part V). Read over the following chapters, take notes, and compare them to your textbook and class notes as preparation to take Practice Test 2 in the back of this book, and then Practice Test 3 (even farther into the back of the book) and Practice Tests 4 and 5 (found online). Once you've mastered what's in this book and learned from your mistakes on the practice tests, you'll be ready to ace the real AP Exam.

Looking For More Help with Your APs?
We now offer specialized AP tutoring and course packages that guarantee a 4 or 5 on the AP. To see which courses are offered and available, visit www.princetonreview.com /college/ap-test-prep

REFLECT

Think about what you have learned in Part IV, and respond to the following questions:

- How much time will you spend on multiple-choice questions?

- How will you change your approach to multiple-choice questions?

- What is your multiple-choice guessing strategy?

- How much time will you spend on free-response questions?

- How will you change your approach to the free-response questions?

- Will you seek further help, outside of this book (such as from a teacher, tutor, or AP Students), on how to approach multiple-choice questions, free-response questions, or a pacing strategy?

Part V
Content Review for the AP Computer Science A Exam

Chapter 3
Primitive Types

Computer Science (CS) is an official name used for many aspects of computing, usually on the developing end; its areas include computer programming, which is exactly what you will be doing in AP Computer Science A (APCS). APCS focuses on the language Java and its components, and in many cases, you will be the programmer. Although the person using your program (the user) will typically see only the end result of your program, CS gives you the tools to write statements (code) that will ideally make the user's experience both functional and enjoyable.

PROGRAMMING STYLE

Computer programming is similar to a foreign language; it has nouns, verbs, and other parts of speech, and it has different forms of style, just like verbal languages. Just as you might use different words and ways of speaking—tone, expressions, etc.—with your family versus your friends, CS has many different languages and, within each language, its own ways of getting the job done. In both the CS world and the APCS world, a particular **programming style** is expected in order to show fluency in the language. A company that might hire you for a CS job will likely expect you to conform to its own unique programming style; similarly, the College Board will expect you to conform to its accepted programming style based on its research of CS styles accepted at universities around the world.

Comments, Identifiers, White Space

Commenting is an extremely vital style technique in the programming world. Comments do not actually cause the program to behave any differently; however, comments serve many purposes, including:

- allowing programmers to make "notes" within the program that they may want to reference later
- allowing the person reading and/or using the program ("the reader" and/or "the user") to understand the code in a less cryptic way, when applicable
- revealing to the programmer/reader/user aspects of the program that are required to make the program operate as intended and/or are produced as a result of the program's execution

There are two types of commenting in Java. **In-line,** or **short, comments** appear after or near a statement and are preceded by two forward slashes ("//") followed by the comment. **Long comments** that extend beyond a single line of code are surrounded by special characters; they begin with ("/*") and end with ("*/").

For example,

    //   This is a short comment
    /*   This is a
          long comment */

Identifiers are names that are given to represent data stored in the memory of the computer during the program's execution. Rather than using a nonsensical memory address code to reference data, Java allows the programmer to name an identifier to perform this job. When we name identifiers in Java, there are guidelines that we *must* use and guidelines that the College Board *expects* us to use:

- An identifier may contain any combination of letters, numbers, and underscore ("_"), but *must* begin with a letter and may not contain any other characters than these, including spaces.
- An identifier *should* be a logical name that corresponds to the data it is associated with; for example, an identifier associated with the side of a triangle would be more useful as `side1` instead of `s`.
- An identifier *should* begin with a lowercase letter and, if it is composed of several words, should denote each subsequent word with a capital letter. If we decided to create an identifier associated with our triangle's number of sides, `numberOfSides` or `numOfSides` would conform to this style; `NumberOfSides` and `numofsides` would not.

White space is another element of style that does not affect the overall functionality of the program. Rather, it enhances the readability of the program by allowing the programmer to space out the code to separate specific statements or tasks from others. Much like a book may leave empty space at the end of a chapter and begin the next chapter on the next page without affecting the overall story, white space has a similar effect.

Compiling & Errors

When the programmer writes Java code, statements are written that are understood within a Java development environment. The computer, however, does not understand this language, much like you would likely not understand a foreign language that you have never studied, spoken in its native environment. Therefore, an **interpreter** is used within the developer environment, enabling the computer to understand the Java code. A computer operates using code written only in **binary** (zeroes and ones, literally!), and so the interpreter "translates" your Java code into binary. This process is called **compiling**. As a result, in most instances as well as on the AP Exam, modern computer programmers do not need to understand binary code directly.

When an interactive development environment ("IDE") is used to compile your code, the code will be automatically checked for basic programming errors. If an error is found within the code, the compiling is halted, and an error message is produced (this feedback is where the "interactive" part comes in); this situation is called a **compile-time error**. Although the error message/code is not always helpful in a direct way, it does allow the programmer to troubleshoot the issue in a more directed way. Unfortunately, since the AP Exam is a pencil-and-paper test, you will have access to neither a computer nor a compiler. Your code must be absent of errors in order to receive full credit for the response (or any credit if it's a multiple-choice question).

A **logical error** is more difficult to troubleshoot, as opposed to a problem with the syntax of the Java code itself. A logical error lies in the desired output/purpose of the program. Similar to ordering dinner and receiving a perfectly prepared dessert instead, you are getting a good result, but it is not appropriate for the desired task.

A **run-time error** is an error that is not caught by the compiler, yet produces an error during the execution of the program. In many ways, this is the worst (and most embarrassing) error for the programmer, because it is not realized until the task is supposedly "done." An example might be a crash that occurs when you are editing your favorite image in a graphics program. It's frustrating for the user and annoying for the programmer when you leave negative feedback on the company's website!

---

1. Assuming all other statements in the program are correct, each of the following statements will allow the program to compile EXCEPT

   (A) // This is a comment
   (B) /* This is a comment */
   (C) // myName is a good identifier name
   (D) // myname is a good identifier name
   (E) All of the above statements will compile.

Here's How to Crack It

Choices (A), (B), and (C) are all valid comments in Java, regardless of their contents and the fact that (B) is not actually any longer than a single line. Choice (D) uses a poor identifier name, not a good one, but this situation will not result in a non-compiling program. Therefore, (E) is correct.

OBJECTS & PRIMITIVE DATA

Output (and Some Input)

In order for your program to "do anything" from the user's perspective (at this level, anyway!), it must produce output to the screen. A program may produce output to many devices, including storage drives and printers, but APCS requires us to produce output only to the screen.

There are two similar statements that we use to produce output to the screen in this course:

```
System.out.print(…);
System.out.println(…);
```

The ellipses in these statements stand for the data and/or identifiers that will be displayed on the screen. We will see the difference between these statements in a minute.

For example, if a triangle has a side length of 2 stored in the memory using the identifier side1 and we wanted to output that information to the screen, we could use one of the following two commands:

```
System.out.print(2);
System.out.print(side1);
```

Since both 2 and side1 represent numerical values, they can be outputted to the screen in this way. If we wanted to display non-numerical data, however, we would use a **string literal** (or simply a **string**) to accomplish this task. A string literal is simply one or more characters combined into a single unit. The previous sentence, and this sentence, can be considered string literals. In a Java program, string literals must be surrounded by double quotes ("") to avoid a compile error. In our triangle example, we can use a string literal to make the output more user-friendly:

```
System.out.println("The length of side 1 is:");
System.out.print(side1);
// side1 may be simply substituted with 2, in this case
```

Note the usage of the println statement rather than the print statement. While print will display the next output on the same line, println will output the string literal and then put the cursor at the beginning of the next line for further output. Note, also, that the statement

```
System.out.print(side1);
```

will display the *value* stored using the side1 identifier, 2. In contrast, the statement

```
System.out.print("side1");
```

will literally display

```
side1
```

Bonus Tips and Tricks…
Check us out on YouTube for additional test-taking tips and must-know strategies at www.youtube.com/ThePrincetonReview

because the double quotes create a string literal here. The College Board loves to ask multiple-choice questions that determine whether you understand these differences.

If quotation marks are how programmers signal the beginning and end of a string literal, how would they display quotation marks? For example, what if an instructional program was intended to display

```
Be sure to display the value of side1, not "side 1".
```

The command below might seem like an appropriate solution but would actually cause a compile-time error.

```
System.out.print("Be sure to display the value of side1, not
"side 1".");
```

The complier will interpret the quotation mark in front of side1 as the close of the string and will not know what to do with the rest of it. To display a quotation mark, the programmer must use an **escape sequence**, a small piece of coding beginning with a backslash (\) used to indicate specific characters. To successfully display the above live, use the command

```
System.out.print("Be sure to print the value of side1, not
\"side1\".");
```

Similarly, the escape sequence \n can be used to create a line break in the middle of a string. For example the command

```
System.out.print("The first line\nThe second line");
```

will display

```
The first line

The second line
```

So if a backslash indicates an escape sequence, how does a programmer print a backslash? This is done using another escape sequence, \\. The following command

```
System.out.println("Use \\n to indicate a new line.");
```

will display

```
Use \n to indicate a new line.
```

There are other escape sequences in Java, but only these three appear on the AP Computer Science A Exam.

2. Assuming all other statements in the program are correct, each of the following statements will allow the program to compile EXCEPT

(A) `System.out.print(1);`
(B) `System.out.print("1");`
(C) `System.out.print(side1);`
(D) `System.out.print("side1");`
(E) All of the above statements will compile.

Here's How to Crack It

Choices (A) and (B) will both display 1, although (A) is numerical and (B) is a string literal. Choice (D) will display the string literal side1. Since there is no indication in the question that side1 has been associated with any data, (C) will generate an error because Java does not know what to display. Therefore, (C) is the answer. Be very careful when choosing "all of the above" or "none of the above" answer choices, as these are often trap answers!

As you might imagine, input is also important in programming. Although you may learn some techniques for getting user input (the Scanner class, for example), the AP Exam will not test any input methods or classes. Instead, the input will be assumed and given as a comment in the coding. It may be similar to this.

```
int k = ..., //read user input
```

You will not be asked to prompt the user for input, unless there is pre-existing code in the task that does it for you. Nice.

Variables & Assignment

Let's put those identifiers to work.

In order to actually "create" an identifier, we need to **assign** a data value to that identifier. This task is done by writing an assignment statement.

The syntax of an assignment statement is

type identifier = data;

Continuing with our triangle example, if we wanted to actually assign the data value of 2 to a new identifier called side1, we could use this statement:

```
int side1 = 2;
```

This statement tells the compiler that (1) our identifier is called `side1`, (2) the data assigned to that identifier should be 2, and (3) our data is an integer (more on this in the next section). The equals sign ("=") is called an **assignment operator** and is required by Java. The semicolon, which we also saw in the output statements above, denotes that the statement is finished. Note that an assignment statement does NOT produce any output to the screen.

When data is associated with an identifier, the identifier is called a **variable**. The reason we use this term is that, as in math, the value of the variable can be changed; it can *vary*! Look at the following code:

```
int myFavoriteNumber = 22;
myFavoriteNumber = 78;
System.out.print ("My favorite number is " +
myFavoriteNumber);
```

Can you predict the output? The variable `myFavoriteNumber` is first assigned the value of 22, but it is then reassigned to the value 78. Therefore, the original value is no longer stored in the computer's memory and the 78 remains. The output would be

```
My favorite number is 78
```

A few items to note in this example:

- Once a variable is given a type (again, more on this later), its type should not be restated. This fact explains why the second assignment statement is missing `int`.
- The string literal is outputted as written, but the variable's *value*, not its name, is outputted.
- In order to output a string literal and a numerical value using the same output statement, use the **concatenation operator** between the two items. Although this operator looks like a typical + sign, it does not "add" the values in the traditional sense; instead, it simply outputs the two values next to each other. For example, two plus two equals four in the mathematical sense, but 2 concatenated with 2 produces 22.

---

3. Assuming all other statements in the program are correct, each of the following statements will allow the program to compile EXCEPT

(A) `System.out.print("Ilove Java");`
(B) `System.out.println("Ilove" + "Java");`
(C) `System.out.print(1 + "love" + Java");`
(D) `System.out.println(1 + "love" + "Java");`
(E) `System.out.print("I love" + " " + "Java");`

Here's How to Crack It

Choices (A) and (B), although their output may not look grammatically correct (they love to do this on the AP Exam—remember, it's not a grammar test!), will compile without error. Choice (D) is fine because the numerical value is concatenated with the string literals, producing a string literal that can be displayed. Choice (E) uses a string literal that is simply an empty space, which is valid. Therefore, (C) is the answer because "Java" is missing the left-hand quotation mark.

The Four Data Types—`int`, `double`, `boolean`, `char`

When programmers want to assign data to a variable, they must first decide what *type* of data will be stored. For the AP Exam, there are four data types that make up the **primitive data** forms—i.e., the basic types of data. More complex data forms will be discussed later.

integer (`int`) represents an integer number: positive numbers, negative numbers, and zero, with no decimals or fractions. Integers can store non-decimal values from –2,147,483,648 to 2,147,483,647, inclusive. That's a lot of values.

double (`double`) represents a number that can be positive, negative, or zero, and can be a fraction or decimal…pretty much any number you can think of. It also has a much bigger breadth of upper and lower limits than an integer; it can express numbers with decades of significant digits. If you have to store an integer that is larger than the limits listed above, you must store the data as a double.

On the AP Exam, you do not have to memorize the upper and lower limits of these numerical data types; you do, however, need to know that a double must be declared for a number that is larger than an integer can store.

boolean (`boolean`) represents a value that is either `true` or `false`. In machine code, `true` is represented by 1 (or any nonzero value) and `false` is represented by 0. This data type is excellent for storing or using yes/no data, such as the responses to: Are you hungry? Are you excited about the AP Exam? Is this chapter boring?

character (`char`) represents any single character that can be represented on a computer; this type includes any character you can type on the keyboard, including letters, numbers, spaces, and special characters such as slashes, dashes, and the like. `char` values are stored using a single quotation mark or apostrophe ('). The values of the capital letters A through Z are 65–90 and lowercase letters are 97–122 (browse <u>unicode-table.com/en</u> for a fancier, more complete listing of these values). Although the AP Exam does not require the memorization of these codes (thankfully), you should know their relative placement in the table. For example, you should know that character "A" comes before (has a lower numerical value) than character "B"; you should also note that every capital letter character comes before the lowercase letters. Therefore, "a" actually comes *after* "Z."

You've Got Character, The Test Doesn't
It's useful to know how `char` works, but it won't be on the AP Exam, so don't stress over it!

Arithmetic Operations

The most primitive uses for the first computers were to perform complex calculations. They were basically gigantic calculators. As a result, one of the most basic operations we use in Java involves arithmetic.

The symbols +, -, *, and / represent the operations addition, subtraction, multiplication, and division, respectively. The operator % is also used in Java: called the "modulus" operator, this symbol will produce the numerical remainder of a division. For example, 5 % 2 would evaluate to 1, since 5 divided by 2 yields 2, with 1 as a remainder. These operations can be performed intuitively on numerical values; they can also be performed on variables that store numerical values.

Speaking of math, back to our triangle example....

Consider the following statement in a program:

```
int side2 = 2, side3 = 3;
```

(Note that you can write multiple assignment statements in a single line, as long as the data types are the same.)

If we wanted to write a statement that found the sum of these data and assigned the result to another variable called sumOfSides, we could easily write

```
sumOfSides = 2 + 3; // method 1
```

But this statement is less useful than

```
sumOfSides = side2 + side3; // method 2
```

Since the data is assigned to variables, for which values can vary, method 2 will reflect those changes while method 1 will not.

This same technique can be applied to all of the mathematical operators. Remember that a mixture of mathematical operations follows a specific order of **precedence**. Java will perform the multiplication and division operations (including modulus), from left to right, followed by the addition and subtraction operations in the same order. If programmers want to change the order of precedence of the operators, they can use parentheses.

Consider these lines of code:

```
System.out.print(3 - 4/5); // statement 3
System.out.print(3 -(4/5)); // statement 4
System.out.print((3 - 4)/5); // statement 5
```

In statement 3, the division occurs first, followed by the subtraction (3 minus the answer).

In statement 4, the same thing happens, so it is mathematically equivalent to statement 3.

In statement 5, the parentheses override the order of operations, so the subtraction occurs, and then the answer is divided by 5.

Okay, here's where it gets crazy. Can you predict the output of these statements? Believe it or not, the output of statements 3 and 4 is 3; the output of statement 5 is 0. These results demonstrate the fact that data in Java is **strongly typed**.

When you perform a mathematical operation on two integers, Java will return the answer as an integer, as well. Therefore, although 4/5 is actually 0.8, Java will return a value of 0. Likewise, Java will evaluate 5/4 to be 1. The decimal part is cut off (not rounded), so that the result will also be an integer. Negative numbers work the same way. Java will return −4/5 as 0 and −5/4 as −1. Strange, huh?

As is true with all computer science, there is a workaround for this called **casting**. Casting is a process through which data is forced to "look like" another type of data to the compiler. Think of someone who is cast in a show to play a part; although actors have personal identities, they assume new identities for the audience. The following modifications to statement 3 demonstrate different ways of casting:

```
System.out.print(3 - (double)(4)/5); // statement 3.1
System.out.print(3 - 4/(double)5); // statement 3.2
```

These statements will cast 4 and 5, respectively, to be double values of 4.0 and 5.0. As a result, the division will be "upgraded" to a division between double values, not integers, and the desired result will be returned. The following statements, although they will compile without error, will not display the desired result of 2.2.

```
System.out.print((double)3 - 4/5); // statement 3.3
System.out.print(3 - (double)(4/5)); // statement 3.4
```

Casting has a higher precedence than arithmetic operators, except parentheses, of course. Therefore, statement 3.3 will first convert 3 to 3.0, but will then perform integer division before completing the subtracting. The result is 3.0. In statement 3.4, the result of dividing the integers is cast to a double; since the integer division evaluates to 0, the cast will simply make the result 0.0, yielding an output of 3.0 once again. Very tricky!

The **increment operator (++)** is used to increase the value of a number by one. For example, if the value of a variable x is 3, then x++ will increment the value of x to 4. This has the exact same effect as writing x = x + 1, and is nothing more than convenient shorthand.

Conversely, the **decrement operator (--)** is used to quickly decrease the value of a number by one. For example, if the value of a variable named x is 3, then x-- decreases the value of x to 2. This has the exact same effect as writing x = x - 1.

Other shortcut operators include +=, -=, *=, /=, and %=. These shortcuts perform the indicated operation and assign the result to the original variable. For example,

```
a += b;
```

is an equivalent command to

```
a = a + b;
```

If `int a` has been assigned the value 6 and `int b` has been assigned the value 3, the following table indicates the results of the shortcut operations.

Shortcut Command	Equivalent Command	Resulting value of a
a += b	a = a + b	9
a -= b	a = a - b	3
a *= b	a = a * b	18
a /= b	a = a / b	2
a %= b	a = a % b	0

4. Consider the following code segment:

```
int a = 3;
int b = 6;
int c = 8;
int d = a / b;
c /= d;
System.out.print(c);
```

Which of the following will be output by the code segment?

(A) 4
(B) 8
(C) 12
(D) 16
(E) There will be no output because of a run-time error.

Here's How to Crack It

Go through the coding one step at a time. The first three lines initialize a as 3, b as 6, and c as 8. The fourth line initializes d as a / b, which is 3 / 6. However, note that this is integer division, so the result must be an integer. In normal arithmetic 3 / 6 = 0.5. In Java, integer division cuts off the decimal part, so that d is 0. The command c /= d is equivalent to c = c / d. However, this requires dividing by 0, which is not allowed in Java (or normal arithmetic, for that matter). In Java, dividing by 0 will cause an ArithmeticException, which is a type of run-time error, so the answer is (E).

Give Me a Break

Humans are pretty smart when it comes to guessing intent For instance, you might have noticed that there's a missing period between this sentence and the one before it. (If not, slow down: AP Computer Science A Exam questions require close reading when looking for errors.) Computers, on the other hand, are literal—more annoyingly so, probably, than those teachers who ask whether you're physically capable of going to the bathroom when you ask whether you *can* go. To that end, then, it's crucial that you end each complete statement (i.e., sentence) with a semicolon, which is our way of telling the Java compiler that it's reached the end of a step. This doesn't mean that you need to place a semicolon after every line—remember that line breaks exist only to make code more readable to humans—but you must place one after any complete declaration or statement.

Study Break
Speaking of breaks, don't burn yourself out and overdo it with your AP Comp Sci preparation. Take it day by day and read a chapter, then work the end-of-chapter drills each day, then every so often, give yourself a break! Go for a walk, call a friend, listen to a favorite song.

KEY TERMS

Computer Science
programming style
commenting
in-line comments (short comments)
long comments
identifiers
white space
interpreter
binary
compiling
compile-time error
logical error
run-time error
string literal (string)
escape sequence
assign
assignment operator
variable
concatenation operator
primitive data
integer
double
boolean
character
precedence
strongly typed
casting
increment operator (++)
decrement operator (−−)

CHAPTER 3 REVIEW DRILL

Answers to the review questions can be found in Chapter 13.

1. Consider the following code segment:

```
1   int a = 10;
2   double b = 10.7;
3   double c = a + b;
4   int d = a + c;
5   System.out.println(c + " " + d);
```

What will be output as a result of executing the code segment?

(A) 20   20

(B) 20.0 30

(C) 20.7 31

(D) 20.7 30.7

(E) Nothing will be printed because of a compile-time error.

2. Consider the following code segment:

```
1   int a = 10;
2   double b = 10.7;
3   int d = a + b;
```

Line 3 will not compile in the code segment above. With which of the following statements could we replace this line so that it compiles?

```
I.    int d = (int) a + b;
II.   int d = (int) (a + b);
III.  int d = a + (int) b;
```

(A) I only

(B) II only

(C) III only

(D) I and III only

(E) II and III only

3. Consider the following code segment.

```
1    int a = 11;
2    int b = 4;
3    double x = 11;
4    double y = 4;
5    System.out.print(a / b);
6    System.out.print(", ");
7    System.out.print(x / y);
8    System.out.print(", ");
9    System.out.print(a / y);
```

What is printed as a result of executing the code segment?

(A) 3, 2.75, 3
(B) 3, 2.75, 2.75
(C) 2, 3, 2
(D) 2, 2.75, 2.75
(E) Nothing will be printed because of a compile-time error.

4. Consider the following statement:

```
int i = x % 50;
```

If x is a positive integer, which of the following could NOT be the value of i after the statement above executes?

(A) 0
(B) 10
(C) 25
(D) 40
(E) 50

Summary

o   Good use of commenting, identifiers, and white space does not affect the execution of the program but can help to make the program coding easier to interpret for both the programmer and other readers.

o   Compilers turn the Java code into binary code. Invalid code will prevent this and cause a compile-time error.

o   Logical errors do not prevent the program from compiling but cause undesired results.

o   Run-time errors also do not prevent the program from compiling but instead cause the program to halt unexpectedly during execution.

o   The AP Computer Science A Exam uses `System.out.print()` and `System.out.println()` for output. Any input is assumed and does not need to be coded by the student.

o   Variables must be initialized with a data type. They are assigned values using the "=" operator.

o   The primitive data types that are tested are `int`, `double`, and `boolean`. `String` is a non-primitive type that is also tested extensively.

o   The `int` and `double` operators +, −, *, /, and % are tested on the AP Computer Science A Exam.

o   Additional math operations can be performed using the `Math` class.

o   The "+" is used to concatenate strings.

Chapter 4
Using Classes and Objects

An **object** is an entity or data type we create in Java. To do so, we use a **class** built specifically for this purpose. Classes contain instance fields (data) belonging to the object and methods to manipulate that data. We will review this in more detail in a later chapter. For now, let's dive into the `Math` class.

THE `Math` CLASS

Part of the AP Computer Science Java subset is the `Math` class. The `Math` class stores common numbers used in mathematical calculations (`Math.PI` and `Math.E`) and methods to perform mathematical functions. The methods of the `Math` class are static. There will be more on static methods later, but, for now, understand that to call the methods of the `Math` class, the programmer must type `Math.` before the name of the method. The `Math` class contains many methods, but only a few are part of the AP Computer Science Java Subset. Unlike most classes that we use to create an object, we normally do not create `Math` objects.

Common `Math` Methods

Method	Return
`Math.abs(x)  //x` is an int	An `int` equal to the absolute value of `x`
`Math.abs(x)  //x` is a double	A `double` equal to the absolute value of `x`
`Math.pow(base, exponent)`	A `double` equal to the base raised to the exponent
`Math.sqrt(x)`	A `double` equal to the square root of `x`
`Math.random()`	A random `double` in the range (0, 1)

Understanding operator precedence is essential for multiple-choice questions on the AP Exam and, perhaps more importantly, for showing off on social media when those "solve this problem" memes pop up and everyone argues over the right answer.

---

1. A math teacher is writing a program that will correctly calculate the area of a circle. Recall that the area of a circle is pi times the radius squared (πr^2). Assuming `Math.PI` returns an accurate decimal approximation of pi, which of the following statements WILL NOT calculate an accurate area of a circle with radius 22 ?

   (A) `r*r*Math.PI; //` r is the int 22
   (B) `r*r*Math.PI; //` r is the double 22.0
   (C) `(double)r*r*Math.PI; //` r is the int 22
   (D) `(double)(r*r)*Math.PI; //` r is the int 22
   (E) All of the above choices will calculate an accurate area.

Here's How to Crack It

Choice (A) will use integer multiplication for `r*r` but will then convert everything to doubles when it multiplies by `Math.PI`, a double. Choice (B) is obviously correct. Choices (C) and (D) will cast some of the values to `double`, but as stated above, this will not impact the result in an undesired way. Therefore, the answer is (E).

It is important to note that `Math.PI` is a static variable of the `Math` class. Therefore, it can be called only if the class has been imported by putting the following statement at the top of the class coding:

```
import java.lang.Math;
```

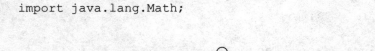

THE `String` CLASS

`String` is an object data type, meaning it has a class with many methods describing the behavior of the object. Below is a table of common methods utilized in the `String` class.

Common <code>String</code> Methods

Method	Return
`length()`	An `int` equal to the length of the string
`substring(int beginIndex)`	A `String` that is a substring of this string starting at the character at the `beginIndex`, through to the end of the string
`substring(int beginIndex, int endIndex)`	A `String` that is a substring of this string starting at the character at the `beginIndex`, up to but not including the character at the `endIndex`

`equals(Object anObject)`	A `boolean` reflecting the status after comparing this string to the specified object.
	
	`String str1 = "frog";`
	`String str2 = "frog";`
	`boolean isEqual = str1.equals(str2);`
	`// returns true`

`compareTo(String anotherString)`	An `int` reflecting the status after comparing two strings lexicographically.
	   - Returns an integer < 0 if `string1` comes before `string2`
	   - Returns an integer 0 if `string1` is the same as `string2`
	   - Returns an integer > 0 if `string1` comes after `string2`
	
	`String str1 = "cat";`
	`String str2 = "dog";`
	`str1.compareTo(str2);   // returns -1`
	`str1.compareTo("cat"); // returns 0`
	`str2.compareTo(str1);   // returns 1`

While the `char` data type is not directly tested, it can be useful to understand that the data in the `String` class is an array of characters. Therefore, strings have many analogous tools to arrays. Consider the coding below.

```
String sample = "Sample"

System.out.print(sample.length());
```

The coding will output the number 6. The `length()` method of the `String` class will output the number of characters in the string, much as length is the number of elements in an array. Furthermore, the strings use indices in much the same way. The index of the first character in a string is 0, and the index of the last character is `length() - 1`.

Indices are useful when dealing with substrings, which are portions of strings. The `String` class has two substring methods. One has two integer parameters

```
String substring (int from, int to)
```

This method returns, as a `String` object, the substring starting at index `from` and ending at index `to - 1`. Note that the character at index `to` will NOT be included in the substring. Therefore, using the `String` sample from above, the command

```
System.out.print(sample.substring(1, 4));
```

will display

```
amp
```

Note that

```
System.out.println(sample.substring(1, 7));
```

will result in an `IndexOutOfBoundsException` since the index 7 – 1 = 6 is outside the bounds of the string.

The other substring method works similarly but uses only one parameter, to indicate the starting index. The resulting substring will continue to the end of the string. Therefore, the command

```
System.out.print(sample.substring(1));
```

will display

```
ample
```

This process can be reversed using the `indexOf` method of the `String` class. This method takes a substring as a parameter and returns the first occurrence of that substring. For example,

```
sample.indexOf("amp")
```

will return 1, as the substring first occurs at index 1. However,

```
sample.indexOf("amb")
```

will return –1, as this substring does not occur.

The `String` class is an **immutable** class. In other words, it has no mutator methods. Thus, if you wish to change the contents of a `String` object, the new contents must be reassigned to the variable.

Let's look at the following code:

```
String sample = "Sample";
sample.substring(1, 4);
```

While this code will not cause an error, `"amp"` is not stored, making it rather useless. Instead, we assign the `String` obtained from the substring command back into the original variable so that `sample` will now contain the literal `"amp"`.

```
sample = sample.substring(1, 4);
```

> When using methods of any class, you should remember that the parameters used to call the method must match the data types of the arguments of the defined method.

For example, `substring` is defined as:

```
substring(int beginIndex, int endIndex)
```

Therefore, the following code would cause a compiler error because the parameters are expected to be `int` data types.

```
sample = sample.substring(1.0, 4.0);
```

---

2. Consider the following code segment:

```
String s = "This is the beginning";
String t = s.substring(5);
int n = t.indexOf("the");
```

Which of the following will be the value of n ?

(A) –1
(B) 3
(C) 7
(D) 9
(E) n will have no value because of a run-time error.

Here's How to Crack It

The question asks for the value of n, which is IndexOf "the" in String t, which is a substring of s. First determine t, which is the substring beginning at the index 5 of s. Remember to start with 0 and to count the spaces as characters. Index 0 is 'T', index 1 is 'h', index 2 is 'i', index 3 is 's', and index 4 is the space. Therefore, index 5 is the 'i' at the beginning of "is." There is only one parameter in the call of the substring method, so continue to the end of String s to get that String t is assigned "is the beginning." Now, find the index of "the." Since index 0 is 'i', index 1 is 's', and index 2 is the space, the substring "the" begins at index 3. Therefore, the value of n is 3, which is (B).

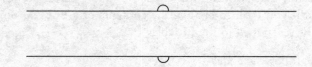

3. Given the following code, what line will cause a compiler error?

```
1   String word = "Sunday Funday Celebration 1.0";
2   word.substring(7);
3   word.substring(3, 6);
4   word.indexOf("day");
5   word.indexOf(1.0);
6   word.compareTo("day");
```

(A) line 2
(B) line 3
(C) line 4
(D) line 5
(E) line 6

Here's How to Crack It

When looking for a compiler error, syntax is usually the culprit. At first glance, it appears all the method names have been spelled correctly, so next move on to the number and data types of the parameters, ensuring they match the expected arguments for each method. The substring method can have 1 or 2 arguments, as long as they represent integers that are valid indices of the string in question. Thus, lines 2 and 3 are fine. The compareTo method compares the string invoking the method to some other string (or String variable) in the parentheses, so line 6 is fine. The indexOf method looks for a specific string. Line 4 uses a string but line 5 attempts to use a double data type. Thus, line 5 (choice D) will cause an error.

KEY TERMS

object
class
immutable

CHAPTER 4 REVIEW DRILL

Answers to the review questions can be found in Chapter 13.

1. Given the following code, which of the following would cause a run-time error?

```
String s1 = "pizza";
```

   (A) `String s2 = s1.substring(0, 2);`
   (B) `String s2 = s1.substring(1, 3);`
   (C) `String s2 = s1.substring(3, 3);`
   (D) `String s2 = s1.substring(2, 3);`
   (E) `String s2 = s1.substring(4, 6);`

2. Given the following code, what is the final value stored in s3?

```
String s1 = "kangaroo";
String s3 = s1.substring(1, 2);
```

   (A) `"k"`
   (B) `"ka"`
   (C) `"a"`
   (D) `"an"`
   (E) `"kn"`

3. Given the following code, what is the final value stored in s4?

```
String s1 = "tango";
String s4 = s1.substring(s1.length() - 2);
```

   (A) `"g"`
   (B) `"go"`
   (C) `"o"`
   (D) `"og"`
   (E) A compiler error will occur.

4. Given that "A" comes before "a" in the dictionary and the following variables have been defined and initialized, which is true?

```
String str1 = "january";
String str2 = "June";
String str3 = "July";
```

(A) str1.compareTo(str3) < 0

(B) str3.compareTo(str2) > 0

(C) str1.compareTo(str2) < 0

(D) str1.compareTo(str2) > 0

(E) str2.compareTo(str3) < 0

5. Given the following code, what is the final value stored in p?

```
1    String word = "boottool";
2    int p = word.indexOf("oo");
3    word.substring(p + 2);
4    p = word.indexOf("oo");
```

(A) 0

(B) 1

(C) 2

(D) 5

(E) 6

Summary

o   When invoking a method, pay close attention to the number and type of parameters the method is expecting, as well as what is being returned.

o   Immutable objects cannot be modified. The variable holding the object can only be assigned a new value.

o   Indices of characters within a string start at `0` and extend to `length() - 1`.

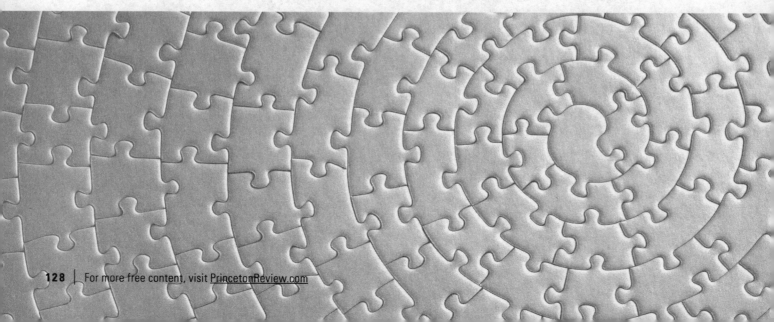

Chapter 5
Boolean Expressions
and if Statements

Now that we have some tools to make the computer accomplish a simple task, let's discuss how to make our programs a little more…interesting.

When you wake up in the morning, some tasks occur automatically, while others may depend on a decision. For example, if your alarm clock sounds at 6:00 A.M.…wait, what if it doesn't? If it sounds at 6:00 A.M., you proceed with your morning rituals; if it does not sound, you wake up late and have to speed up or change, your routine. When you sit down to eat your favorite breakfast cereal… none is left! Now what?

Most, if not all, of the actions we perform depend on decisions. These decisions affect whether or not we perform the actions or even how we perform the actions. Programs possess this exact ability to make decisions and react accordingly. In this way, the programmer can *control the flow* of the program.

THE `if` STATEMENT

If you read the above examples closely, you will literally find the word *if* as a pivotal word in your decisions of what actions to perform next. The reserved word `if` is a **conditional statement** used in Java when programmers want to control the flow of the programs—e.g., if they want Line 2 to occur ONLY if a condition in Line 1 is true. This is referred to as **flow control.**

The syntax of a simple `if` statement is

    if (condition) statement;

Syntax statements in this book will be presented in *pseudocode* in order to illustrate the general form, and then further examples will be given. Pseudocode is not Java code that will compile, but it shows the format of the Java statements that we will write later.

Consider an instance when you are asking a parent whether you can go out to the mall with a friend on Friday night. The (classic) parent response usually looks something like this: *If you clean your room, you can go to the mall on Friday.*

In pseudocode, the parent's response could be written as

    if (you clean your room) go to the mall;

In this example, "you clean your room" is the **condition** of the `if` statement and "go to the mall" is the *statement*. The condition in an `if` statement must have a boolean result. Note that if you do clean your room (true), you will go to the mall; however, if you do not clean your room (false), you will not go to the mall. The `if` statement is written in this way; the programmer is now controlling the flow of the program. Thus, "go to the mall" will occur if the condition is true, but will be skipped if the condition is false. Another popular (pseudocode) way to write this statement is

> if (you clean your room)
>   go to the mall;

This construction simply uses white space to make the code more readable. The AP Exam may present an `if` statement in either of these formats.

Let's try a code example. Consider the following lines from a Java program:

```
int num1 = 4, num2 = 5;
if (num1 == num2)
    System.out.print("The numbers are the same.");
```

Since we have an `if` statement, one of two possibilities can occur based on whether `num1` has the same value as `num2`: (1) the program will display the string literal `"The numbers are the same."` if the condition is true, or (2) the program will not display any output if the condition is false.

Note the use, here, of the **boolean operator ==** (also known as the equality operator); do not confuse this boolean operator with the assignment operator =. A boolean operator asks a question, while an assignment operator executes a command. `num1 = 4` *assigns* the value 4 to the variable `num1`, while `num1 == num2` *determines whether* the two values are equal. The assignment statement produces no other result, while the boolean statement returns a **truth value** based on the comparison.

Wouldn't it be nice if conditions in life depended on just one comparison, as our previous code example did? If we dig a bit deeper into our alarm clock example from before, there are probably a few more decisions that need to be made in order to begin your morning rituals; a few of these decisions might be, "is it a school day?"... "do I feel healthy?"... "is my blanket glued to my mattress, trapping me between them?" Note that each of these questions, regardless of its plausibility, has a true or false (boolean) answer.

If (see how many times we use this word?) we want to incorporate a more complicated condition into our code, we must create a **compound condition**. Compound conditions include at least one boolean operator; all of these and their meanings are as follows:

&&	logical *and*
||	logical *or*
!	logical *not*
==	is equal to
!=	is not equal to

Let's explore how each of these can be incorporated into a program.

Consider a situation in which you need a study break and decide to visit your local bakery for a snack. Your favorite dessert is typically Italian cannoli, but you will also accept an apple turnover. But apple turnovers are somewhat dry, so you will buy one only if they are selling coffee that day.

Since this example is relatively complicated, let's break it into chunks.

> When attacking a complicated programming situation, break it into chunks and tackle each part, one by one.

We will use pseudocode for this example.

Let's outline the conditions presented in this example, in order:

- The bakery has cannoli.

- The bakery has apple turnovers.

- The bakery has coffee.

The complication here is that some of these decisions depend on others. For example, if the bakery DOES have cannoli, then it doesn't matter whether it has apple turnovers. Again, step by step: start with condition (1).

> if (bakery has cannoli) buy dessert;

Now, another decision must be made based on this decision; if the bakery DOES have cannoli, we get our desired dessert. If it does NOT have cannoli, we must try the apple turnover.

if (bakery has cannoli)

> buy dessert; // occurs only if bakery has cannoli

else if (bakery has apple turnovers) // occurs only if bakery has no cannoli

> buy dessert; // occurs only if bakery has apple turnovers

Note the *else* keyword used here. `else` is used if the programmer wants a statement to execute if the condition is false.

It's not that easy, though…we must consider the coffee. Since you will buy an apple turnover only if there is ALSO coffee for sale, the && operator is appropriate here:

1 if (bakery has cannoli)

2   buy dessert; // bakery has cannoli

3 else if (bakery has apple turnovers && bakery has coffee) // no cannoli

4   buy dessert; // bakery has apple turnovers AND coffee

This pseudocode seems to work, but we must check for logical errors.

Using the numbered lines of pseudocode, let's trace the possibilities using a **trace table**.

has cannoli: line 1, condition is true -> line 2, buy dessert

no cannoli, no turnovers, no coffee: line 1, false -> line 3, false -> no dessert

no cannoli, yes turnovers, no coffee: line 1, false -> line 3, false -> no dessert

no cannoli, no turnovers, yes coffee: line 1, false -> line 3, false -> no dessert

no cannoli, yes turnovers, yes coffee: line 1, false -> line 3, true -> line 4, buy dessert

Moral of the story: This bakery had better get itself together.

There is a lot of pseudocode here! Controlling the flow of a program can be difficult and confusing, which is why it is a popular topic on the AP Exam. But it is also important because most programs, like most things we do in life, rely on conditions and react accordingly.

If we look at the bakery example one more time, the line

        buy dessert;

occurs twice. Good programming style attempts to repeat the same lines of code as little as possible, if ever. Therefore, we can rearrange the boolean operators in the following way, creating the same result:

if (bakery has cannoli OR (bakery has apple turnovers AND bakery has coffee))

        buy dessert;

That is a hefty boolean condition; however, it (1) eliminates the repetition of code and (2) provides a more "elegant" programming solution. "Elegant" is a relative term, of course, but the AP Exam often uses this subjective term to write code and to confuse you. Either way, you should be familiar with both ways.

Got a Question?
For answers to test-prep questions for all your tests and additional test-taking tips, subscribe to our YouTube channel at www.youtube.com/ThePrincetonReview

> The AP Exam free-response questions do not require you to write code with "elegance"; in the free-response questions they will accept any code solution as long as it fulfills the specifications of the question.

To make things more complicated (or more life-like), consider a further idea. What if we want to execute *several* commands when a condition is true (or false) instead of just one? For example, using the bakery case, let's say that buying cannoli is so exciting that we must devour it right away. In other words, if the conditions are met for the bakery having cannoli, we want to buy it AND eat it. The pseudocode would look something like:

1 if (bakery has cannoli)

2 {

3   buy dessert; // bakery has cannoli

4   eat dessert;

5 }

6 else if (bakery has apple turnovers && bakery has coffee) // no cannoli

7   buy dessert; // bakery has apple turnovers AND coffee

The { and } symbols in lines 2 and 5 indicate **blocking**, a technique used in flow control statements that allows the programmer to execute a series of commands (instead of just one) when a given condition is satisfied.

Use blocking to execute more than one statement based on a condition.

Here is a summary for evaluating boolean expressions:

- An && (and) expression is true if BOTH A and B are true.
- An || (or) expression is true if EITHER A or B is true, or if they are both true.
- The ! (not) operator simply reverses the truth value of the variable.

The truth value of an expression is often abbreviated to a single letter. Thus, A may represent an expression such as x >= 0. The expression will either be true or false depending on the value of x, but for simplicity's sake we just refer to the whole expression as A.

Consider the following three expressions:

To evaluate A && B

First evaluate A. If A is false then stop: the whole expression is false. Since false && anything is false, there is no need to continue after the first false has been evaluated. This idea is called **short-circuit evaluation**. This idea is used (and tested) frequently. However, if A is true, then you must evaluate B to determine the truth value of the whole expression.

To evaluate A || B

First evaluate A. If A is true then stop: the whole expression is true. Since true || anything is true, there is no need to continue after the first true has been evaluated. This is short-circuit evaluation again. However, if A is false, then you must evaluate B to determine the truth value of the whole expression.

To evaluate !A

First evaluate A. If A is true, the whole expression is false. If A is false, the whole expression is true.

---

1. Consider the following code.

```
int x = 0;
if (x == 0)
    System.out.print("1");
else
    System.out.print("2");
    System.out.print("3");
```

Which of the following best describes the result of executing the code segment?

(A) Since the value of x is 0, the first print statement will be performed, producing 1 as the output.

(B) Since the value of x is 0, the first print statement will be performed, producing 13 as the output.

(C) Since the value of x is 0, the first print statement will be performed, producing 123 as the output.

(D) == is not the correct boolean operator, so a syntax error will be produced by the compiler prior to execution.

(E) == is not the correct boolean operator, so a logical error will be produced by the compiler prior to execution.

Here's How to Crack It

Since x is assigned to 0, the condition of the if statement will be true, so the first print statement will be performed, and the output will be 1. The else statement will then be skipped, so 2 will not be outputted, eliminating (C). The trick here, however, is that the third print statement is NOT part of the else statement since it is not blocked with {}, even though it is (incorrectly) indented. This will output 3, eliminating (A). Furthermore, == is a valid boolean operator so (D) and (E) are clearly incorrect (and a compiler will never produce a logical error). The correct answer is (B).

2. Consider the following boolean expression.

```
(X && !Y) || (!X && Y)
```

Which of the following condition(s) will always cause the expression to evaluate to `true`?

(A) X is `true`
(B) Y is `false`
(C) X and Y are both `true`
(D) X and Y have the same truth values
(E) X and Y have opposite truth values

Here's How to Crack It

The || indicates that either (X && !Y) is true or (!X && Y) is true. Each of these expressions uses a combination of X and Y, thus ruling out (A) and (B). In the first expression, X is true while Y is false. In the second expression, the reverse is true: Y is true and X is false. This eliminates both (C) and (D) because the truth values of X and Y cannot match and certainly cannot be both true. Since X and Y have opposite truth values, (E) is the correct answer.

To sum up, let's create a truth table of various combinations of boolean conditions, simply called A and B, and the truth possibilities based on those combinations. Since there are two variables, there are four possible combinations of their truth values: they are both true, only one of them is true (both ways), and neither is true. These possibilities are shown in the first two columns below. In subsequent columns, the truth values are shown for the boolean statements shown in the first row.

A	B	A && B	A || B	!A	!B	!(A && B)	!A || !B
T	T	T	T	F	F	F	F
T	F	F	T	F	T	T	T
F	T	F	T	T	F	T	T
F	F	F	F	T	T	T	T

Note that the truth values of the last two expressions are identical; these results are an illustration of DeMorgan's Law, which might be thought of as the "distributive property" of boolean expressions. Applying a ! (not) operator to an expression reverses the truth value of each variable and changes an && to an ||, or vice versa. If this law is applied to !(A && B), the result is !A || !B, as shown in the last column.

The intricacies of `if` statements that we just explored will apply to all flow control statements, so understand them here before you move on to the next section.

Augustus De Morgan was a British mathematician and logician in the 19th century. De Morgan's Law can be used to simplify complicated boolean expressions. The basic concept is to know that an expression can be rewritten to simplify and logically hold the same value. For example, logically speaking:

!true = false

!false = true

So the two forms of the law are stated as follows:

1. !(a && b) is equivalent to !a || !b
2. !(a || b) is equivalent to !a && !b

In other words, when you apply a negation to an expression inside parentheses, negate each expression and swap the operator.

Applying De Morgan's Law:

Example 1   `!(x >= 0 && y < 0)`

First, handle the negation and swap && to || `!(x >= 0) || !(y < 0)`

Now simplify each expression.

- If x is NOT >= 0 then it must be < 0
- If y is NOT < 0 then it must be >= 0   `x < 0 || y >= 0`

Example 2   `!(x == 0 && !(y == 0))`

First, handle the negation and swap && to || `!(x == 0) || !!(y == 0)`

Now simplify each expression.

- If x is NOT == 0 then it must be != 0
- Two negations eliminate each other   `x != 0 || y == 0`

3. Consider the following code segment.

```
boolean a = true, b = false;
if (/ * missing code * /)
    System.out.print("Nice job.");
else
    System.out.print("Nicer job.");
```

Which of the following could be used to replace / * missing code * / so that the output of this block of code is "Nicer job."?

I. `a && !b`
II. `!a || b`
III. `!a && b`

(A) I only
(B) I and II only
(C) I and III only
(D) II and III only
(E) I, II, and III

Roman numeral problems are only as annoying as their hardest option; look at the options and do the easiest one first, which is often not I. Then use Process of Elimination.

Here's How to Crack It

Ahh, the dreaded "Roman numeral" problems that the College Board loves to torture us with. If "Nicer job." has to be displayed, then the condition must evaluate to `false`.

Create a truth table.

a	b	a && !b	!a || b	!a && b
true	false	true && !false true && true true	!true || false false || false false	!true && false false && false false

Only the last two expressions result in a false outcome; thus (D) is the correct answer.

4. Suppose p and q are declared as boolean variables and have been initialized to unknown truth values.

What does the following boolean expression evaluate to?

`(!p && !q) || !(p || q)`

(A) The expression always evaluates to `true`.

(B) The expression always evaluates to `false`.

(C) The expression evaluates to `true` whenever p is `false`.

(D) The expression evaluates to `true` whenever q is `false`.

(E) The expression evaluates to `false` whenever p and q have opposite truth values.

Here's How to Crack It

Using De Morgan's Law, we can see that the truth value of the expression on the right, `!(p || q)`, simplifies to the expression on the left, `!p && !q`. Since trial and error is a useful strategy, set up a truth table to evaluate the potential answers.

p	q	!p && !q
T	F	!T && !F F && T F
F	T	!F && !T T && F F
T	T	!T && !T F && F F
F	F	!F && !F T && T T

Eliminate (A) and (B) because sometimes the expression evaluated `true` and sometimes `false`.

Eliminate (C): in the second row, p was `false` but the expression did not evaluate to `true`.

Eliminate (D): in the first row, q was `false` but the expression did not evaluate to `true`.

(E) is correct. Checking the first two rows, p and q had opposite truth values and both rows evaluated to `false`.

KEY TERMS

`if`
conditional statement
flow control
condition
boolean operator (==)
truth value
compound condition
`&&` (logical *and*)
`||` (logical *or*)
`!` (logical *not*)
`==` (is equal to)
`!=` (is not equal to)
trace table
blocking
short-circuit evaluation

CHAPTER 5 REVIEW DRILL

Answers to the review questions can be found in Chapter 13.

1. Consider the following code segment:

```
for (int i = 200; i > 0; i /= 3)
{
    if (i % 2 == 0)
        System.out.print(i + "  ");
}
```

What is the output as a result of executing the code segment?

(A) 200 66 22 7 2
(B) 66 22 7 2
(C) 200 66 22 2
(D) 200 66 22
(E) 7

2. Suppose p and q are declared as boolean variables and have been initialized to unknown truth values.

What does the following boolean expression evaluate to?

```
(p && !q) || (p && q)
```

(A) The expression always evaluates to the same value as p.
(B) The expression always evaluates to the same value as q.
(C) The expression always evaluates to true.
(D) The expression always evaluates to false.
(E) The expression evaluates to true only if p and q have opposite truth values.

Summary

o   Values can be compared to form boolean statements using == (equals), != (not equal), < (less than), <= (less than or equal to), > (greater than), and >= (greater than or equal to).

o   Boolean statements can be combined using && (and), || (or), and ! (not).

o   If statements can be used to allow a command or series of commands to be executed once only if a certain boolean statement is true. Else statements can be used to execute a different command if that condition is not met.

Chapter 6
Iteration

THE `while` STATEMENT

When programmers want a statement (or multiple statements) to occur repeatedly, they have two options: (1) copy and paste the statement as many times as necessary (inefficient and ugly), or (2) write a conditional statement called a **loop** (efficient and "elegant").

> On the AP Exam, you will be expected to know two types of loops:
> `while` and `for`.

The syntax of a **while loop** is as follows:

while (condition) statement;

Note its similarity to the `if` statement. The `while` statement is a loop that does exactly what its name implies: the loop cycles again and again, *while* the condition is true. Consider a paint-soaked paintbrush that you just used to paint your bedroom. Hopefully, you will not store the paintbrush away until it is no longer dirty. A `while` loop that could represent this situation in pseudocode would look like:

1 while (paintbrush is dirty)

2   do not put away paintbrush;

3 put away paintbrush;

Note that if the condition is true (paintbrush is dirty), line 2 will continue to execute, over and over again, until the condition is false (paintbrush is not dirty). Once the condition is false, line 2 is skipped and line 3 is finally executed.

Unfortunately, this loop is fundamentally flawed. Although its logic *seems* to be correct, it is not. Within the statement(s) of a loop, the variable(s) in the condition must be modified so that there is a chance that the truth value of the condition will be changed. How will the paintbrush become less dirty—is this a self-cleaning paintbrush? Probably not. Therefore, the paintbrush will actually remain dirty, and Java will keep executing line 2, forever. When this happens, the programmer has written an **infinite loop**, which is a logical error and is therefore undesirable. Ever have your computer randomly "freeze" in the middle of your work, leaving it unresponsive and causing you to lose that perfectly sculpted digital picture that you just spent an hour perfecting? That is an infinite loop and definitely not desirable.

On the AP Exam, you must trace code in multiple-choice questions and detect infinite loops. In free-response questions, you must write code that is free of infinite loops.

While loops, like if statements, are therefore dependent on their conditions. If a condition is more intricate, as it usually is (Do we put the paintbrush away if it is not dirty, but it is wet? Not dirty but it is still not *clean*?), we can use the techniques outlined in the previous section. Boolean operators are mandatory and compound conditions and/or blocking are appropriate when necessary. A more realistic pseudocode representation of our paintbrush example could be

1   while (paintbrush is dirty && paintbrush is wet) // ! means NOT wet

2   {

3   clean paintbrush; // is it COMPLETELY clean?

4   dry paintbrush; // is it COMPLETELY dry?

5   do not put paintbrush away;

6   }

7   put paintbrush away;

In this example, the paintbrush will continue to be cleaned and dried (and not put away) until it is either NOT dirty or NOT wet, or both, at which point the condition will be false and the paintbrush will be put away. Remember that an && condition is true only if both conditions are true; therefore, if the paintbrush is not dirty but is still wet (or vice versa), it will be put away. Is this the desired result? Who cares?! Reading code is not about logical understanding of a situation; rather, it is about understanding the code and its result.

It is also worth noting here that an && statement may be **short-circuited**. Since both boolean statements on either side of the && must be true, a false result from the first statement will automatically render the condition false. As a result, Java will completely skip the second condition, bypassing the rest of the condition.

1. Consider the following code segment.

```
int val1 = 2, val2 = 22, val3 = 78;
while (val2 % val1 == 0 || val2 % 3 == 0)
{
    val3++;
    val2--;
}
```

What will `val3` contain after the code segment is executed?

(A) 77

(B) 78

(C) 79

(D) 80

(E) None of the above

Here's How to Crack It

When tracing loops, make a table of values for each variable to organize your work.

Tracing the loop is the best way to handle this type of problem. Remember that `%` returns the remainder of the division between the two numbers. In order for the condition to be true, there first must be no remainder when dividing `val2` by `val1`. Since 22/2 = 11, there is no remainder, and the condition will be true (an "or" statement will be true if its first condition is true), and the loop statements will execute, incrementing `val3` to 79 and decrementing `val2` to 21. Since there are no visible statements that would decrement `val3` below 79, we can eliminate (A) and (B). Execution then returns to the condition; this time, we have 21/2, which does yield a remainder, so we check the rest of the division, and 21 `%` 3 does not yield a remainder, so the condition is true overall and the loop statements execute again. We now have `val3` = 80 and `val2` = 20, eliminating (C). Again we try to evaluate the condition, which will be true since 20/2 has no remainder, increasing `val3` to 81 and decreasing `val2` to 19. We can now eliminate (D). By Process of Elimination, (E) is the answer.

THE for STATEMENT

A `for` statement is another type of loop. **For loops** and `while` loops are equally effective in controlling the flow of a program when a statement (or set of statements) is to be executed repeatedly. The syntax is quite different, however:

for (initializer; condition; incrementer) statement;

Since the `for` loop requires more components, it can potentially avoid an infinite loop situation, although there is no guarantee. Let's try a pseudocode example. Consider a younger sibling who is learning to count to 22. The child will start with 1 and continue counting until reaching 22, and then stop. The counting process repeats until the condition is met. Pseudocode may look like:

for (start with 1; not yet reached 22; go to the next number)

count the number;

The execution of a `for` loop is more difficult to understand. Here are the steps:

1. The initializer will occur first, beginning the process.
2. The condition will be checked to make sure it is true.
3. The statement(s) will execute.
4. The incrementer will occur, changing the number.
5. See step (1) and keep repeating (1) to (4), until (2) is false.
6. The loop ends.

A code example of this situation, outputting the current number to the screen, could be:

```
for (int num = 1; num <= 22; num++)

    System.out.println(num);
```

This code will produce each counting number and output it to the screen, each on a separate line. Once again, remember that boolean operators are mandatory and compound conditions and/or blocking are appropriate when necessary.

> **Take Note:** `for` loops and `while` loops are interchangeable, although one method may look more elegant than the other.

Go Online!
For answers to test-prep questions for all your tests and additional test-taking tips, subscribe to our YouTube channel at www.youtube.com/ThePrincetonReview

On the AP Exam, multiple-choice questions may show you several loop structures in both formats and ask you questions that compare the results, so you should practice working between them. On a free-response question that asks you to write a loop, you will be equally correct whether you decide to write a `for` loop or a `while` loop.

For and while statements are loops; if statements are not.

The following two code examples involving loops have identical results:

```
int num = 1;
while (num <= 3)
{
    System.out.println(num);
    num++;
}
System.out.println("Done");

---
for (int num = 1; num <= 3; num++)
    System.out.println(num);
System.out.println("Done");
```

Each set of code is equally effective and equally respected in both the programming world and on the AP Exam. But multiple-choice questions can use either format, or both, so you should familiarize yourself with both.

> `While` loops perform the blocked statement(s) once, and then evaluate the condition to determine whether the loop continues; `for` loops evaluate the condition first and then perform the blocked statement(s) if the condition is initially true.

2. What will be the output when the following code is evaluated?

```
for (int k = 0; k < 3; k++)
{
    for (int j = 1; j < 4; j++)
    {
        System.out.print(j + " ");
    } System.out.println();
}
```

(A) 1 2 3 4
     1 2 3 4
     1 2 3 4

(B) 0 1 2
     0 1 2
     0 1 2
     0 1 2

(C) 1 2 3
     1 2 3
     1 2 3

(D) 1 2 3
     1 2 3
     1 2 3
     1 2 3

(E) 1 2 3 4
     1 2 3 4
     1 2 3 4
     1 2 3 4

Here's How to Crack It

One glance at the condition in the outer `for` loop reveals that it will iterate a total of 3 times (k = 0, 1, and 2). The same will occur for the inner loop (j = 1, 2, and 3). Answers that involve loops of 4 can be eliminated, ruling out every choice except (C). There is no need to continue. However, to see why (C) works, work through the two loops. The outer loop sets k = 0, then j = 1. It prints 1 and a space and then increments j to 2. It prints 2 and a space and then increments j to 3. It prints 3 and a space and then increments j to 4. Since 4 is not less than 4, it terminates the inner loop. `System.out.println()` prints a line break. Then k is incremented to 1. Since k does not affect the output or the value of j, the loop again prints 1 2 3 before printing a line break. The value of k increments to 2, printing a third line of 1 2 3. Finally, k is incremented to 3, which terminates the outer loop, leaving (C) as the result of the print. The answer is (C).

3. Consider the following code fragments. Assume someNum has been correctly defined and initialized as a positive integer.

```
I.    int i;
      for (i = 0; i < someNum; i++)
      {
              someNum--;
      }
II.   int i;
      for (i = 1; i < someNum - 1; i++)
      {
              someNum -= 1;
      }
III.  int i = 0;
      while (i < someNum)
      {
              i++;
              someNum--;
      }
```

All the following statements are true about these code fragments EXCEPT

(A) The `for` loops in I and II do not have the same number of iterations.
(B) The `for` loops in I and III have the same number of iterations.
(C) The value of `someNum` after the execution of I and III is the same.
(D) The value of `i` after the execution of II and III is the same.
(E) I, II, and III produce identical results in `someNum`.

Here's How to Crack It

For an EXCEPT question, cross out the original question and rewrite it without the negative so that it's easier to keep your task in mind. In this case, rewrite the question to say, "Which is false?"

The loops in I and III accomplish the same task. In each loop, `i` is initialized to 0, executes while `i < someNum`, then increments `i` by 1 and decrements `someNum` by 1 within the loop. Thus, any choice indicating the iterations or results of loops I and III are the same should be eliminated, because these conditions are true. Eliminate (B) and (C).

The loop in II will have fewer iterations than the loops in I and III (initializing `i` to 1 instead of 0, ending the loop when `i < someNum - 1` instead of `i < someNum`). As a result, the loop in II will be executed fewer times. Choice (A), indicating that I and II do not have the same number of iterations, is true, so eliminate it.

For the remaining choices, let `someNum` equal a positive (nonzero) value (not too big)…let's try 5.

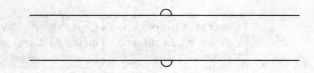

I	i	SomeNum
	0	5
	1	4
	2	3
	3	2

II	i	SomeNum	SomeNum − 1
	1	5	4
	2	4	3
	3	3	2

III	i	SomeNum
	0	5
	1	4
	2	3
	3	2

From these trace tables of values, you can see that the final value of `i` after the execution of II and III is 3, demonstrating that (D) is true. Eliminate (D). The value of `someNum` is only the same for I and III, so (E) is false, and is the correct choice.

———————◯———————

———————◯———————

4. Consider the following code segment:

```
for (int i = 1; i < 100; i = i * 2)
{
    if (i / 50 == 0)
        System.out.print(i + " ");
}
```

What is printed as a result of executing the code segment?

(A) 1 2 4 8 16 32 64
(B) 1 2 4 8 16 32
(C) 2 4 8 16 32 64
(D) 2 4 8 16 32
(E) 4 8 16 32 64

Here's How to Crack It

The initial condition for execution to enter the loop is i = 1. Since 1/50 = 0 in integer division, 1 will be displayed, so eliminate (C), (D), and (E). The difference between (A) and (B) is the 64 at the end, so let's skip the output in between and focus on the 64. If i = 64, the if statement will be false, and thus 64 will not be printed. Therefore, the answer is (B).

Synopsis

Here's a quick synopsis of which concepts from the chapters so far you can expect to find on the exam, and which you won't.

Don't Forget This!
Head over to your free online student tools to download a printable version of this chart and other important pages from within this book.

	Concepts Covered on the AP Computer Science A Exam	Concepts Not Covered on the AP Computer Science A Exam
Primitives	• `int` • `double` • `boolean`	• `short` • `long` • `byte` • `char` • `float`
Increment/Decrement Operators	• `x++` • `x--`	• `++x` • `--x`
Logical Operators	• `==` • `!=` • `<` • `<=` • `>` • `>=` • `&&` • `||` • `!`	• `&` • `|` • `^` • `<<` • `>>` • `>>>`
Conditional Statements	• `if/else` • `for` • `while`	• `do/while` • `switch` • plain and labeled `break` • `continue`
Miscellaneous		• `?:` (ternary operator) • User input • JavaDoc comments

KEY TERMS

loop
while loop
infinite loop
short-circuited
for loop

CHAPTER 6 REVIEW DRILL

Answers to the review questions can be found in Chapter 13.

1. Consider the following output:

```
0   1
0   2   4
0   3   6   9
0   4   8   12   16
```

Which of the following code segments will produce this output?

(A)
```java
for (int x = 1; x < 5; x++)
{
    for (int z = 0; z <= x; z++)
    {
        System.out.print(x * z + "   ");
    }
    System.out.println(" ");
}
```

(B)
```java
for (int x = 1; x <= 5; x++)
{
    for (int z = 0; z < x; z++)
    {
        System.out.print(x * z + "   ");
    }
    System.out.println(" ");
}
```

(C)
```java
for (int x = 1; x < 5; x++)
{
    for (int z = 0; z <= 4; z++)
    {
        System.out.print(x * z + "   ");
    }
    System.out.println(" ");
}
```

(D)
```java
for (int x = 1; x < 5; x++)
{
    for (int z = 0; z <= 4; z += 2)
    {
        System.out.print(x * z + "   ");
    }
    System.out.println(" ");
}
```

(E)
```java
for (int x = 1; x <= 5; x++)
{
    for (int z = 0; z <= x; z++)
    {
        System.out.print(x * z + "   ");
    }
    System.out.println(" ");
}
```

2. The speed limit of a stretch of highway is 55 miles per hour (mph). The highway patrol issues speeding tickets to any- one caught going faster than 55 miles per hour. The fine for speeding is based on the following scale:

Speed	Fine
greater than 55 mph but less than 65 mph	$100
greater than or equal to 65 mph but less than 75 mph	$150
greater than or equal to 75 mph	$300

If the value of the `int` variable `speed` is the speed of a driver who was pulled over for going faster than 55 mph, which of the following code segments will assign the correct value to the `int` variable `fine`?

I.
```
if (speed >= 75)
   fine = 300;
if (speed >= 65 && speed < 75)
   fine = 150;
if (speed > 55 && speed < 65)
   fine = 100;
```

II.
```
if (speed >= 75)
   fine = 300;
if (65 <= speed < 75)
   fine = 150;
if (55 < speed < 65)
   fine = 100;
```

III.
```
if (speed >= 75)
   fine = 300;
if (speed >= 65)
   fine = 150;
if (speed > 55)
   fine = 100;
```

(A) I only
(B) II only
(C) III only
(D) I and II
(E) I and III

3. Consider the following code segment:

```
int x = 10;
int y = 3;
boolean b = true;
for (int i = 0, i < 15; i += 5)
{
    x = x + y;
    b = (x % y == 2);
    if (!b)
    {
        y++;
        i += 5;
    }
}
```

What is the value of x after the code segment executes?

(A) 10
(B) 15
(C) 17
(D) 22
(E) 25

4. In the following statement, a and b are boolean variables:

```
boolean c = (a && b) || !(a || b);
```

Under what conditions will the value of c be true?

(A) Only when the value of a is different than the value of b
(B) Only when the value of a is the same as the value of b
(C) Only when a and b are both true
(D) Only when a and b are both false
(E) The value of c will be true for all values of a and b.

5. Consider the following code segment:

```
while ((x > y) || y >= z)
{
    System.out.print("*");
}
```

In the code segment above, x, y, and z are variables of type int. Which of the following must be true after the code segment has executed?

(A) x > y || y >= z
(B) x <= y || y > z
(C) x > y && y >= z
(D) x < y && y <= z
(E) x <= y && y < z

6. Consider the following code segment:

```
int a = 0;
for (int i = 0; i < 10; i++)
{
    for (int k = 0; k <= 5; k++)
    {
        for (int z = 1; z <= 16; z = z * 2)
        {
            a++;
        }
    }
}
```

What is the value of a after the code segment executes?

(A) 31
(B) 180
(C) 200
(D) 300
(E) 400

7. Consider the following code segment:

```
int x = 10;
int y = x / 3;
int z = x % 2;
x++;
System.out.println(x)
```

What is printed as a result of executing the code segment above?

(A) 2
(B) 4
(C) 10
(D) 11
(E) 15

8. Consider the following code segment:

```
int a = 10;
double b = 3.7;
int c = 4;
int x = (int) (a + b);
double y = (double) a / c;
double z = (double) (a / c);
double w = x + y + z;
System.out.println(w);
```

What is printed as a result of evaluating the code above?

(A) 10

(B) 15

(C) 15.5

(D) 17

(E) 17.5

9. Consider the following code segments:

I.
```
int x = 10;
int y = 20;
int z = 0;
if (x < y && 10 < y/z)
{
        System.out.println("Homer");
}
else
{
        System.out.println("Bart");
}
```

II.
```
int x = 10;
int y = 20;
int z = 0;
if (x > y && 10 < y/z)
        System.out.println("Homer");
else
  System.out.println("Bart");
```

III.
```
int x = 10;
int y = 20;
int z = 0;
if (x < y || 10 < y/z)
        System.out.println("Homer");
else
        System.out.println("Bart");
```

Which of the code segments above will run without error?

(A) I only
(B) II only
(C) III only
(D) II and III
(E) I, II, and III

Summary

- `While` statements can be used to cause a command or series of commands to execute while a certain boolean statement is true.

- `For` statements are similar to `while` statements but include the initialization of a variable before the looping and a modification of the variable after each execution of the loop.

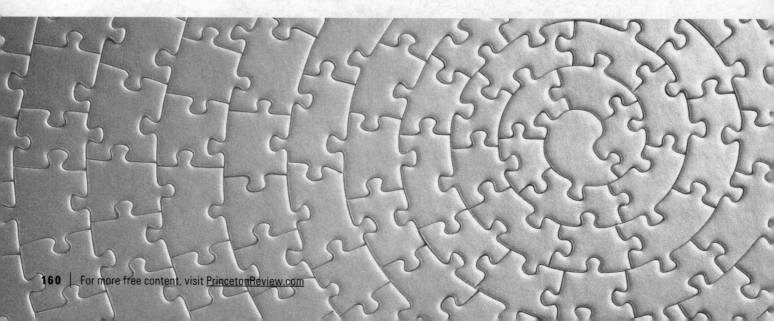

Chapter 7
Writing Classes

When a group of statements, including control structures, is assembled into a single unit, the unit is called a **class**. Similar to a word processing document or a picture file stored on your computer, a class is stored on your computer in a file. Unlike a word processing document, however, a class must follow specific rules in order to conform to Java and, as a result, to be understood by the compiler. Remember that your brilliantly constructed program is useless unless the compiler can successfully translate it into machine code.

DESIGN & STRUCTURE

The structure of a class, at this level anyway, is straightforward. Take all of the statements you've written before this chapter, put curly brackets around them, kind of like a huge block, name it, and save it. The naming conventions for a class are similar to those of a variable, except that they should begin with a capital letter. The name of the class should reference the purpose or function of the class. For example, a class that calculates a GPA might be called `GPA` or `GradePointAvg`. The way we declare a class in Java is using the header:

```
public class GradePointAvg
{
    // statements not shown
}
```

Well, Actually...
This is a convention but not a rule. You can have all of the code on a single line if your heart so desires, but that would be very bad form.

Note that the statements in the class reside at least one tab stop across the page. If the programmer would like to use more white space within the structures of the class, they will be tabbed further into the page:

```
public class GradePointAvg
{
    // other code and variable declarations not shown

    while (/* condition not shown */)
    {
        // looped statements not shown
    }
}
```

Typically, variable declarations are placed into the code first, right after the class header, as a sort of "setup" for the rest of the class. Of course, this is not a rule, but it is a good guideline in order to keep your code readable.

On the AP Exam, your code must be readable (not just legible), quickly and easily.

This class would be saved to the computer as GradePointAvg.java; the .java extension helps the compiler to recognize the file as containing Java code. If the code compiles (there are no syntax errors), the compiler will create another file in the same folder called GradePointAvg.class; this file is unreadable to the programmer because it is encoded in machine language. The computer, however, uses this file to execute the program. The .java file is called the **source code** of the program, since it defines the program's actions and functions.

Remember that classes are executed top-down—i.e., line 1 followed by line 2, etc. If programmers want to alter top-down execution, they must use a flow control structure, as we studied before.

---

1. Which of the following class declarations would cause a compile-time error? Assume the rest of the code compiles as intended.

    (A) `public class Calculus`
    (B) `public class apCalculus`
    (C) `public class APCalculus`
    (D) `public class 4APCalculus`
    (E) `public class APCalculus extends Calculus`

Here's How to Crack It

Choices (A) and (C) follow the format as discussed above. The naming convention for class names is that they *should* begin with a capital letter; however, this is not required by the compiler, so (B) does not cause an error. Be careful when the College Board uses programming techniques in the answer choices that you may not know; in this case, the *extends* keyword comes in a later section of this book, so you may choose it here if you have never seen it. However, it is used properly, so (E) does not cause an error, but you would not be able to use POE if you didn't know this. The real problem with (D) is that it begins with a numerical character, which is not allowed in a class name. The answer is (D).

POE is a great tool, but it isn't always enough on an AP Exam. Know your stuff!

METHODS

Picture a Java class as a closet, with essentially limitless possibilities. If you were to declare a single shelf to hold, say, board game boxes…that would be a great way to organize your collection of games, toys, and other sophisticated possessions.

A class is organized in this way using methods.

> A **method** is a group of code that performs a specific task.

Although a class can simply contain a list of commands, any program that accomplishes a task could easily balloon to 100 lines of code or more. Instead of writing a class that contains a giant list of disorganized code, writing separate methods for each small task (within the overarching task) is an excellent way to make your code more readable. In addition, method-based classes enable easier flow control.

To understand this concept, let's break down a bright, sunny Saturday in the middle of the summer (don't worry—you will make it). Perhaps some of the activities you would do might include getting out of bed (obviously), eating breakfast, taking a shower, getting ready for the beach, driving to the beach, enjoying the beach, and eating lunch. Each of these activities has its own specific components; for example, part of eating breakfast includes drinking orange juice and taking a daily vitamin supplement. The pseudocode of a program that simulates this Saturday's activities might look like this:

```
public class Saturday1
{
        hear alarm;
        turn off alarm;
        get out of bed;
        make breakfast;
        eat breakfast; ...
```

You get the idea…. A long list of commands that occur top-down. Now, consider each of these general activities as a separate grouping of smaller activities, called a method. Each small activity will be defined later, but your Saturday class would look much cleaner:

```
public class Saturday2
{
        wake up method;  // includes alarm
        eat breakfast method; // includes preparation, OJ,
                              // vitamin, etc.
        take a shower method; // includes preparing for the
                              // shower, etc.
        beach method;  // includes prep for the beach, driving
                       // to the beach, etc.
        eat lunch method;
}
```

The result is a cleaner, more structured class that is easier to read. A class that is created to control a larger program, such as Saturday2, is called a **driver class** because it *drives* the program through its general structure which will, in turn, execute the smaller commands. Note also that if, for some reason, the programmer wanted the simulation to take a shower before eating breakfast, the two lines would be switched in Saturday2 and the job would be done. Performing the same change in Saturday1 would involve switching multiple lines of code. Even more poignant would be a simulation that repeats method calls, such as one that represents your extra-hungry older brother, who eats breakfast twice. The driver would simply call the breakfast method twice (or use a loop to call it more than twice) and the job would be completed.

An **object class** is a different kind of class which houses the "guts" of the methods that the driver class calls. As you understand this setup, you will see that your driver classes begin to shorten, while your object classes expand. For example, the driver of a car truly performs a relatively small set of actions in order to drive the car: start the engine, buckle the seatbelt, check the mirrors, accelerate, brake, steer. The driver does not actually understand (nor does he need to) exactly how these operations work: he just does them. How does the accelerator pedal *actually* make the car move more quickly? Doesn't matter. The "driver" just operates the pedal, and the rest happens under the hood. The object class is the "under the hood" class. It defines all of the aspects of an object; more specifically, it defines what the object *has* and what the object *does*.

The object class referred to in this section should not be confused with the Object class in the Java language which is the Parent class of all classes. The Object class is part of the Java.lang package. Every class in Java is a descendent of this class. Every class in Java inherits the methods of the Object class.

> For the AP Exam, you must be able to write, troubleshoot, and understand object AND driver classes, as well as understand how they interact. These skills are HUGE in the free-response questions!

Back to the breakfast example....

Pseudocode for the object class might look something like this:

```
public class Saturday3
{
    wake up(...)
    {
        hear alarm;
        turn off alarm;
        get out of bed;
    }


    breakfast(...)
    {
        make breakfast;
        eat breakfast;
    }
}
```

Since our object class could be used for any day of the week, not just Saturday, `BeachDay` might be a more appropriate name for this class. The driver class from before, which executes a series of actions for this particular day, might be called `Saturday`.

———————◦———————

2. Which of the following statements would best describe an efficient design to represent a pair of sunglasses?

(A) Three classes: `UnfoldGlasses`, `CleanGlasses`, and `WearGlasses`

(B) An `UnfoldGlasses` class with methods `CleanGlasses` and `WearGlasses`

(C) A `PairOfSunglasses` class with boolean variables `unfolded`, `cleaned`, and `worn`

(D) A `PairOfSunglasses` class with methods that `unfold`, `clean`, and `wear` the objects in the class

(E) A `UseSunglasses` class with statements that `unfold`, `clean`, and `wear` the sunglasses

Here's How to Crack It

Design questions must account for efficiency and "beauty," since the former isn't formally tested on the multiple-choice questions and the latter is not tested in the free-response questions. Since a pair of sunglasses is best represented as an object—it has attributes and can do tasks—eliminate (A), (B), and (E). Since the tasks of a `PairOfSunglasses` object would best be performed in a method, (C) is not appropriate. The answer is (D).

———————◦———————

One more item that needs to be mentioned…do you see how each method in the object class has a "title," or **header**? The header is used to indicate the overall function of a method.

This is a Java book, right? So let's look at some Java. These two classes are designed to simulate a phone downloading and opening a new app.

```java
1 import Phone;
2 public class UsePhoneApp
3 {
4   public UsePhoneApp()  // just do it, we'll explain later
5   {
6       Phone myPhone = new Phone();
7       myPhone.downloadApp();
8       myPhone.openApp();
9       myPhone.closeApp();
10  }
11 }
```

```java
1 public class Phone
2 {
3   private boolean hasApp;
4   public Phone()
5   {
6       hasApp = false;
7   }
8   public void downloadApp()
9   {
10      hasApp = true;
11  }
12
13  public void closeApp()  // closes the app
14  {
15      if (hasApp)
16          System.out.println ("App is closed.");
17  }
18
19  public void openApp()  // opens the app
20  {
21      if (hasApp)
22          System.out.println ("App is running...");
23  }
24 }
```

OUTPUT:

```
App is running...
App is closed.
```

There are many components in this program; first, note that we now have two classes that make up a single program. In isolation, neither of these classes would produce a useful result. The UsePhoneApp class would not compile because the compiler does not understand the methods if they are not present (compiler: what does openApp mean?); the Phone class would compile but would not actually perform any actions without UsePhoneApp (compiler: when do I openApp, and on which phone?). In order to allow the UsePhoneApp class to access the Phone class, the line

```java
import Phone;
```

must be used at the top of the file above the class declaration.

Lines 4–7 in `Phone` make up a special kind of method called a **constructor**. An object must be constructed before it can perform any actions, just as a car must be built before it can be driven. Line 6 in `UsePhoneApp` calls this constructor method, which "builds" the `Phone` object; this command must occur before the non-constructor methods are called; otherwise, the compiler will return an error. Imagine someone pressing an imaginary accelerator pedal and trying to drive somewhere without a car. Interesting, but not possible.

Line 3 of `Phone` defines whether the `Phone` has an app (true) or does not (false). This is the sole attribute of a `Phone` object in our program; more complex programs may have dozens or even hundreds of attributes (a phone, in reality, has many more attributes, such as a screen, volume buttons, etc.). The programmer should write these attributes, called **instance variables** or **fields**. Following the data fields is the constructor, as we stated before, and then a series of methods that control what the `Phone` *can do*.

> An object class defines what an object HAS and DOES.

A method has several components. The method header is built in a very specific way; its syntax is as follows:

visibility returnType methodName (param1, param2, …)

The visibility of a method can be public or private, depending on the situation (more on this later). The **return type** identifies what type of data, if any, will be returned from the method after its commands are executed. The name of a method, similar to the name of a variable, should be an intuitive name that summarizes the function of the method; it should conform to the same specifications as a variable name (begin with a lowercase letter, etc.). The **parameters**, which are optional, are the data that the method needs in order to perform its job.

In our previous example, the method header for `closeApp` was:

```
public void closeApp()
```

This is functional, but it is also relatively simple for the example. Its visibility is public, its return type is void (there is no information returned), and it does not have parameters. A more realistic method to close an app on a phone might require information regarding when it should be closed, and might return data, such as whether or not it was closed successfully. Thus, the revised method header might look like

```
public boolean closeApp (int minutes)
```

Note that the single parameter, minutes, is defined with its type. Since minutes will be a temporary variable that exists only during the execution of this method, it must be defined as new, right in the header. A method can have any number of parameters, depending on the programmer's design decisions for the program.

A method must begin with a header containing a visibility modifier (private or public), a return type or void if no information will be returned, and a method name. Parameter(s) are optional, depending on the method's requirements to perform its task.

The ultimate purpose of a method is to perform some sort of task with respect to the object. Note that `openApp()` and `closeApp()` simply access the data field `hasApp` and react accordingly; i.e., the message is displayed only if the value `hasApp` is `true`. `downloadApp()` is more profound, in a way; rather than simply accessing data, it actually changes the value of a data field—in this case, updates `hasApp` to `true` once the "app" is "downloaded." As a result, it is common in Java to label methods like `openApp()` and `closeApp()` as **accessor methods** and to label methods like `downloadApp()` as **mutator methods**.

We have used an analogy to a car several times already in this chapter, but it's a great way to understand these concepts. When you want to start a car, you have to go through a series of steps. Since all of those steps perform, ultimately, a single action—the car starting—a method would be a great way to keep the "car starting" commands in a single, convenient unit. As a programmer, you would have to decide what data the method would need in order to work (parameter(s)) and what data, if any, the method would return. Does the car need a key to start? A password code? Does the brake pedal have to be depressed? This information would all be accepted through parameters. Should the method return whether the car has started? How long it took to start? A code that represents whether it needs an oil change? These are all examples of possible return data.

In some cases, there may be a situation in which the car can be started multiple ways—for example, the owner has a push-button starter and a remote starter. The designer could write two `startCar` methods (or three, or four…), each one performing the same task but requiring different information (parameters) to do the task. This process is called **overloading** and can be accomplished by writing two or more methods with identical names but different types and/or numbers of parameters.

Precondition

A **precondition** is a comment that is intended to inform the user more about the condition of the method and guarantees it to be true.

On the AP Exam, the precondition shows up as a comment immediately above the method. It is the responsibility of the program that calls the method not to pass parameters that violate the precondition.

```
/***   preconditon—a and b are positive integers

*/

public int sum(int a, int b)

{

}
```

Postcondition

A **postcondition** is a condition that must always be true just after the execution of some section of code or after an operation in a formal specification.

On the AP Exam, the postcondition is written as a comment either before or within the method as shown in the example below. The method designer is responsible for making sure that these conditions are met.

```
public int sum100(int a, int b)

{

<code>

// postcondition—returns 100, if sum is greater than 100, or the value of sum

if (sum < 100)

        return sum;

else

        return 100;}
```

> A method may accept any number of parameters, but may return only one data value or object.

As a final example for this section, consider a programmer who is trying to write an object class that represents a book (like this book, only arbitrarily more interesting). Some of the data the programmer may consider are:

- What does a book *have*? A cover, pages, words, …

- What can a book *do*? It can be read, be skimmed, be put away, …

From this information, the programmer can begin to write the object class. The programmer must first determine which item(s) are relevant to the situation so as to keep the object class as efficient as possible. For example, if the programmer is designing a book to be used as a paperweight, it is probably not important to discuss how many words are in the book, so that data field would not be incorporated into the program. Likewise, if the programmer is not a student studying a ridiculous number of books in a short amount of time (sound familiar?), then it may not be relevant to have a method that skims the book, rather than reading it closely. The class will then be built based on these decisions.

As you can see, the **planning** of the program is just as important as, if not more important than, the actual writing of the program. In some classes, your teacher may remind you to "write an outline" or "write a first draft" before you compose the final product, and you might skip that step and go right to the end unit and still be successful. For programming at any profound level, which is required in this course to some extent, planning is essential in order for your program to work well and in order to increase your efficiency. Remember, the AP Exam is strictly timed.

> The AP Exam tests the planning of a class by presenting a *lengthy* description of the requirements, along with other interacting classes in the project.

COMPOSITION

Now that we have written classes to run a program, we must get these classes to interact correctly in order to create a functioning program. We have the driver, we have the car, now we need to put the driver into the car to eagerly drive to the AP Computer Science A Exam on exam day.

The driver and object classes must reside in the same folder on the computer. If you are using an interactive development environment (as opposed to command line programming), you often have to create a "Project" or some similar structure in the software that will hold all of the program's files in one place. Remember that the driver depends on the object class in order to compile, and the object class depends on the driver to make it actually do anything.

Consider a program that will take "flower" objects and "plant" them into a garden. The flower objects might be outlined in an object class called `Flower`. One class will perform the planting, so we can call it `MakeGarden`.

Suppose the `Flower` constructor method has the following header:

```
public Flower(int xPosition, int yPosition)
```

where `xPosition` and `yPosition` are the horizontal and vertical coordinates in the garden, respectively, where the flower object will be planted. Our driver would have to first "create" the flowers, and then plant them accordingly.

> In order to create an object, we must instantiate the object using its corresponding class.

Each time we instantiate a flower object, we must assign it an **object reference variable**; as the fancy name implies, this is just a variable name. Some lines in `MakeGarden` might look like this:

```
Flower f1 = new Flower(2, 1);
Flower f2 = new Flower(2, 2);
Flower f3 = new Flower(2, 3);
```

These lines will instantiate three different flower objects, each containing its own instance data. `f1`, `f2`, and `f3` are used to distinguish between the objects. We can then use these objects to perform methods. Consider a plant method in the `Flower` class; this method would "plant" the flower and might have the following header:

```
public void plant()
```

In `MakeGarden`, we must invoke this method through the objects. Let's say we want to plant only `f1` and `f3`, but not `f2`. We would add the following lines:

```
f1.plant();
f3.plant();
```

Now let's say the plant method, instead, returns whether or not the plant was successfully planted. This altered plant method might have the header:

```
public boolean plant()
```

Now we can use the returned data to output an appropriate message in the driver:

```
if (f1.plant())

  System.out.print("Planted successfully.");

else

  System.out.print("There was a problem.");
```

Because we are invoking `f1.plant`, `f1` should be planted as requested. Since the plant method returns a boolean value, we can place `f1.plant` in the context of an `if` statement (it produces a truth value so it is considered a condition), and now it also functions as part of a control structure. Awesome!

Let's add to our garden situation. As you know, other items can appear in a garden besides flowers. Plants, bushes, and weeds can appear in gardens. Each of these items would probably have its own object class, since their instance data and methods would be different from those of flowers. For example, a flower has flower petals, while a plant does not; weeds often grow on their own without water, whereas most flowers and plants do not. Regardless, separate object classes can be created for each of these object types, and the driver can hold them all together, as long as they are all stored in the same folder on the computer.

Assuming each of these object classes has been created and each corresponding object class has a plant method as outlined above, `MakeGarden` might include these lines:

```
Flower f1 = new Flower();
Flower f2 = new Flower();
Plant p1 = new Plant();
Plant p2 = new Plant();
Weed w1 = new Weed();
if (f1.plant())
System.out.println("Planted successfully");
if (f2.plant())
System.out.println("Planted successfully");
if (p1.plant())
System.out.println("Planted successfully");
if (w1.plant())
System.out.println("You have a weed.");
```

Note that `MakeGarden` does not instantiate any `Bush` objects, and does not attempt to plant the `p2` object. Note also that we cannot see the entire class! The programmer has the task of deciding which objects to instantiate of which type, when and whether to use them, and how to use them appropriately, based on their class specifications. Still think you can go directly to the final draft?

Let's add another layer. Programmers often recognize that an object is actually composed of many smaller, or more basic, objects. If you think about a flower, it actually has several parts, each of which *has* data and *does* particular actions. As a result, we could write object classes for, say, the stalk and the root system. The `Stalk` class and the `RootSystem` class, then, would reside as attributes of each flower. Their classes, again, must be placed in the same folder as the rest of the program's classes. The programmer can then set up the `Flower` class as follows:

```
public class Flower
{
    // other data not shown
    private Stalk st;
    private RootSystem rootSys;

    public Flower()
    {
        st = new Stalk();
        rootSys = new RootSystem();
        // other commands not shown
    }

    // other methods not shown
}
```

This means that every `Flower` object *has* a stalk and a root system. The `Flower` class, then, is called an **aggregate class** because it is made up of, among other data, instances of other classes. This setup is more realistic; think of any object in your room, and you can probably see pretty quickly that it is made of smaller objects, each with its own data and methods. A laptop computer has keys, ports, and a screen, which can all be considered objects because they *have* stuff and *do* stuff. A dresser has drawers, but we can go even deeper…a drawer has walls and a floor and can be opened or closed…the floor of a drawer has a shape and is made of a certain material and can be broken if the drawer is overstuffed…you get the idea. Luckily, as programmers, we get to decide the detail of the object classes, and the answer typically lies in the desired function of the program, as we stated before. Do you *really* need to know what material the floor of the drawer is made of? Most people do not, although a furniture retailer might. Again, it all depends on the application.

> The free-response questions on the AP Exam will present some sort of context and will often tell you exactly what class(es) and/or method(s) to write, so they don't get a wild variety of solutions from test takers around the world.

Otherwise, they could literally be forced to read thousands of completely different approaches to a given task. This fact is not good for our creativity, but it's great for scoring a 5; save your creative juices for those extra college classes you can take when you AP out of CS!

Use class `Chair` and method `sitOnChair` to answer Questions 3 and 4.

```
public class Chair
{
    private int numberOfLegs = 4;
    private boolean padded;

    public Chair(boolean soft)
    {
        if (soft) padded = true;
        else padded = false;
    }
}

public void sitOnChair( )
{
        <implementation not shown>
}
```

3. The method `sitOnChair` belongs to another class and is supposed to allow the user to "sit" on a `Chair` if the chair is padded. Which of the following code segments could be used to replace <implementation not shown> so that `sitOnChair` will work as intended?

    I.   `Chair c = new Chair(true);`
         `c.sit();`
    II. `Chair c = new Chair(true);`
    III. `Chair c = new Chair(true);`
         `if (c.padded) System.out.print("You are sitting.");`

    (A) I only
    (B) II only
    (C) III only
    (D) I, II, and III
    (E) None

Here's How to Crack It

Since (A), (B), and (C) each allow the selection of only one option, we must check all of them. We've got this! Remember that an object must (1) be instantiated in the executing class, and (2) be associated only with methods that are defined in its class. Option I instantiates a `Chair` correctly, but then attempts to invoke a `sit()` method, which is not defined in `Chair` (or anywhere); eliminate (A) and (D). Option II correctly instantiates a `Chair` but does not attempt to "sit"; eliminate (B). Option III is incorrect because it also attempts to access `padded`, which is private data in `Chair` and therefore not accessible directly; eliminate (C). Since no option is valid, (E) is the answer.

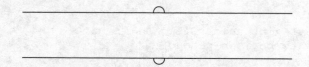

4. Which of the following modifications, if any, would help to make the `Chair` class MOST useful to the `sitOnChair` method, based on the task attempted in Question 3?

   (A) Adding an accessor method that returns the value of `numberOfLegs`
   (B) Adding an accessor method that returns the value of `padded`
   (C) Adding a mutator method that changes the value of `numberOfLegs`
   (D) Adding a mutator method that changes the value of `padded`
   (E) Adding an accessor method that returns the values of both `numberOfLegs` and `padded`

Here's How to Crack It

The situation presented in Question 4 requires the information regarding whether the chair is padded. `numberOfLegs` is irrelevant here, regardless of your personal bias; eliminate (A), (C), and (E). Since the `padded` attribute of the chair does not have to be changed, eliminate (D). The answer is (B).

Do not get "emotional" about a situation presented; follow the specifications carefully and don't assume the programmer's intentions.

5. Consider the following method:

```
public int halfRoot(int n)
{
        return Math.sqrt(n) / 2;
}
```

Which of the following method calls would cause a run-time error?

(A) `halfRoot(-2)`
(B) `halfRoot(3)`
(C) `halfRoot((int)2.0)`
(D) `halfRoot(3.0)`
(E) None will cause a run-time error.

Here's How to Crack It

The heading of the method definition requires an integer parameter. Choices (A) and (B) directly use integers. Even though (A) uses a negative, this doesn't result in an error. In math class, this doesn't result in a real number. However, in Java, this results in `NaN`. While this is not a preferred result, it is not strictly an error. Choice (C) casts a double as an integer and thus would compile and run correctly. Choice (D) gives a double parameter when an integer is required. This would cause an error. While this error would appear to cause an `IllegalArgumentException`, it will instead cause a compile-time error rather than a run-time error. The `IllegalArgumentException` would arise only if the programmer deliberately throws it, if an argument is legal in Java terms but inappropriate for the purposes of the program. (For example, a program intended to find the factorial of an integer might be designed to throw an `IllegalArgumentException` if it takes a negative parameter.) Since none of these results in a run-time error, the answer is (E).

REFERENCES

All of this data that is passed from driver classes to object classes and vice versa creates a complicated operation that's occurring behind the scenes. Consider this example: the programmer decides to write a class that represents a vinyl record player (for music), or "turntable." The driver class will then operate the turntable, turning it on and off, controlling it, and putting on/taking off the desired record. For this program, we will have three classes: `Turntable` and `Record`, which represent each of these objects, and `PlayRecord`, which will be the driver that relates them.

In theory, we would have to perform the following steps in the driver:

- create (instantiate) a turntable object
- create one or more record objects
- place the record onto the turntable
- switch on the turntable

Some code from these classes might look like this:

```
public class Record
{
    // data not shown

    public Record()
    // constructor code and other methods not shown
}
public class Turntable
{
    private Record r;
    // other data not shown

    public Turntable(Record r1)
    {
        r = r1;
        // other statements not shown
    }

    // other methods not shown
}
public class PlayRecord
{
    public static void play()
    {
        Record rec = new Record();
        Turntable tt = new Turntable(rec);
        // other statements not shown
    }

    // other methods not shown
}
```

In this example, note that `Turntable` is an aggregate class, since part of its instance data involves another object. More importantly for this section, note the instantiation of the `Record` object in the driver, the "passing" of that object to the `Turntable` class, and the assignment `r = r1`. When an object is passed to another class and, as a result, received through a parameter, a **reference** is created to the object. Think of it this way: if you just picked up your favorite Taylor Swift record (you know you love her) and wanted to play it, you wouldn't need two copies of the album. In the same way, we don't have to create a copy of the `Record` object; we just need to create another reference to it in order for it to be used in the `Turntable` class. This is the only way the `Turntable` class can use this record, since it was instantiated in the driver. The record can then be used in context (in this case, assigned to the data field `r`) and then the reference will disappear once the constructor is over. Since the reference is not an actual copy of the object, its life is not affected.

Another way to think of references is to think of superheroes and their secret identities. Clark Kent was just another name for the person; he was still Superman the whole time. They were the same guy with the same superpowers, the same attributes, and the same ability to perform cool superhero actions. Therefore, "Clark Kent" was simply a reference created to *refer* to the same guy.

It is extremely important to know that primitive data is not copied by reference; it is copied by value itself.

> When received as a **parameter**, primitive data is actually copied, while object data will simply receive **a** new reference to the object itself. Primitives are copied by value; objects are copied by reference.

Here's the really confusing part—or maybe not really. If a copy of a primitive data value is made, then the two copies (the original and the new one) exist exclusively. Therefore, if you change the value of one copy, the other is not affected. On the other hand, if a new reference to an object is made, then a modification of the object through the reference will be reflected by all references. Again, the superhero example: if Superman dyed his hair blond because it was all the rage, then both Clark Kent and Superman will have blond hair. They are two names that reference the same guy, so any changes will be reflected in all the references. If we suddenly decided that Superman/Clark Kent should be called "Blue Guy" instead of either of these two names, we are still referring to the same guy; he now has three *aliases* instead of two.

This is important for understanding object equality. Two objects are considered equivalent only if they are, in fact, the same object. In the superhero example above, Clark Kent is equal to Superman since they are the exact same person.

Now imagine that Superman has an identical twin brother named Duperman with alter ego Klarc Tenk. Since Duperman and Klarc Tenk are the same person, Duperman is equal to Klarc Tenk. Therefore, in Java `Duperman == Klarc Tenk` is true. However, even though they are identical twins, Superman and Duperman are different people. Therefore, Superman is not equal to Duperman. In Java, Superman and Duperman could be identified as identical twins using the `equals` method of the Object class. The `equals` method takes an Object parameter and returns `true` if and only if the two object have identical data, regardless of whether they are the same object. While the boolean statement `Superman == Duperman` is false, the statement `Superman.equals(Duperman)` is true.

`this` Keyword

Sometimes to call a method it may be necessary for the calling object to be able to refer to itself. When an object calls a method, an implicit reference is assigned to the calling object. The name of this implicit reference is `this`. The keyword `this` is a reference to the current calling object and may be used as an object variable. For example:

```
this.mySize
```

Use the following incomplete class declarations to answer Questions 6 and 7.

```
public class Number
{
    private int value;

    public Number(int someNum)
    {
        if (someNum >= 0)
            value = someNum;
    }

    public int changeVal(int newVal)
    {
        /* missing code */
    }

    public int getValue()
    {
        return value;
    }
}

public class NumChanger
{
    public void change()
    {
        Number n1 = new Number(5);
        Number n2 = new Number(5);
        int sum1 = n1.getValue() + n2.getValue();
        int oldn1Val = n1.changeValue(10);
        n2 = n1;
        int sum2 = n1.getValue() + n2.getValue();
        System.out.print(sum1 + " " + sum2);
    }

    //other methods not shown
}
```

6. The `changeVal` method in `Number` should reassign `value` to be the value taken as the parameter and return the original value. Which of the following code segments should be used to replace / * *missing code* * / so that `changeVal` will work as intended?

   (A) ```
   value = newVal;
   return value;
   ```
   (B) ```
   value = newVal;
   return 5;
   ```
   (C) ```
   int oldVal = value
   value = newVal;
   ```
   (D) ```
   int oldVal = value;
   value = newVal;
   return value;
   ```
   (E) ```
   int oldVal = value;
   value = newVal;
   return oldVal;
   ```

## Here's How to Crack It

To accomplish the task, two events must occur: `value` must be reset to the parameter value and the old value must be returned. Choice (C) does not attempt to return any value, so it cannot be correct. The remaining answer choices attempt to accomplish both events; however, if `value` is reset and its new value is returned, the second event is done incorrectly. The original value must be stored, so eliminate (A) and (B). Choice (D) stores the old value but returns the new value, since it has been reassigned to `newVal`, so it is not correct. Since (E) stores the old value, reassigns `value`, and returns the old value, (E) is the answer.

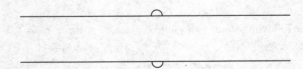

7. What will be printed as a result of executing the `change` method? Assume `changeVal` in the `Number` class works as intended.

   (A) 5 5
   (B) 5 10
   (C) 10 5
   (D) 10 10
   (E) None of these
   ```

Here's How to Crack It

The College Board *loves* to write multiple-choice questions with confusing object references like this. Remember that setting an object "equal" to another object merely means that the two identifiers reference the same object (like Superman and Clark Kent). sum1 will be assigned to the sum of the values of n1 and n2, which is 10, so the first number printed will be 10. Eliminate (A) and (B). oldn1Val is irrelevant here but n1.changeValue(10) makes n1 have a value of 10. n2 = n1 will now have variable n2 reference the same object as n1, which has a value of 10 from the previous statement. Therefore, n1.getValue and n2.getValue will both return 10, so sum2 will be 10 + 10 = 20. As a result, the second number printed will be 20 and (C) and (D) can be eliminated. The answer is (E).

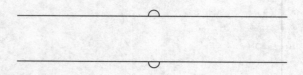

8. The following method is intended to output "Strings match." if the two strings contain identical data and otherwise print "Strings do not match."

```
public void match(String s, String t)
{
    if (/* missing code */)
        System.out.println("Strings match.");
    else
        System.out.println("Strings do not match.");
}
```

Which of the following statements could replace /* *missing code* */ to allow the method to work as intended?

I.   s.compareTo(t) == 0
II. compareTo(s, t) == 0
III. s == t

(A) I only
(B) III only
(C) I and III only
(D) II and III only
(E) I, II, and III

Here's How to Crack It

This question is testing the proper way to determine whether two strings contain identical data. Go through each statement one at a time. Statement I uses the `compareTo` method. The `compareTo` method of the `String` class takes on another string as a parameter and returns an `int`. If the two strings contain identical data, the return is `0`. (Note that this can also be applied to other objects, as the `Object` class has a similar `compareTo` method.) Therefore, Statement I will cause the method to work as intended. Eliminate (B) and (D), which do not include Statement I. Statement II also uses `compareTo`. However, since `compareTo` is a non-static method of the `String` class, it must be invoked by a `String` object. Also, the `compareTo` method takes only one parameter. Therefore, Statement II would cause a compile-time error. Eliminate (E), which contains it. Now, look at Statement III. When the `==` operator is applied to objects, the result is `true` only if the references are the same. If two objects have different references but contain identical data, the return will be `false`. The above method needs for the return to be `true` in this case. Although this does not cause a compile-time or run-time error, the method will not work as intended. Therefore, eliminate (C), which contains Statement III. The answer is (A).

STATIC MODIFIER

The **static** keyword can appear in two contexts at this level. A **static variable** is an attribute that is shared among all instances of a class. When the value of this variable is changed, the alteration is reflected by all of the objects instantiated through that class. A classic example of a static variable is the high score list on a video game. Consider the video game Tetris. After you launch the game, you start a new game and play until you lose... then, since you are obsessed with Tetris, you start over. If each game that you play is considered an object of the same class, a static variable might be the high score. Every time you start (or instantiate) a new game, the high score remains the same as it was when it was initially set. Once a new high score is set, every new game will reflect the new high score, rendering the old high score non-existent (or second best, etc.).

In an object class, a static variable is declared with the rest of the instance data at the top of the class, preceded by the keyword static. Static variables are often used for identification numbers or for counters. Consider this short program:

```
public class Box
{
    private static int boxNumber = 0;
    // other data fields not shown

    public Box()
    {
        boxNumber++;
        // other statements not shown
    }
}
public class BoxCreator
{
    public BoxCreator()
    {
        Box box1 = new Box();
        Box box2 = new Box();
    }
}
```

As each Box object is instantiated in BoxCreator, the static variable in the Box class will be updated. That way, the next time a box is created, the box number value is incremented for all box objects. The static variable is not an attribute of each individual box; rather, it is a shared value among all boxes. Contrast this set-up with a non-static declaration of boxNumber; every time a box is instantiated, its boxNumber would start as 0 and then be incremented, making every box have the same boxNumber value of 1.

In order to show that this structure is actually working, let's create an accessor method to let the driver "see," or access, the value of boxNumber. This method is necessary for this result since boxNumber has been declared private. A non-constructor method that is designed to access and/or modify a static variable is a **static method** and must be declared as such. To add this functionality and test it, here are our new object and driver classes:

```
public class Box
{
    private static int boxNumber = 0;
    // other data fields not shown

    public Box()
    {
        boxNumber++;
        // other statements not shown
    }

    static public int getBoxNum()
    {
        return boxNumber;
    }
}
public class BoxCreator
{
    public BoxCreator()
    {
        Box box1 = new Box();
        Box box2 = new Box();
        System.out.print (Box.getBoxNum() + " boxes
        created so far.");
    }
}
```

Notice the method call from BoxCreator does not use an object reference variable; rather, the class is used directly. Since static variables are shared among all instances, the programmer needs to access static methods (and therefore, static variables) through the class itself.

9. A class called ComputerMouse has a static variable connector and a static method getConnector. Which of the following statements is true based on this information?

(A) In order to invoke getConnector, a new ComputerMouse object does not need to be instantiated; getConnector must be called directly through the object class.

(B) In order to invoke getConnector, a new ComputerMouse object must be instantiated and then getConnector must be called through that object.

(C) Since connector is declared static, getConnector is shared among all objects in the program.

(D) Since connector is declared static, ComputerMouse objects cannot be mutated during execution.

(E) Since connector is declared static, all of the methods in ComputerMouse must also be declared static.

Here's How to Crack It

The AP Exam tests rote knowledge as well as reasoning; this question can be answered correctly only if you know how static works. A static method must be called directly through the class, so (A) looks good so far, but eliminate (B). Choice (C) is incorrect because getConnector will be shared among all ComputerMouse objects, not all objects in general. Choice (D) is nonsensical since static is not related to mutations. Choice (E) would be correct if it said "all of the methods in ComputerMouse that access or mutate connector...." The answer is (A).

Do not be afraid of answer choices (A) or (E).

KEY TERMS

class
source code
method
driver class
object class
header
constructor
instance variables (fields)
return type
parameters
accessor methods
mutator methods
overloading
precondition
postcondition
planning
object reference variable
aggregate class
reference
static
static variable
static method

CHAPTER 7 REVIEW DRILL

Answers to the review questions can be found in Chapter 13.

1. A development team is building an online bookstore that customers can use to order books. Information about inventory and customer orders is kept in a database. Code must be developed that will store and retrieve data from the database. The development team decides to put the database code in separate classes from the rest of the program. Which of the following would be an advantage of this plan?

   I.   The database access code could be reused in other applications that also need to access the database.
   II. The database access code can be tested independently. It will be possible to test the database access code before the interface is developed.
   III. A team of programmers can be assigned to work just on the code that is used to access the database. The programmers can work independently from other programmers, such as those who develop the user interface.

   (A) I only
   (B) II only
   (C) III only
   (D) I and II only
   (E) I, II, and III

2. In Java, instance fields (also known as instance variables) and methods can be designated public or private. Which of the following best characterizes the designation that should be used?

   (A) Instance fields and methods should always be public. This makes it easier for client programs to access data fields and use the methods of the class.
   (B) Instance fields should be either public or private, depending on whether or not it is beneficial for client programs to access them directly. All methods should be public. A private method is useless because a client program can't access it.
   (C) Keep all methods and instance fields private. This enforces encapsulation.
   (D) Instance fields should always be private so that clients can't directly access them. Methods can be either public or private.
   (E) All instance fields should be public so client programs can access them, and all methods should be private.

3. Which of the following are signs of a well-designed program?

   I.   Clients know how data is stored in the class.
   II. Classes and methods can be tested independently.
   III. The implementation of a method can be changed without changing the programs that use the method.

   (A) I only
   (B) II only
   (C) II and III
   (D) I and II
   (E) I, II, and III

4. Consider the following classes:

```
public class Sample
{
    public void writeMe(Object obj)
    {
        System.out.println("object");
    }
    public void writeMe(String s)
    {
        System.out.println("string");
    }
}
```

What will be the result of executing the following?

```
Sample s = new Sample( );
String tmp = new String("hi");
s.writeMe(tmp);
```

(A) Compile-time error

(B) "hi"

(C) "object"

(D) "string"

(E) Run-time error

5. Consider the following class:

```
public class Sample
{
    public void writeMe(Object obj)
    {
        System.out.println("object");
    }
    public void writeMe(String s)
    {
        System.out.println("string");
    }
}
```

What will be the result of executing the following?

```
Sample s = new Sample( );
Object tmp = new Object( );
s.writeMe(tmp);
```

(A) Compile-time error

(B) "string"

(C) "object"

(D) "tmp"

(E) Run-time error

6. Consider the following class:

```
public class Sample
{
    public void writeMe(Object obj)
    {
        System.out.println("object");
    }
    public void writeMe(String s)
    {
        System.out.println("string");
    }
}
```

What will be the result of executing the following?

```
Sample s = new Sample( );
Object tmp = new String("hi");
s.writeMe(tmp);
```

(A) Compile-time error
(B) "hi"
(C) "object"
(D) "string"
(E) Run-time error

7. Consider the following class:

```
public class Sample
{
    public void writeMe(Object obj)
    {
        System.out.println("object");
    }
    public void writeMe(String s)
    {
        System.out.println("string");
    }
}
```

What will be the result of executing the following?

```
Sample s = new Sample( );
String tmp = new Object( );
s.writeMe(tmp);
```

(A) Compile-time error
(B) "hi"
(C) "object"
(D) "string"
(E) Run-time error

8. Consider the following class:

```
public class Sample
{
    int val = 0;
}
```

Is `val` an attribute or a method?

(A) Neither: a compile-time error occurs when we try to execute this code.
(B) `val` is an attribute.
(C) `val` is a method.
(D) `val` is both an attribute and a method.
(E) Neither: `val` is a primitive.

9. Consider the following class:

```
public class Sample
{
    public String writeMe(String s)
    {
        System.out.println("object");
    }
    public void writeMe(String s)
    {
        System.out.println("string");
    }
}
```

What will be the result of executing the following?

```
Sample s = new Sample( );
Object tmp = new Object( );
s.writeMe(tmp);
```

(A) Compile-time error
(B) `"hi"`
(C) `"object"`
(D) `"string"`
(E) Run-time error

Summary

o   A class is an assembly of control statements. A class can contain methods and variables. On the AP Computer Science A Exam, all class methods are public and can be accessed by other classes, and all class variables are private and cannot be accessed by other classes.

o   A method is a group of code that performs a specific task.

o   A method can take any number of variables of specified types as input parameters and return one value of a specified type as output. However, methods need not take any parameters or return any values.

o   An object is a specific instance of a class. An object is identified by one or more references.

o   For static class, all methods and variables must be called by the class name. For non-static variables, all methods and variables must be called by object references.

o   On the AP Computer Science A Exam, all object variables are private and thus cannot be called by other classes, and all object methods are public and thus can be called by other classes.

Chapter 8
Array

An **array** is a data structure that makes handling like (as in similar) data easier. An array may store primitive data values or object references. Each piece of data is called an element, and an index is used to specify the location of the element we wish to access. Imagine an airline that sells more than a thousand tickets a day. If we want to process that data to accumulate statistics on origin cities or prices of tickets, each ticket could be instantiated separately, using a unique object reference variable for each ticket. Imagine then invoking a method on each of those object reference variables. By putting the data into an array, and then using a loop to access each element of the array, the code becomes much more efficient.

PRIMITIVES & OBJECTS

In order to instantiate an array, you must first decide what type of data will be contained in the array. Suppose you are creating a program that will keep track of your test grades in your APCS class. Since grades are usually represented by integer numbers, you will create an array of integers. The syntax for instantiating an array of integers is

```
int [] <identifier> = new int [<array size>];
```

This format is used if you do not yet know the values that will be stored in the array. Alternatively, if you already know the data values, you can instantiate the array using an **initializer list**:

```
int [] <identifier> = {<data1>, <data2>, …, <data n>};
```

Notice the square brackets—these are standard symbols in Java that signify an array is present. The braces (curly brackets) indicate an initializer list. In the beginning of the semester, you do not yet know your grades. In order to create an array called `testGrades` that will eventually store your first five test grades, you could write a statement like this:

```
int [] testGrades = new int[5];
```

This array object will store your test grades and keep them organized using **index numbers** (or locations). Just as your tests might be organized as Chapter 1 Test, Chapter 2 Test, etc., your data will be accessed through the identifier of the array and index number. The tricky part is that array indices start with the number 0 instead of 1. Therefore, if your Chapter 1 Test is the first test score in the array, it will be stored at index 0. If the first test you have in APCS reviews a previous course, then it's Chapter 0 instead of Chapter 1. If you did not instantiate the array using an initializer list, then you will assign data values using the index numbers; you will do the same process to access the data regardless of how you created the array. For example, if you scored a 95 on the first test, you could write the line:

```
testGrades[0] = 95;
```

Creating an array with five scores at once might look like this,

```
int [ ] testScores = {90, 80, 100, 85, 92};
```

Let's say that, after looking over your test, you realize that your teacher made a grading error, and you actually scored a 98. You can either increment the data value or reassign it:

```
testGrades[0] += 3;
```

or

```
testGrades[0] = 98;
```

You can also perform any integer operation and also display the value to the user with that same format.

Let's step it up a notch. Suppose, after all five tests are complete, your teacher feels that the scores are too high and decides to deflate the grades. (You didn't think this book would discuss only *nice* teachers, did you?) The programmer can use a simple loop in order to **traverse** the array and change every value accordingly, rather than writing 5 separate lines. Since an array's length is well-defined, a `for` loop is usually appropriate for arrays. Provided that the array is **full**, meaning all 5 values are assigned, the following loop will traverse the array and subtract 2 points from every grade:

```
for (int index = 0; index < 5; index++)
    testGrades[index] -= 2;
```

Note the values of `index` will be 0, 1, 2, 3, and 4, even though it stores five elements. Since the index numbers start at 0, you must stop traversing the array before index 5, or your will receive an **ArrayIndexOutOfBoundsException** and the program execution will be interrupted. Free-Response Questions on the AP Exam often test your ability to write code that does not go out of bounds.

An array also has a constant value returned by <arrayName>.`length` that will return the number of elements in the array. The above loop could be written:

```
for (int index = 0; index < testgrades.length; index++)
    testGrades(index) -= 2;
```

Much better than writing multiple lines, right? The loop systematically changes every value in the array. We are just scratching the surface of the usefulness of arrays, and we have already improved our coding efficiency.

> The AP Exam will require you to create, traverse, and modify arrays; free-response questions are loaded with arrays and will specifically state that an array must be created. The Course and Exam Description states, specifically, that free-response questions 3 and 4 have to do with arrays (3 is Array/ `ArrayList` and 4 is 2D Array).

The programmer needs to ensure that every element of the array contains a meaningful value, or undesired results may occur. In an array of integers, the value of an unassigned element will default to 0. Consider the following code segment that will calculate the average of your five test grades:

```
int total = 0, len = testGrades.length;
double average;
for (int index = 0; index < len; index++)
    total += testGrades[index];
average = (double) total / len;
```

If all five of your test grades are stored in the array, this code segment will calculate the average correctly. If you did not input one of your scores, however, it will remain stored as 0 and incorrectly drag down your average, which is (definitely) an undesired result.

There is an alternative way to execute the previous code segment. This involves using an **enhanced-for loop**. An enhanced-for loop can be used to automatically go through each element of an array.

```
int total = 0, len = testGrades.length;
double average;
for (int grade : testGrades)
    total += grade;
average = (double) total / len;
```

In the enhanced-for statement, a previously declared array or an ArrayList (more on ArrayLists later) must be referenced after the colon. The loop will iterate for each element in the list, from index 0 to index length - 1. However, no variable is used to refer to the current index. Instead, the element located at the current index is stored as the variable declared before the colon. (The variable must be of the same type stored in the array.) Therefore, the enhanced-for loop above stores each element—one at a time in increasing order by index—of the array testGrades as grade. It then adds grade to total. Thus, the enhanced-for loop has the same functionality as the for loop in the previous example. The benefits of the enhanced-for loop are that it will not cause an ArrayIndexOutOfBoundsException when traversing an array and that it shortens the notation of the element considerably.

---

1. Consider the following code segment:

```
final int[] a1 = {1, 2};
int[] b1 = {3, 4};
a1 = b1;
System.out.print(a1[1]);
```

What is printed as a result of executing the code segment?

(A) 2

(B) 3

(C) 4

(D) Nothing is printed due to a compile-time error.

(E) Nothing is printed due to a run-time error.

Here's How to Crack It

This is an easy one if you know your compiler. Since a1 is declared final, its reference cannot be changed. In the third line, the programmer attempts to change a1 to reference the second array, which is not allowed. The answer is (D).

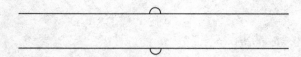

2. Consider the following code segment:

```
int [] a = {1, 2, 3};
int [] b = {4, 5, 6};
a = b;
for (int i = 0; i < b.length; i++)
{
        b[i] *= 2;
}
System.out.println(a[0]);
```

What is printed as a result of executing the code segment?

(A) 1
(B) 4
(C) 8
(D) Nothing is printed due to a compile-time error.
(E) Nothing is printed due to a run-time error.

Here's How to Crack It

Remember arrays are objects. An assignment statement assigns the object reference so both a and b are pointing to the same array. If b is changed, a is changed as well. After the loop, b = {8, 10, 12}. Since a is pointing at b, a[0] = 8.

3. Consider the following incomplete method:

```
public static int mod3(int[] a)
{
    int count = 0;

        // code not shown

    return count;
}
```

Method `Mod3` is intended to return the number of integers in the array that are evenly divisible by 3. Which of the following code segments could be used to replace *// code not shown* so that `Mod3` will work as intended?

I.
```
for (int i = 0; i < a.length; i++)
{
    if (i % 3 == 0)
    {
        count++;
    }
}
```

II.
```
for (int i = 0; i < a.length; i++)
 {
    if (a[i] % 3 == 0)
    {
        count++;
    }
}
```

III.
```
int i = 0;
while (a[i] % 3 == 0)
{
    count++;
    i++;
}
```

(A) I only
(B) II only
(C) III only
(D) I and II
(E) II and III

Here's How to Crack It

The `while` loop in option III has two problems. It will either only execute while encountering an integer in the array that is divisible by 3 (possibly stopping before traversing the entire array) or, if all the entries in the array are divisible by 3, it will go beyond the bounds of the array, causing a run-time error. This eliminates (C) and (E). Option I checks whether the index (or location) is divisible by 3. This eliminates (A) and (D). Option II checks whether the element is divisible by 3. Choice (B) is the answer.

Since objects are typically used to represent real-world phenomena, arrays are also commonly used to organize and manipulate objects. Suppose you have an object class that represents a pair of sneakers. The following code segment would instantiate an array that would store five of these objects:

```
PairOfSneakers collection[] = new PairOfSneakers[5];
```

Since each element is an object, however, the default value for each object is **null**. Since null is not a valid object, operations performed on null will result in a **NullPointerException**, another error that will halt the execution of the program. Without getting into the specifics of the PairOfSneakers class, a statement that could assign an instantiated pair of sneakers called jordans is

```
collection[0] = jordans;
```

Now, suppose PairOfSneakers has a tie() method that will tie the laces of the corresponding pair of sneakers; i.e., jordans.tie() will tie that pair. At this point, index 0 references the jordans object—remember that objects are referenced, not copied—but elements at indices 1–4 are null. To avoid a NullPointerException, check that each object is not equal to null.

```
for (int i = 0; i < collection.length; i++)
    if (collection[i] != null)
      collection[i].tie();
```

> When using a loop to traverse an array of objects, be sure the array is full to avoid undesired results.

4. Consider the following code:

```
public int[] someMethod (int[] array, int value)
{
    for (int i = 1, i < array.length - 1; i++)
        array[i - 1] += value;
    return array;
}
```

Which of the following statements is true about the method someMethod?

(A) The method will not return the first value in the array.
(B) The method will return the last value in the array.
(C) The method will cause a run-time error.
(D) The method will not increment the first element of the array by value.
(E) The method will not increment the last element of the array by value.

Here's How to Crack It

The return value must be an array of integers, so eliminate (A) and (B) because `array[i]` is an integer. The loop traverses the array without going out of bounds and no illegal operations are performed on the elements in the array. There will be no run-time error, so eliminate (C). The `array[0]` is incremented because the variable `i` is initialized with a starting value of 1. The method then increments `array[i - 1]`. By the same reasoning, the last element will not be incremented. The final value of `i` will be `array.length - 1`, which is normally used to find the last index within the array, but the assignment statement uses `i - 1` (which is now representing the second to the last index of the array). The loop terminates without accessing the last element, so the answer is (E).

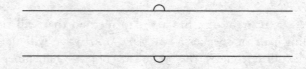

5. Consider the following code:

```
public int[] mystery (int[] array, int num)
{
    for(int i = 1, i < array.length - 1; i++)
        array[i] = 0;
    return array[0];
}
```

There is an error in method `mystery`. Which of the following modifications is needed to correct the compiler error?

(A) Change `int[] array` in the method header parameter to `int[] numbers`.
(B) Change `array.length - 1` to `array.length` in the loop statement.
(C) Change `array[i] = 0;` to `array[i - 1] = 0;`.
(D) Change the `return` statement to `return array;`.
(E) None of these choices will make the method compile.

Here's How to Crack It

The problem with this method is the discrepancy between the return type `int[]` and the type of value that the method attempts to return, `int`; (D) addresses this issue. Choice (A) will have no effect on the outcome of the method because `array` is simply the name of the variable that references the array. Choices (B) and (C), although valid, will not correct the return type issue. Choice (E) is incorrect, again, because the return type issue is keeping the method from compiling. The answer is (D).

SEARCHES

Once data is stored in an array, a common task is to methodically search the array for given data. Consider a line of parked cars in the "Curbside To Go" section of your local chain restaurant. When the server is taking the food to a particular car, she must use a given attribute—say, a license plate number—to find the correct car. Once the correct car is found, the server can deliver the food and then go back inside for the next order, beginning the process all over again…and again…and again.

This same technique is used for searching an array. In APCS, we have two methods of searching arrays, the **sequential search** and the **binary search**. Since each of these search methods uses a distinct formula to search through the arrays, they are commonly referred to as **search algorithms**.

The chain restaurant example given above is an example of a sequential search. All of the cars are "lined up" and the server begins with the first car, checking its license plate number against the one she is looking for. If it's correct, the server delivers the food and returns. If not, she moves on to the next car and repeats the process; this all ends when either (1) the correct car is found or (2) the correct car is not in the line at all. This sequential process works just fine, although it can be very tedious. The server would have to do much more work if the desired car were at the end of the line, as opposed to at the beginning. Remember, we are programming a computer; the server cannot simply "look" at all of the plates at once, as we might in real life. The computer does not know how to "look," unless we know how to write the program that enables it!

A code segment that performs a linear search for a number `target` in an array of integers `nums` might look like this:

```
for (int i = 0; i < nums.length; i++)
    if (nums[i] == target)
        System.out.print("Found at " + i);
```

This segment will correctly traverse the array, searching for `target`, starting with index `0` and continuing to index `length - 1`, as desired. Remember that `nums.length` is the size of the array and therefore `nums[length]` would be out of bounds. When `target` is found, the print statement displays its index number. This process will continue until the end of the array is reached. Note that if `target` is never found, there will be no output.

When writing algorithms that traverse arrays, programmers often implement the enhanced-`for` loop, which is designed specifically for traversing entire arrays. In cases in which traversing the *entire* array is not the intent or would cause a run-time error, the enhanced-`for` loop should not be used. Assuming `nums` from the previous example would not cause such a problem, the same code segment can be written as an enhanced-`for` loop structure like this:

```
int loc = 0;
for (int num : nums)
{
    if (num == target)
      System.out.print("found at " + loc);
    i++;
}
```

Each time the loop iterates, `num` will be assigned the value of the next element in the array. This structure automatically ensures that the loop does not go out of bounds. In this case, `loc` is the location or index in which the target is found.

> It is important to note that the enhanced-`for` loop provides a variable that will hold each element of the array. It will NOT automatically provide the index of that element. You will have to add code to keep track of the index if you want to use it. If the variable created to hold each element is modified in any way, the array will **not** be modified.

A binary search is much more efficient; think of it as a "divide-and-conquer" mechanism. Instead of our restaurant server starting with the beginning of the line of cars, she will start with the middle car. Depending on whether the license plate is "greater" or "less" than the car she is looking for, the server will move in the appropriate direction.

There is a huge obstacle with binary searches, however, or at least, for us with our current level of Java knowledge: these searches work only when there is an inherent order in the data. Suppose the top 21 students in the senior class are lined up in a row. You are looking for a student within that top 21 named Kathy, whom you have never met, and you are not sure where she is in the line. If the students are not lined up in a particular order, a sequential search is your only option, and you might need all 21 tries to find her if she is the last person in the lineup. If they are sorted in alphabetical order by first name, though, you can divide and conquer. Go to the middle person and find out her name…if her name is Sara, you would move toward the front of the line and ignore the back. You then perform the same process, asking the name of the person halfway between the front of the line and Sara, and then ignore the appropriate side. Within a few tries, you will have Kathy.

Here is a code example of how a binary search might look for array `nums` when searching for `target`, assuming `nums` is sorted:

```
int front = 0, back = nums.length - 1, middle = 0;
boolean isFound = false;
while((front <= back) && (!isFound))
{
    middle = (front + back) / 2;
    if (nums[middle] < target)
    {
        front = middle + 1;
    }
    else if(nums[middle] > target)
    {
        back = middle - 1;
    }
    else
    {
        isFound = true;
    }
}

if (isFound)
{
    System.out.println("Found at " + middle);
}
else
{
    System.out.println("Target Not Found");
}
```

On the AP Exam, you will not be required to *write* a search algorithm; however, you will be required to *recognize* a search algorithm and trace it, which can be done the easy way if you understand the algorithm, or the hard way by actually tracing the code, step by step. Try to identify the key characteristics of each search; for example, the "sum divided by 2" line is a good indicator of a binary search. The enhanced-`for` loop will traverse the entire array, which may indicate a sequential search.

6. Which of the following statements is true regarding search algorithms?

(A) Searching for a Twix in a row of unsorted candy is most efficient using a sequential search.

(B) Searching for a Twix in a row of unsorted candy is most efficient using a binary search.

(C) Searching for a Twix in a row of sorted candy is most efficient using a sequential search.

(D) Searching for a Twix in a row of sorted candy is most efficient using a binary search.

(E) None of these

Here's How to Crack It

Searching is usually more efficient using a binary search, provided the array is sorted—eliminate (B), since you can't use a binary search on unsorted data. However, a binary search will require more than one comparison if the target is not in the middle, whereas a linear search (also called a sequential search) will need only one comparison if the target is first in line. Therefore, each of the three situations presented in (A), (C), and (D) could be the most efficient, depending on the position of the Twix. The answer is (E).

7. Assuming `target` is in array a, which of the following methods will correctly return the index of `target` in sorted array a?

I.
```java
public int findTarget(int[] a, int target)
{
for (int x = 0; x < a.length; x++)
  if (a[x] == target)
     return x;
}
```

II.
```java
public int findTarget(int[] a, int target)
{
  int k = 0;
  for (int x : a)
  {
      if (x == target)
          return k;
      k++;
  }
  return -1;
```

III.
```java
public int findTarget(int[] a, int target)
{
  int f = 0, h = a.length, g = 0;
for (int i = 0; i < h; i++)
{
      g = (f + h)/2;
      if (a[g] < target)
            f = g + 1;
      else if (a[g] > target)
            h = g - 1;
}
if (a[g] == target)
      return g;
return -1;
}
```

(A) I only
(B) II only
(C) I and II only
(D) II and III only
(E) I, II, and III

Here's How to Crack It

Notice that Options I and II look like linear searches, while III looks like a binary search. Option I will not compile because a non-void method must return data. An `if` statement without an `else` implies data may not be returned—even though the assumption states that will not occur—so the compiler will stop here. Eliminate (A), (C), and (E). Both (B) and (D) include Option II, so it must be correct; skip to Option III. Note that the variables are a bit confusing—but front/middle/back correspond to f/g/h, so they are in alphabetical order. Option III is a nice binary search, and it avoids the return problem in Option I by returning −1 if `target` is not found, a common practice when writing search algorithms. Therefore, Options II and III are correct and (D) is the answer.

Read Carefully!
This question is about a sorted array! Be sure you read the entire question carefully before you dive in.

SORTS

Probably the most useful algorithms you will learn in AP Computer Science A are **sorting algorithms**—but they are also probably the most difficult to understand. If you've been keeping up within this book so far, then you have a good start.

As the name implies, sorting algorithms will take data in an array and rearrange it into a particular order. We already know that this technique is useful if we want to search for data using the binary search algorithm. But imagine this automated process in real life: a process that automatically sorts the cups in your cabinet in height order, a process that automatically takes your homework assignments and arranges them in time order, and a process that sorts your to-do list in priority order. Needless to say: sorting algorithms are extremely powerful.

The **selection sort** is the first sorting algorithm we will discuss, and one of the three sorting algorithms you need to know for the AP Exam. This is a search-and-swap algorithm, so you should remember that the selection sort searches and swaps. Similar to a sequential search, the sort will first traverse the array for the lowest value. Once it finds the lowest value, it will swap its position in the array with the data at index 0. Now the first element is sorted. The process then repeats for index 1. The rest of the array will be searched for the lowest value and swapped with the data at index 1. Note that if the lowest value is already in position, it will stay there.

Consider the array below. We would like to sort this array from least to greatest.

8	6	10	2	4

Our strategy will be to first find the smallest element in the array and put it in the first position. We will then find the smallest of the remaining elements and put that in the second position. We will continue to do this until the array is ordered.

We can start by looking at every element in the array (starting with the first element) and finding the smallest element. It's easy for a person to quickly glance through the array and see which element is smallest, but the sorting algorithm that we will implement can compare only two elements at once. So here's how we can find the smallest element: take the number in the first cell in the array and assign it to a variable called `smallestSoFar`. We'll also assign the position of that value to a variable called `position`. In this case, `smallestSoFar` will equal 8 and `position` will be 0. Note that even though we are assigning 8 to `smallestSoFar`, the first cell of the array will contain 8; we didn't actually remove it.

```
smallestSoFar = 8;
position = 0;
```

8	6	10	2	4

Next we'll walk through the array and compare the next value to `smallestSoFar`. The next value is 6, which is less than 8, so `smallestSoFar` becomes 6 and `position` becomes 1.

```
smallestSoFar = 6;
position = 1;
```

8	6	10	2	4

Now let's look at the next value in the array. 10 is larger than 6, so `smallestSoFar` remains 6.

```
smallestSoFar = 6;
position = 1;
```

8	6	10	2	4

The next value in the array is 2: 2 is smaller than 6.

```
smallestSoFar = 2;
position = 3;
```

8	6	10	2	4

And finally, we look at the last element, 4. Because 4 is greater than 2, and we are at the end of the array, we know that 2 is the smallest element.

```
smallestSoFar = 2;
position = 3;
```

8	6	10	2	4

Now we know that 2 is the smallest element in the array. Because we want to order the array from least to greatest, we need to put 2 in the first cell in the array. We don't simply want to overwrite the 8 that is in the first cell, though. What we'll do is swap the 2 with the 8 to get

2	6	10	**8**	4

We now have the smallest element in place. Next we'll need to find the second smallest element in the array. We can do this using the same approach we employed to find the smallest element. Because we know that 2 is the smallest element, we have to look at the elements only in positions 1 to 4 for the second smallest element.

Start by assigning 6 to `smallestSoFar` and 1 to `position` and then compare 6 to 10. Six is the smaller element. Next, compare 6 to 8; 6 is still the smaller element. Finally, compare 6 to 4; 4 is smaller, and because we have no more elements in the array, 4 must be the second smallest element in the array.

Swap 4 with the second element in the array to get

2	4	10	8	6

Make another pass through the array to find the third smallest element, and swap it into the third cell. The third smallest element is 6.

2	4	6	8	10

Finally, we look at the last two elements. Eight is smaller than 10, so we don't need to do anything. Our array is now sorted from least to greatest.

Implementation of a Selection Sort

Here is how a selection sort can be implemented in Java. The following implementation will sort the elements from least to greatest and will begin by sorting the smallest elements first.

```
//precondition: numbers is an array of ints
//postcondition: numbers is sorted in ascending order
1        public static void selectionSort1(int[] numbers)
2        {
3          for (int i = 0; i < numbers.length - 1; i++)
4          {
5            int position = i;
6            for (int k = i + 1; k < numbers.length; k++)
7            {
8              if (numbers[k] < numbers[position])
9              {
10                   position = k;
11             }
12           }
13           int temp = numbers[i];
14           numbers[i] = numbers[position];
15           numbers[position] = temp;
16         }
17       }
```

How could this be useful? Consider a case in which you have an unsorted array of 1,000 `Student` objects, and each `Student` object has a method that returns a grade point average for that `Student`. What if you would like to find the five students with the highest grade point average? In this case, it would be a waste of time to sort the entire array. Instead, we can just run through five cycles of the second implementation of the selection sort shown above, and the top five students will be sorted.

The **insertion sort** is a little less intuitive. Rather than traversing the entire array, it compares the first two elements and, depending on the comparison, inserts the second value "in front" of the first value into index 0, moving the first value to index 1. The first two elements are now sorted. Then the third element is checked, and the inserting continues. Note that here, also, an already sorted element will remain in its position.

Below is an array with 9 elements. This array is sorted from least to greatest except for the last element.

2	3	5	8	11	14	17	22	15

We would like to move 15 so that the entire array is in order. First, we'll temporarily assign 15 to a variable. This will give us room to shift the other elements to the right if needed.

```
temp = 15
```

2	3	5	8	11	14	17	22	

We then compare 15 to the first element to its left: 22. Because 22 is larger than 15, we shift 22 to the right.

```
temp = 15
```

2	3	5	8	11	14	17	->	22

We then compare 15 to the next element: 17. Because 17 is larger, we shift that to the right also.

```
temp = 15
```

2	3	5	8	11	14	->	17	22

Next we compare 15 to 14. Because 15 is larger, we don't want to shift 14 to the right. Instead, we insert 15 into the empty cell in the array. Now the array is correctly sorted.

Insert 15:

2	3	5	8	11	14	15	17	22

Now we'll look at how we can use the idea illustrated above to sort an entire array. This example will start at the beginning of the sorting process.

Here is the array that we are going to sort.

8	6	7	10

First, we'll look at just the first two elements of the array to make sure that they are sorted relative to each other.

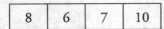

To do this, we'll pull 6 (the number that is farthest to the right in our subarray) out of the array and temporarily assign it to a variable. We'll then compare 6 to 8. Because 8 is larger, shift 8 to the right and then put 6 in the cell where 8 was.

`temp = 6`

8	->	7	10

Here's what the array looks like.

6	8	7	10

Now we need to put 7 in the proper place relative to 6 and 8. We start by assigning 7 temporarily to a variable.

`temp = 7`

6	8		10

We then compare 7 to the first number to its left: 8. Because 7 is less than 8, we shift 8 one place to the right.

`temp = 7`

6	->	8	10

Next, we'll compare 7 to the next number in the array: 6. Because 6 is less than 7, we don't want to shift 6 to the right. Instead, we will put 7 in the second cell. Our array now looks like the following:

6	7	8	10

Now we need to put 10 in its place relative to the first 3 elements in the array.

6	7	8	10

`temp = 10`

6	7	8	

First we compare 10 to 8; because 8 is smaller than 10, we don't need to shift 8 to the right. In fact, we can put 10 right back into the cell from which it came.

6	7	8	10

Implementation of an Insertion Sort

Here is how an insertion sort can be implemented in Java.

```
//precondition: x is an array of integers; x.length >= 0
//postcondition: x is sorted from least to greatest
1   public static void insertionSort(int[] x)
2   {
3       for (int i = 1; i < x.length; i++)
4       {
5           int temp = x[i];
6           int j = i - 1;
7           while (j >= 0 && x[j] > temp)
8           {
9               x[j + 1] = x[j];
10              j--;
11          }
12          x[j + 1] = temp;
13      }
14  }
```

Note that like the selection sort, the insertion sort contains nested loops. In this case, we have a `while` loop nested within a `for` loop.

The `for` loop, beginning on line 3, proceeds from index 1 to the end of the array. The `while` loop goes through the array from i to 0 and shifts elements that are larger than `temp` to the right on line 9. On line 12, we put the value of `temp` into its proper place in the array.

Another type of sort used on the AP Exam is the **merge sort.** This is a more complex type of sort that uses **recursion,** which is the technique that uses a method to call itself. (Recursion will be further discussed in Chapter 12.) A merge sort is like a divide-and-conquer. An array is split into two pieces. Each piece is sorted. The two sorted pieces are then merged together into one sorted list. In order to sort each of the two pieces, the same divide-and-conquer method is used.

Below is an array with 8 elements:

14	8	9	3	5	4	21	12

The merge sort will divide this array into two pieces:

Let's look at just the left half of the array. This array is divided into two pieces:

14	8		9	3

Each of these pieces is similarly divided into two pieces:

14		8		9		3

Since each remaining piece contains only one element, simply order the two from left to right:

8	14

3	9

Now merge the two sorted segments. Compare the first element in each piece. The smaller is 3, so this is the first element of the merged array. Now compare the first element in each piece that hasn't already been copied. These are 8 and 9. The smaller is 8, so this is the second element of the merged array. Again, compare the first element in each piece that hasn't already been copied. These are 14 and 9. The smaller is 9, so this is the third element of the merged array. Since the second array has no remaining elements that haven't already been copied, add the remaining element(s) from the first array into the merged array. The only remaining element is 14, so this is the fourth element:

3	8	9	14

Follow a similar process for the right half of the first array. Divide into two pieces:

5	4

21	12

Each of these pieces is similarly divided into two pieces:

5		4		21		12

Since each remaining piece contains only one element, simply order the two from left to right:

4	5

12	21

Now merge the two sorted segments. Compare the first element in each piece. The smaller is 4, so this is the first element of the merged array. Now compare the first element in each piece that hasn't already been copied. These are 5 and 12. The smaller is 5, so this is the second element of the merged array. Since the first array has no remaining elements that haven't already been copied, add the remaining elements from the second array into the merged array. The remaining elements, 12 and 21, become the third and fourth elements of the merged array:

4	5	12	21

Thus, the two sorted pieces of the original array look like this:

3	8	9	14

4	5	12	21

Merge the two sorted arrays. Compare 3 and 4 to get that the first element is 3. Compare 8 and 4 to get that the second element is 4. Compare 8 and 5 to get that the third element is 5. Compare 8 and 12 to get that the fourth element is 8.

Compare 9 and 12 to get that the fifth element is 9. Compare 14 and 12 to get that the sixth element is 12. Compare 14 and 21 to get that the seventh element is 14. Since the first array has no uncopied elements, 21, which is the only remaining uncopied element in the second array, becomes the eighth element of the merged array. Below is the final array:

3	4	5	8	9	12	14	21

Implementation of a Merge Sort

Here's how a merge sort can be implemented in Java.

```
//precondition: x is an array in integers; x.length >= 0
//postcondition: x is sorted from least to greatest
1    public static void mergeSort (int[] x)
2    {
3        int[] temp = new int[x.length];
4        mergeSortHelper(x, 0, x.length - 1, temp);
5    }
6    public static void mergeSortHelper (int[] x, int lowIndex,
     int highIndex, int temp)
7    {
8        if (lowIndex < highIndex)
9        {
10           int mid = (lowIndex + highIndex) / 2;
11           mergeSortHelper(x, lowIndex, mid, temp);
12           mergeSortHelper(x, mid + 1, highIndex, temp);
13           merge(x, lowIndex, mid, highIndex, temp);
14       }
15   }
16   public static void merge(int[] x, int lowIndex, int
     mid, int highIndex, temp)
17   {
18       int l = lowIndex;
19       int m = mid + 1;
20       int n = highIndex;
21       while (l <= mid && m <= highIndex)
22       {
23           if (x[l] < x[m])
24           {
25               temp[n] = x[l];
26               l++;
27           }
28           else
29           {
30               temp[n] = x[m];
31               m++;
32           }
33       n++;
34       }
35       while (l <= mid)
36       {
37           temp[n] = x[l];
38           l++;
39           n++;
40       }
```

```
41     while (m <= highIndex)
42     {
43         temp[n] = x[m];
44         m++;
45         n++;
46     }
47     for (n = lowIndex; n <= highIndex; n++)
48     {
49         x[n] = temp[k];
50     }
51 }
```

This is clearly a more complex sort than the other two and it involves the use of multiple methods. The first method splits the array into two pieces, the second sorts the individual pieces, and the third merges the two pieces into one sorted array.

KEY TERMS

array

initializer list

index numbers

traverse

full

`ArrayIndexOutOfBoundsException`

enhanced-`for` loop

`null`

`NullPointerException`

sequential search

binary search

search algorithms

sorting algorithms

selection sort

insertion sort

merge sort

recursion

CHAPTER 8 REVIEW DRILL

Answers to review questions can be found in Chapter 13.

1. What is the length of the array `numbers` after the following code executes?

```
String word = "Bear";
int[] numbers = new int[word.length() - 1];
```

(A) 1

(B) 3

(C) 4

(D) 6

(E) The array will not be created due to a compile-time error.

2. Consider the following code segment:

```
String[] s = new String[2];
String[] t = {"Michael", "Megan", "Chelsea"};
s = t;
System.out.print(s.length);
```

What is printed as a result of executing the code segment?

(A) 1

(B) 2

(C) 3

(D) Nothing will be printed due to a compile-time error.

(E) Nothing will be printed due to a run-time error.

3. Consider the following code segment:

```
final int[] a1 = {1, 2};
int[] b1 = {3, 4};
a1 = b1;
System.out.print(a1[1]);
```

What is printed as a result of executing the code segment?

(A) 2

(B) 3

(C) 4

(D) Nothing will be printed due to a compile-time error.

(E) Nothing will be printed due to a run-time error.

4. Consider the following code segment:

```
final int[] myArray = {1, 2};
myArray[1] = 3;
System.out.print(myArray[1]);
```

What is printed as a result of executing the code segment?

(A) 1

(B) 2

(C) 3

(D) Nothing will be printed due to a run-time error.

(E) Nothing will be printed due to a compile-time error.

5. Consider the following incomplete method:

```
public static int mod3(int[] numbers)
{
    int count = 0;
    for (int i = 0; i < numbers.length; i++)
    {
        /* mystery code */
    }
    return count;
}
```

Method `mod3` is intended to return the number of integers in the array `numbers` that are evenly divisible by 3. Which of the following code segments could be used to replace /* *mystery code* */ so that `mod3` will work as intended?

I.
```
if (i % 3 == 0)
{
    count++;
}
```

II.
```
if (numbers[i] % 3 == 0)
{
    count++;
}
```

III.
```
while (numbers[i] % 3 == 0)
{
    count++;
}
```

(A) I only
(B) II only
(C) III only
(D) I and II
(E) II and III

6. Assume that an array `arr` of integer values has been declared and initialized with random numbers. Which of the following code segments correctly swaps the values stored in `arr[0]` and `arr[3]`?

(A)
```
arr[0] = 3;
arr[3] = 0;
```

(B)
```
arr[0] = arr[3];
arr[3] = arr[0];
```

(C)
```
int k = arr[3];
arr[3] = arr[0];
arr[0] = k;
```

(D)
```
int k = arr[3];
arr[0] = arr[3];
arr[3] = k;
```

(E)
```
int k = arr[0];
arr[3] = arr[0];
arr[0] = k;
```

7. Consider the following code segment:

```
int [] scores = {75, 63, 52, 80};

for (int s : scores)
{
    if (s < 75)
    {
        s += 5;
    }
}
for (int s : scores)
{
    System.out.print(s + " ");
}
```

What is printed as a result of executing the code segment?

(A) 75 63 52 80
(B) 75 68 57 80
(C) 80 68 57 80
(D) 80 68 57 85
(E) Nothing will be printed due to a compile-time error.

8. Consider the following code segment:

```
String [] names = {"Abi", "Brianna", "Jada", "Kiara", "Tiffany", "Vanessa"};
int middle = names.length/2 - 1;

for (int x = 0; x < middle; x++)
{
    String hold = names[x];
    names[x] = names [names.length - x - 1];
    names[names.length - x - 1] = hold;
}

for (String n: names)
{
    System.out.print(n + "   ");
}
```

What is printed as a result of executing the code segment?

(A) Abi   Brianna   Jada   Kiara   Tiffany   Vanessa
(B) Abi   Jada   Brianna   Vanessa   Kiara   Tiffany
(C) Vanessa   Tiffany   Kiara   Jada   Brianna   Abi
(D) Vanessa   Tiffany   Jada   Kiara   Brianna   Abi
(E) Vanessa   Brianna   Jada   Kiara   Tiffany   Abi

Summary

- An array is a grouping of a fixed length of variables of the same data type or objects of the same class.

- Arrays are indexed beginning at 0 and ending at length −1.

- An enhanced-`for` loop automatically performs the loop for each element of an array.

- A sequential search looks for an element of an array beginning at index 0 until the desired element is found and returns the index. If the element is not found, it returns −1.

- A binary search begins searching in the middle of an array and moves to higher or lower indices to find the desired element. A binary search tends to be more efficient but can be used only on an ordered list.

- A selection sort orders an array by swapping the smallest elements to the first index and then repeatedly finding the second smallest element to swap into the second index, and so on.

- An insertion sort orders an array by finding the appropriate location for an element, shifting other elements to take its place, and then placing the element into the appropriate location.

- A merge sort orders an array by recursively dividing the array into smaller pieces. The smaller pieces are sorted and merged with other pieces.

Chapter 9
ArrayList

LISTS & ArrayLists

There are two big limitations of the powerful array structure in Java: an array has a fixed length, and it can store only one type of data. If you wanted to represent, say, a friend's collection of action figures, an array would require all of the action figures to be the same type. Generally speaking, they must *all* be flying superheroes, or they must *all* have protective body armor, etc.

Likewise, a collection of action figures represented as an array could store only a fixed number of action figures, no more and no less. If there are extra, unused slots, they stay there, which could be problematic if you have an array of helmeted heroes, and you try to remove the helmet from every element in every index of the array. Once you reach the first empty spot, there is no hero and therefore no helmet, so the directions do not make sense; in Java, the compiler will return a `NullPointerException` for this situation.

> There are advantages and disadvantages to every structure that we study in Java.

An `ArrayList` addresses both of these issues. An **ArrayList object** is **dynamically sized**, expanding and compressing as elements are added and removed. An `ArrayList` can also store multiple types of data, without limit.

Let's use an example to understand the advantages and disadvantages of arrays versus `ArrayLists`. Consider your lunch bag that you take to school. If you wanted to represent your lunch bag using an array or `ArrayList` structure, which would be more accurate?

Naturally, the answer to this question depends on (1) the details of the objects in the bag—in this case, the types of lunch items—and (2) the programmer's choice of which is more appropriate. If your lunch contains a sandwich object, a fruit object, and a drink object, the `ArrayList` structure might be a better choice. Furthermore, as the components of the lunch are removed, the lunch bag theoretically shrinks (or can shrink). An `ArrayList` seems appropriate.

Let's consider the same lunch example, but this time, suppose the items are stored in a plastic container with compartments. Regardless of whether you have not yet eaten your lunch, you are done with your lunch, or it's currently anytime in between, the number and setup of the compartments do not change. We will discuss a workaround for "tricking" the array into thinking the lunch objects are all the same type. These facts and abilities render an array structure more appropriate than an `ArrayList`.

To further demonstrate the usefulness of an `ArrayList` structure, note that it is also possible to create a **typed ArrayList,** which allows only objects of the same type to be stored in the list. This structure combines useful aspects of both arrays and `ArrayLists`.

In order to instantiate an `ArrayList` called `lunchBag` that will store the various components of our lunch, we use the following line of code:

```
ArrayList lunchBag = new ArrayList();
```

Note that, unlike the syntax we use for instantiating an array, neither the type of object nor the length of the list is defined initially.

In order to access data from within the list, particular methods must be invoked; unlike for array structures in Java, there is not a convenient bracket notation available with lists. To return the second object, an `Apple` object, in the `ArrayList` and store it using the variable `food`, the line of code would be

```
Apple red = lunchBag.get(1);
```

There are several other useful methods available in the `List` class, and they are all mentioned in the AP Exam Quick Reference, although their functionality is (obviously) not given. These methods include `add`, `set`, `remove`, and `size`.

> Bracket notation can be used only with array objects; lists must use the appropriate methods.

If the programmer decides it is more appropriate to keep the dynamic sizing ability of the `ArrayList` while fixing the type of data it can hold (as in an array), it would be instantiated as follows:

```
ArrayList<Apple> lunchBag = new ArrayList<Apple>();
```

One of the drawbacks of using `ArrayList` is that only objects can be stored in an `ArrayList`. The primitive data types `int` and `double` cannot be stored in `ArrayLists`. If programmers want to store integer and double data types, they must use the `Integer` or `Double` wrapper classes. `Integer` and `Double` objects can be created using integers and doubles, respectively, as parameters. For example,

```
Integer n = new Integer(5);
Double x = new Double(6.1);
```

To call the values, use the `intValue()` and `doubleValue()` methods. The following commands

```
int a = n.intValue();
double y = x.doubleValue();
```

assign a = 5 and y = 6.1.

Additionally, the AP Computer Science Java Subset includes the static variables `MIN_VALUE` and `MAX_VALUE` of the `Integer` class. These store the minimum and maximum possible values of the integer data type.

Array	ArrayList
After an array is created, it cannot be resized.	`ArrayLists` will automatically resize as new elements are added.
No import statement is needed to use an array, unless the array holds elements that require an import statement.	You must import `java.util.ArrayList`, or use the full package name whenever you use an `ArrayList`.
Elements are accessed using index notation (e.g., `myArray[2]`).	Elements are accessed using methods of the `ArrayList` class (e.g., `myList.get(2)`, `myList.add("George")`).
Arrays can be constructed to hold either primitives or object references.	`ArrayList` instances can hold only object references, not primitives. The `Integer` and `Double` wrapper classes must be used to store integer and double primitives in an `ArrayList`.

Each array can be declared for only one type of element. For example, if an array is declared to hold strings, you cannot store an integer in it.	An `ArrayList` can hold a heterogeneous collection of objects. For example, the following is perfectly legal (though not recommended):
	`ArrayList list = new ArrayList( );`
	`list.add(new String("A String"));`
	`list.add(new Integer(4));`

KEY TERMS
ArrayList object
dynamically sized
typed ArrayList

CHAPTER 9 REVIEW DRILL

Answers to review questions can be found in Chapter 13.

1. Consider the following code segment:

```
ArrayList list = new ArrayList( );
list.add("A");
list.add("B");
list.add(0, "C");
list.add("D");
list.set(2, "E");
list.remove(1);
System.out.println(list);
```

What is printed as a result of executing the code segment?

(A) [A, B, C, D, E]
(B) [A, B, D, E]
(C) [C, E, D]
(D) [A, D, E]
(E) [A, C, D, E]

2. Consider the following data fields and method:

```
private ArrayList letters;
// precondition: letters.size( ) > 0
// letters contains String objects
public void letterRemover( )
{
    int i = 0;
    while (i < letters.size( ))
    {
        if (letters.get(i).equals("A"))
            letters.remove(i);
        i++;
    }
}
```

Assume that ArrayList letters originally contains the following String values:

[A, B, A, A, C, D, B]

What will letters contain as a result of executing letterRemover( )?

(A) [A, B, A, A, C, D, B]
(B) [B, C, D, B]
(C) [B, A, C, D, B]
(D) [A, B, A, C, D, B]
(E) [A, A, B, C, D, B, D]

3. Consider the following method:

```
private ArrayList myList;
// precondition: myList.size( ) > 0
// myList contains String objects
public void myMethod( )
{
    for (int i = 0; i < myList.size( ) - 1; i++)
    {
        myList.remove(i);
        System.out.print(myList.get(i) + " ");
    }
}
```

Assume that myList originally contains the following String values:

```
[A, B, C, D, E]
```

What will be printed when the method above executes?

(A) A B C D E
(B) A C E
(C) B D E
(D) B D
(E) Nothing will be printed due to an IndexOutOfBoundsException.

4. Consider the following code segment:

```
ArrayList list = new ArrayList( );
for (int i = 1; i <= 8; i++)
{
    list.add(new Integer(i));
}
for (int j = 1; j < list.size( ); j++)
{
    list.set(j / 2, list.get(j));
}
System.out.println(list);
```

What is printed as a result of executing the code segment?

(A) [2, 4, 6, 8, 5, 6, 7, 8]
(B) [1, 2, 3, 4, 5, 6, 7, 8]
(C) [1, 2, 3, 4]
(D) [1, 2, 3, 4, 1, 2, 3, 4]
(E) [2, 2, 4, 4, 6, 6, 8, 8]

Summary

- `ArrayLists` are lists of objects of variable length.

- An enhanced-`for` loop automatically performs the loop for each element of an array or `ArrayList`.

- A sequential search looks for an element of an array or `ArrayList` beginning at index 0 until the desired element is found and returns the index. If the element is not found, it returns −1.

- A binary search begins searching in the middle of an array or `ArrayList` and moves to higher or lower indices to find the desired element. A binary search is more efficient but can be used only on an ordered list.

- A selection sort orders an array or `ArrayList` by swapping lower elements to lower indices.

- An insertion sort orders an array or `ArrayList` by finding the appropriate location for an element, shifting other elements to take its place, and then placing the element into the appropriate location.

Chapter 10
2D Arrays

2D ARRAYS

Two-dimensional, or **2D, arrays** are structures that have entered, exited, and re-entered the required topics for the AP Exam. They are quite powerful and, at the same time, not too difficult to understand once you have mastered 1D array structures, which we studied in Chapter 8.

A great example of a 2D array is a stand-up soda machine, like you see in the mall or in front of the supermarket. You know the type, the one in which you drop money and hope desperately that the soda actually drops out.

Think of the soda machine as a set of **rows** across the machine, each having a different type of soda (let's say that the first row has cola, second has orange, etc.). Each of those rows can be considered an array. Now consider the vertical **columns** down the machine; each column will have one of each type of soda, since it travels down the rows (first item is cola, second item is orange, etc.). *That* vertical column can also be considered an array. The result is an "array of arrays," which Java quantifies as a 2D array, with index numbers assigned independently to each row and column location.

In the soda machine example, the very first cola in the upper left location of the 2D array would be located at index 0 of the first horizontal array, as well as index 0 of the first vertical array. The code to access this element (soda) in a 2D array (soda machine) already instantiated as `sodaMachine` would be `sodaMachine[0][0]`, with the first 0 being the row and the second 0 being the column. The second cola would be located at `[0][1]`, and the first orange would be located at `[1][0]`, and so on. For an `m` by `n` 2D array, with `m` being the number of rows and `n` being the number of columns, the last element in the lower right corner would be located at `[m - 1][n - 1]`. But you didn't forget that index numbers begin at 0 and end at `(array.length - 1)`, did you?

The methods and constants available for use with array structures are available for 2D array structures as well, because a 2D array is an array—just a fancy one. It's a little tricky, however; in order to, say, return the number of cola slots across the soda machine, you would use `sodaMachine.length`, as expected. In order to access the number of slots down the left side of the machine, however, you would use `sodaMachine[0].length`, meaning you want the length of the first column of the 2D array.

1. Consider the following code segment:

```
int[][] num = new int [4][4];
for (int i = 0; i < num.length; i++)
{
    for (int k = 0; k < num.length; k++
    {
        num[i][k] = i * k;
    }
}
```

What are the contents of num after the code segment has executed?

(A) 0 0 0 0
     0 1 2 3
     0 2 4 6
     0 3 6 9

(B) 0 1 2 3
     1 2 3 4
     2 3 4 5
     3 4 5 6

(C) 0 3 6 9
     0 2 4 6
     0 1 2 3
     0 0 0 0

(D) 1 1 1 1
     2 2 2 2
     3 3 3 3
     4 4 4 4

(E) 0 0 0 0
     1 2 3 4
     2 4 6 8
     3 6 9 12

Here's How To Crack It

2D array questions are always intimidating. The first iteration of the outer loop will occur with i = 0. Looking at the inner loop, the k values will range from 0 to 3 before it terminates. Since i = 0 and each iteration of the inner loop will multiply i by k, the first row of the array will be all zeroes. Eliminate (B), (C), and (D). Wow! Once that finishes, the outer loop will have its second iteration, with i = 1. The inner loop will then start over with k = 0, and i times k will equal 0 as a result. The first number in the second row, then, will be 0. Eliminate (E) because the first number in its second row is 1: and the answer is (A).

Remember that an array, regardless of its dimensions, can store any one type of data, but not multiple types. Also remember that, as is true for most computer programming language rules, there is always a workaround! More on this later.

KEY TERMS

two-dimensional arrays (2D arrays)
rows
columns

CHAPTER 10 REVIEW DRILL

Answers to review questions can be found in Chapter 13.

1. The following class, `Arr2d`, is meant to represent a 2-dimensional array object. The constructor will initialize `Arr2d` using the number of rows and columns that have been passed. Choose the statement that will initialize the array in the constructor.

```
public class Arr2D {
    private int [][] arr;

    Arr2D (int rows, int columns)
    {
        /* missing code */
    }
}
```

(A) `int [] arr = new String [rows][columns];`
(B) `int [][] arr = new String [rows - 1][columns - 1];`
(C) `arr = new String [rows][columns];`
(D) `arr = new String [rows - 1][columns - 1];`
(E) `int arr [][] = new String [rows][columns];`

2. Consider the following code segment:

```
int [][] numbers = {{1, 2, 3, 4}, {5, 6, 7, 8}};
for (int [] nums : numbers)
   for (int n : nums)
      System.out.print(n + " ");
System.out.print("\n");
```

What is printed as a result of executing the code segment?

(A) 1 2 3 4 5 6 7 8
(B) 1 2 3 4
    5 6 7 8
(C) 1 2
    3 4
    5 6
    7 8
(D) 5 6 7 8
    1 2 3 4
(E) A compiler error would occur.

3. Consider the following code segment:

```
int[][] numbers = new int [4][4];
initializeIt(numbers);
int total = 0;
for (int z = 0; z < numbers.length; z++)
{
    total += numbers[z][numbers[0].length - 1 - z];
}
```

The call to `initializeIt()` on the second line initializes the array `numbers` so that it looks like the following:

```
1 2 5 3
7 9 4 0
3 3 2 5
4 5 8 1
```

What will be the value of `total` after the code has executed?

(A) 11
(B) 12
(C) 13
(D) 14
(E) 15

4. Consider the following code segment:

```
int[][] numbers = new int[3][6];
initializeIt(numbers);
int total = 0;
for (int j = 0; j < numbers.length; j++)
{
    for (int k = 0; k < numbers[0].length; k += 2)
    {
        total += numbers[j][k];
    }
}
```

The call to `initializeIt()` on the second line initializes the array `numbers` so that it looks like the following:

```
2 4 6 3 2 1
5 6 7 4 2 9
4 0 5 6 4 2
```

What will be the value of `total` after the code has executed?

(A) 18
(B) 35
(C) 37
(D) 72
(E) 101

5. Consider the following code segment:

```
int[][] num = new int[4][4];
for (int i = 0; i < num.length; i++)
{
    for (int k = 0; k < num[0].length; k++)
    {
        num[i][k] = i * k;
    }
}
```

What are the contents of num after the code segment has executed?

(A) 0 0 0 0
     0 1 2 3
     0 2 4 6
     0 3 6 9

(B) 0 1 2 3
     1 2 3 4
     2 3 4 5
     3 4 5 6

(C) 0 3 6 9
     0 2 4 6
     0 1 2 3
     0 0 0 0

(D) 1 1 1 1
     2 2 2 2
     3 3 3 3
     4 4 4 4

(E) 0 0 0 0
     1 2 3 4
     2 4 6 8
     3 6 9 12

6. Consider the following code segment:

```
int [][] numbers = {{1, 2, 3, 4},{5, 6, 7, 8}};
initializeIt(numbers);
String line ="";
for (int a = 0; a < numbers[0].length; a++)
{
    for (int b = 0; b < numbers.length; b++)
    {
        line += numbers[b][a] + " ";
    }
    line += "\n";
}
System.out.println(line);
```

The call to `initializeIt()` on the second line initializes the array so that it looks like the following:

```
1   2   3   4
5   6   7   8
```

What will be printed after the code has executed?

(A) 1   2   3   4
     5   6   7   8

(B) 5   6   7   8
     1   2   3   4

(C) 8   7   6   5
     4   3   2   1

(D) 1   2
     3   4
     5   6
     7   8

(E) 1   5
     2   6
     3   4
     4   8

7. Consider the following client code and method:

```
int [][] numbers = {{1, 2, 3, 4}, {5, 6, 7, 8}, {9, 10, 11, 12}};
int [] myArr = mystery(numbers, 2);
for (int j: myArr)
    System.out.print(j + " ");

public static int [] mystery(int [][] arr, int n)
{
    int [] m = new int[arr.length];
    for (int i = 0; i < arr.length; i++)
            m[i] = arr[i][n];
    return m;
}
```

What will be printed after the code executes?

(A) 5   6   7   8
(B) 2   6   10
(C) 9   10   11   12
(D) 4   8   12
(E) 3   7   11

8. Consider the following code:

```
int [][] numbers = {{1, 2, 3, 4}, {5, 6, 7, 8}, {9, 10, 11, 12}};

for (int r = numbers.length - 1; r > 0 ; r--)
{
    for (int c = 0; c < numbers[r].length; c++)
    {
    numbers[r - 1][c] = numbers[r][c];
    }
}
```

Which of the following represents the current values in the array?

(A) 1   2   3   4
    5   6   7   8
    9   10   11   12
(B) 9   10   11   12
    5   6   7   8
    1   2   3   4
(C) 1   2   3   4
    1   2   3   4
    1   2   3   4
(D) 9   10   11   12
    9   10   11   12
    9   10   11   12
(E) 12   11   10   9
     8   7   6   5
     4   3   2   1

Summary

- A two-dimensional array is an array of one-dimensional arrays. On the AP Computer Science A Exam, these arrays will always be the same number of columns in each row. Also, arrays of dimensions greater than 2 are not tested.

Chapter 11
Inheritance

Inheritance is the quintessential way—and the only way, for our purposes—to create direct relationships between classes. An **inheritance hierarchy** is designed in order to quantify this relationship, much like a family tree, and it defines the "parent" class and all of its "child" classes. A carefully designed hierarchy implemented as an inheritance relationship between classes is arguably the most powerful programming technique that you will learn in this course.

HIERARCHIES & DESIGN

The designing of the hierarchy is critical in implementing inheritance. As the programmer, you have limitless ways to design a hierarchy, so the importance of the planning process cannot be overstated.

The first decision for the programmer/designer—yes, there are programmers who focus solely on *design*—is to define the parent class of the situation. Typically, the parent class (**superclass**) is the most general form of the objects that will be instantiated in the overall program. Every other class in the program will lie lower in the hierarchy (**subclasses** of the superclass), but their objects will be more specific versions of the overall parent class. This setup creates an IS-A relationship between the parent and the child classes.

Let's use potato chips as our example for this discussion. If we are designing a hierarchy of classes to properly represent potato chips, there are a ridiculous number of possibilities—would the parent class be `PotatoChip`? `Potato`? `Snack`? `SaltySnack`? `JunkFood`? So we have to make a decision based on the situation that we are given; if the programmer receives no context whatsoever, the design is very difficult and will produce unpredictable—yet all viable—results.

In this case, let's use `Snack` as the superclass. A `Snack` object is very general; there may be many subclasses in our situation. Let's define two subclasses for `Snack`, one for our purposes and an extra for practice: `PotatoChip` and `Cookie`. Since a potato chip is a snack (as is a cookie), the setup makes intuitive sense. Note how we define the relationship from the bottom (lowest subclasses) of the hierarchy to the top (highest superclass). Let us then define another, lower set of classes that will be subclasses of `PotatoChip`: `BBQChip` and `OnionChip`.

A visual representation of a hierarchy makes the design much easier to understand:

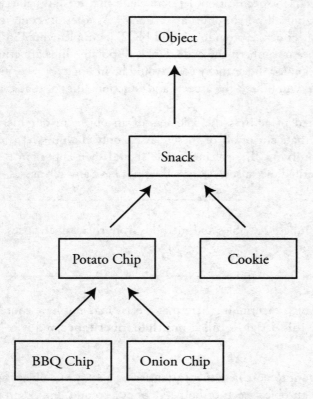

As you can see, there are several IS-A relationships here. A `BBQChip` IS-A `PotatoChip`, which IS-A `Snack`. A `BBQChip` also IS-A `Snack`, by inheritance. All of these relationships as designed in the hierarchy should make intuitive sense and/or conform to the given specifications.

> On the AP Exam, at least one free-response question and at least several multiple-choice questions typically focus on the design and/or implementation of inheritance relationships. Detailed specifications will be given in order to suppress the variety of exam responses to score.

Let's discuss the benefits of the setup we have created. When we are ready to implement code, we should decide which variables and methods should be implemented, as well as their locations within the hierarchy. These variables and methods have a HAS-A relationship with the class to which they belong. This task is more formidable than it might seem; very general variables and methods should be closer to the top of the hierarchy, while more specific variables and methods should reside in lower subclasses. For example, virtually every snack food has some kind of flavor. Therefore, code to address the flavor of the snack food should be implemented in `Snack`, and it will be subsequently inherited by all of the subclasses: Since a `Snack` object HAS-A flavor, and a `PotatoChip` object IS-A `Snack`, a `PotatoChip` object also HAS-A flavor. What about an `OnionChip` object? It also HAS-A flavor, as described above.

Now consider code that addresses the crunch of an object in the hierarchy. Without any detail in specification, let's conclude that it is arguable whether a cookie is crunchy, but all potato chips are crunchy. As a result, code that addresses the crunchy aspect of the program should NOT be implemented in Snack; that way Cookie does not inherit the code. Since all potato chips are crunchy, the appropriate location for the crunchy code would be in PotatoChip, and BBQChip and OnionChip will inherit the aspects and functionalities of that code.

If we wanted to address the spiciness of an object in our hierarchy, we might determine that, out of all of these classes, only the BBQChip has a spice factor worth quantifying. The spiciness code should then appear in BBQChip and will not be inherited, because BBQChip does not have any subclasses.

> Classes inherit variables and methods from their superclasses, not the other way around.

It is also worth mentioning here that a class may not have more than one direct superclass. This design is called **multiple inheritance** and it is NOT allowed in Java.

It is important to note here that instantiating a BBQChip object will automatically instantiate an object each of both PotatoChip and Snack. In order for this to occur correctly, however, Java requires us to address their instantiation explicitly. Therefore, the constructor BBQChip must first make a call to super(), which invokes the constructor of PotatoChip, its superclass. If the super constructor requires (a) parameter(s), then the super() call must include those parameter(s) as well. Java will otherwise invoke super() on its own, often resulting in undesired results and an easily avoided missed point on a free-response question. As a rule, all classes in Java will instantiate the Object class, which is the ultimate generalization—think: if I look around the room right now, what isn't an object?

Consider the following class:

```
public class College extends School
{
        // private data fields not shown

        // the only constructor in this class
        public College (String town, double tuition)
        {
            // code not shown
        }

        // other methods not shown
}
```

1. In order to write `LawAcademy`, a subclass of `College`, which of the following constructors is valid?

   I. ```
       public LawAcademy (String twn, double tuit)
       {
           super.College(twn, tuit);
       }
       ```
   II. ```
       public LawAcademy (String twn, double tuit)
       {
           super(twn, tuit);
       }
       ```
   III. ```
        public LawAcademy (String twn, double tuit, String st)
        {
            super(st, tuit);
        }
        ```

   (A)  II only
   (B)  I and II only
   (C)  I and III only
   (D)  II and III only
   (E)  I, II, and III

### Here's How to Crack It:

The final answer is (D) but let's start with eliminations. This one has an item that's easy to eliminate—I—and one you may be tempted to eliminate—III. `Super.College` is not a valid reference, since the super-dot operator is different from the `super()` method. Segment II is a typical way to handle the situation and so it is fine. Segment III brings in the extra parameter, which ends up being used as the first parameter (the `String` one) in the super call, rendering `twn` unused, but that doesn't matter. As long as the super constructor is called correctly, we are good. So (D) is the correct answer.

Let's tackle another.

2. Consider a class `Recliner` that extends a `Chair` class. Assuming both classes each have a no-parameter constructor, which of the following statements is NOT valid?

   (A)  `Object a = new Recliner();`
   (B)  `Recliner b = new Chair();`
   (C)  `Chair c = new Chair();`
   (D)  `Chair d = new Recliner();`
   (E)  All of the above choices are valid.
        ```

Here's How to Crack It

This question enforces the idea of creating references using hierarchies. According to the question, a `Recliner` is a `Chair`, not the other way around. Likewise, any Java object is an Object. It is valid to declare a variable's type to be more generic than its referenced object, but not the other way around. Choice (B) is the only choice that breaks this rule: declaring a variable requires a `Chair` to be a `Recliner`, not the other way around (the reverse of what the question dictates). The correct answer is (B).

3. Consider the following two classes:

```
public class A
{
    public int method1(int x)
    {
        return 2;
    }
}
public class B extends A
{  /*  code not shown  */  }
```

Which of the following could be the signature of a method in `class B` that correctly overloads `method1` in `class A`?

(A) `public int method1(String x)`
(B) `public int method1(int y)`
(C) `private int method1(int x)`
(D) `public int method2(String x)`
(E) `public int method2(int y)`

Here's How to Crack It

Overloading a method means creating a new method with the same name, visibility, and return type, regardless of whether the method lies in the parent class or the child class. The parameter must be different, however, or the new method overrides the original method. Choice (B) will override `method1`, (C), (D), and (E) will create all new methods that are independent of `method1`, and (C) does not have the same visibility as `method1`. The answer is (A).

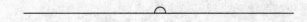

Now, suppose there is functionality in a superclass that is inherited, but should be changed based on the level of inheritance. For example, all snacks can be eaten, so the programmer appropriately implements an `eat()` method in `Snack`. As a result, all subclasses will inherit this method and its functionality. But what if, say, an `OnionChip` must be eaten differently than the other snacks? Perhaps after a few chips, "eaters" have to wipe their hands before continuing to eat. The desired `eat()` method—possessing the identical name, parameters, and return type—would be implemented in `OnionChip`, and all objects of that class (and only that class, in this example) would use this new `eat()` method. The super-class's `eat()` method has been **overridden** by this new version. The workaround for this situation would be to use the **super keyword**: `super.eat()`.

Though no longer part of the official Course Description, it's pretty cool to know that another level of overriding involves **method abstraction**. Suppose that the programmer wants to force all subclasses to have the `eat()` method, but decides that an `eat()` method's code in `Snack` is inappropriate; for example, all `Snack` objects can be eaten but the WAY they are eaten depends so much on the type of snack that superclass code for the method seems inappropriate. (You would not eat a chip the same way you would eat a cookie, would you? Go with it.) The `eat()` method can be declared abstract; in this design, the `Snack` class has now mandated every subclass to either (1) override the abstract method with code or (2) declare the method abstract once again, forcing its subclasses to override the abstract method.

---

4. Consider the following two classes:

```
public class Parent
{
    public void writeMe(String s)
    {
        System.out.println("Object");
    }
}
public class Child extends Parent
{
    public void writeMe(String s)
    {
        System.out.println("Object");
    }
}
```

Which of the following best describes the `writeMe` method of the `Child` class?

(A) An inherited method

(B) An overridden method

(C) An overloaded method

(D) An interface method

(E) An abstract method

Here's How to Crack It

Since the `writeMe` method in `Child` has the same name, return type, and parameter types, it is overriding `writeMe` in `Parent`. The answer is (B).

POLYMORPHISM

Polymorphism is a technique that, in a way, breaks all of the rules we think would happen in inheritance—and yet, it conforms to them at the same time.

Using our `Snack` example from above, including the overridden method in `OnionChip`, suppose several objects from various levels in the hierarchy reside in an untyped `ArrayList`. The programmer would like to, using a simple loop, simulate the user "eating" the chips in the list, regardless of their type. The loop will iterate through the list and automatically invoke the appropriate `eat()` method, including the overridden method for `OnionChip` objects, as desired. This is an example of polymorphism.

The word *polymorphism,* which means "many forms," can also apply to programs in a more profound manner. This process, directly or indirectly, involves virtually every technique we have learned in this book.

Suppose an interface called `Eatable` is implemented by all of the classes in the `Snack` hierarchy. Every class has either overridden the abstract methods from the interface, as normally required, or passed the abstraction to a subclass.

Have you ever seen those snack bags that have multiple forms of snacks (for example, potato chips AND pretzels AND nacho chips…) in them? This example is similar; if you instantiated the "bag" as either a typed `ArrayList` or an array, you could fill the structure with instances of all of these classes by declaring the type as `Eatable`. Once the `eat()` method is invoked on all of the components of the list structure using a loop, each object will automatically invoke its corresponding `eat()` method! Pretty awesome.

Use the information below to answer Questions 5 and 6.

———————————○———————————

Consider the following declaration for a class that will be used to represent a rectangle:

```
public class Rectangle
{
    private double width;
    private double height;
    public Rectangle()
    {
        width = 0;
        height = 0;
    }
    public Rectangle(double w, double h)
    {
        width = w;
        height = h;
    }

    // postcondition: returns the height
    public double getHeight()
    {
        return height;
    }

    // postcondition: returns the width
    public double getWidth()
    {
        return width;
    }
}
```

The following incomplete class declaration is intended to extend the above class so the rectangles can be filled with a color when displayed:

```
public class FilledRectangle extends Rectangle
{
    private String color;
    // constructors go here

    public String getColor()
    {
        return color;
    }
}
```

Consider the following proposed constructors for this class:

```
I.    public FilledRectangle()
      {
          color = "red";
      }
```

```
II.   public FilledRectangle(double w, double h, String c)
      {
          super (w, h);
          color = c;
      }
```

```
III.  public FilledRectangle(double w, double h, String c)
      {
          width = w;
          height = h;
          color = c;
      }
```

5. Which of these constructors would be legal for the FilledRectangle class?

(A) I only
(B) II only
(C) III only
(D) I and II
(E) I and III

Here's How to Crack It

This is an interesting one. II follows all of the rules nicely, invoking the super constructor and initializing the data field in its class, so II is good; eliminate (A), (C), and (E). Note that we do not have to check III now. For I, remember that the superclass's default constructor (the one with no parameters) will be invoked automatically if it is not called. Therefore, I is fine, so eliminate (B). Only one answer choice remains, so there is no need to continue. However, to see why III does not work, note that the variables width and height are private variables in Rectangle and, therefore, not inherited by FilledRectangle. Therefore, this will not compile. The answer is (D).

6. Based on the class declarations for `Rectangle` and `FilledRectangle` given above, which of the following code segments would be legal in a client class? Assume that the constructor that takes no arguments has been implemented for `FilledRectangle`.

I. ```
    FilledRectangle r1 = new Rectangle();
    double height = r1.getHeight();
    ```
II. ```
    Rectangle r2 = new FilledRectangle();
    double height = r2.getHeight();
    ```
III. ```
    Rectangle r3 = new FilledRectangle();
    r3.getColor();
    ```

Which of the code segments above are legal?

(A) None
(B) II only
(C) III only
(D) I and II
(E) II and III

## Here's How to Crack It

Since II appears in the most answer choices, let's check that option first. A `FilledRectangle` may be declared as a `Rectangle` because it is a subclass of `Rectangle`, and a `FilledRectangle` inherits `getHeight` from `Rectangle` as well, so II is legal: eliminate (A) and (C). A `Rectangle` cannot be declared as a `FilledRectangle` for the same reason, so I is illegal and (D) can be eliminated. As for III, a `Rectangle` object can invoke methods only from `Rectangle` (regardless of r3's identity as a `FilledRectangle`), so the second line is illegal. The answer is (B).
    ```

7. Consider the following class:

```
public class Cat
{
    private String name;
    private int age;

    public Cat(String name, int age)
    {
        this.name = name;
        this.age = age;
    }
    public String toString()
    {
        return (name + ": " + age);
    }
}
```

Suppose another class were to include the following code segment:

```
Cat c = new Cat("Billi", 5);
System.out.println(c);
```

Which of the following will be the output of the code segment?

(A) c

(B) 5

(C) Billi

(D) Billi: 5

(E) There would be no output.

Here's How to Crack It

The first line of the code segment creates a Cat object with name initialized as Billi and age initialized as 5. The second line prints the Cat object c. When an object is used as the parameter to a print, the toString method of the Object class is called. In this case, however, that method is overridden by the toString method of the Cat class. This method returns the name of the Cat, concatenated with ": ", concatenated with the age of the Cat. Therefore, it prints Billi: 5, which is (D).

KEY TERMS
inheritance
inheritance hierarchy
superclass
subclasses
multiple inheritance
overridden
super keyword
method abstraction
polymorphism

...VIEW DRILL

...questions can be found in Chapter 13.

...wing two classes:

```
...s Parent

...: String str;

...: void write()

        ...ystem.out.println(str);


    ...lic void write(String greeting)

        System.out.println(greeting + str );


...lic class Child extends Parent

    public void write(String g)
    {
        super.writeMe(g);
    }

}
```

The following statements have been written in a client program and meant to be executed in succession. However, one of them cause a compiler error. Identify the line of code that causes the compiler error.

```
Parent p1 = new Parent();   // statement A
Child c1 = new Child();     // statement B
p1.write();                 // statement C
c1.write();                 // statement D
c1.write(5);                // statement E
```

(A) statement A
(B) statement B
(C) statement C
(D) statement D
(E) statement E

2. How many classes can a given class extend?

(A) None
(B) 1
(C) 2
(D) 3
(E) As many as it needs to

3. Consider the following classes.

```
public class Employee
{
    private String name;
    private String department;

    Employee ()
    {
       name = "";
       department = "";
    }
    Employee (String iName)
    {
       name = iName;
       department = "";
    }
    Employee (String iName, String iDepartment)
    {
       name = iName;
       department = iDepartment;
    }
    public String toString()
    {
       return name + " " + department;
    }
}

public class Manager extends Employee
{
    private double salary;

    Manager()
    {
       salary = 0;
    }
Manager(double iSalary)
    {
       salary = iSalary;
    }
    Manager(String iName, String iDepartment, double iSalary)
    {
       super(iName, iDepartment);
       salary = iSalary;
    }
    public void setSalary(double iSalary)
    {
       salary = iSalary;
    }
    public String toString()
    {
       String str = super.toString();
       return str += " " + salary;
    }

}
```

Which of the following code combinations will NOT cause a compilation error?

(A) `Employee emp1 = new Employee();`

(B) `Employee emp2 = new Employee("Jones", "Sales");`

(C) `Employee emp3 = new Manager("Jones", "Sales", 50000.0);`

(D) `Employee emp4 = new Manager(50000.0);`

(E) `Manager emp5 = new Employee("Jones", "Sales");`

For questions 4–5, consider the following classes:

```
public class Bread
{
    private String name;
    Bread()
    {
        name = "bread";
        System.out.println("Freshly baked bread smells good");
    }
    public String toString()
    {
        return name;
    }
}
public class Pastry extends Bread
{
    Pastry(){
        System.out.println("Baking pastry is an art");
    }
}
public class Croissant extends Pastry
{
    Croissant()
    {
        System.out.println("Croissants taste buttery");
    }
}
```

4. If a client program executes the following statement:

```
Croissant c = new Croissant();
```

Which of the following represents the resulting output?

(A) `Freshly baked bread smells good`

(B) `Croissants taste buttery`

(C) `Croissants taste buttery`
    `Freshly baked bread smells good`

(D) `Freshly baked bread smells good`
    `Baking pastry is an art`
    `Croissants taste buttery`

(E) `Croissants taste buttery`
    `Baking pastry is an art`
    `Freshly baked bread smells good`

5. If a client program executes the following statements:
```
Croissant c = new Croissant();
System.out.println(c);
```

Which of the following is true about the last line of code?

(A) The following will printed:

bread

(B) The following will printed:

croissant

(C) An error will occur because name can be referenced only in `Bread` class.

(D) An error will occur because there is no `toString()` method in the Croissant class.

(E) None of the above are true.

6. An apartment rental company has asked you to write a program to store information about the apartments that it has available for rent. For each apartment, the company wants to keep track of the following information: number of rooms, whether or not the apartment has a dishwasher, and whether or not pets are allowed. Which of the following is the best design?

(A) Use four unrelated classes: `Apartment`, `Rooms`, `Dishwasher`, and `Pets`.

(B) Use one class, `Apartment`, which has three subclasses: `Room`, `Dishwasher`, and `Pet`.

(C) Use one class, `Apartment`, which has three data fields: `int rooms`, `boolean hasDishwasher`, `boolean allowsPets`.

(D) Use three classes—`Pets`, `Rooms`, and `Dishwasher`—each with a subclass `Apartment`.

(E) Use four classes: `Apartment`, `Pets`, `Dishwasher`, and `Rooms`. The class `Apartment` contains instances of the other classes as attributes.

7. Consider the following class declarations:

```
public class Vehicle
{
    private int maxPassengers;
    public Vehicle( )
    {
        maxPassengers = 1;
    }
    public Vehicle(int x)
    {
        maxPassengers = x;
    }
    public int maxPassengers( )
    {
        return maxPassengers;
    }
}
public class Motorcycle extends Vehicle
{
    public Motorcycle( )
    {
        super(2);
    }
}
```

Which of the following code segments will NOT cause a compilation error?

(A) `Motorcycle m1 = new Motorcycle(3);`

(B) `Vehicle v1 = new Motorcycle(4);`

(C) `Motorcycle m2 = new Vehicle( );`

(D) `Vehicle v2 = new Motorcycle( );`

(E) `Vehicle v3 = new Vehicle( );`
    `int max = v3.maxPassengers;`

Summary

o   A subclass inherits from a superclass. A superclass is the most general form of an object. Subclasses are more specific types of the superclass.

o   A superclass can have more than one subclass, but a subclass can have only one superclass.

o   Subclasses inherit methods and variables from superclasses but can override these methods and variables.

o   The reserved word `super` can be used to call an overridden method or variable.

o   An object of a subclass is also an object of its superclass.

Chapter 12
Recursion

Stay Up to Date!
For late-breaking information about test dates, exam formats, and any other changes pertaining to AP Comp Sci A, make sure to check the College Board's website at apstudents.collegeboard. org/courses/ap-computer-science-a

RECURSION

The final flow control structure that appears on the AP Exam is called **recursion**. It is not represented in the free-response questions and appears at least once in the multiple-choice questions (but typically only a few times). This structure has a result similar to a loop, but approaches the task in a different manner.

Remember those little wind-up toys you played with when you were little? You know, the plastic teeth or bunny (or whatever) with the little white knob on the side? You would wind the knob over and over, and when you let go, the little teeth would move across the table. The more you wound the knob, the longer the teeth would walk. Since the winding is the same action repeated, it can be considered a loop. The *unwinding* action, however, differentiates this situation from a `while` or `for` loop. When an unwinding or "winding down" occurs as a result of a "winding up," recursion is lurking in the shadows.

The distinguishing characteristic of a recursive method is a call to the very method itself; this statement is called a **recursive call**. In order to prevent an infinite loop, the recursive method includes a **base case**, which signals execution to stop recursing and return to each prior recursive call, finishing the job for each. Let's use an easy example to illustrate this somewhat confusing topic, and then we'll spice up the example a bit afterward.

Suppose you have a giant bag of small, multicolored, candy-coated chocolates. As a programmer, you naturally do not want to eat these candies in a haphazard manner; instead, you want to use some sort of algorithm. You decide that you will eat random candies, one at a time, until you reach your favorite color; when your favorite color is reached, you will systematically eat the same colors you ate previously, in backward order.

For example, if you eat red -> blue -> orange -> blue -> green, and green is your base case, you will then eat blue -> orange -> blue -> red and the recursion is complete. Pretty tough to remember, right? Well, a recursive method renders this task a cinch. In pseudocode,

```
eatCandy (color of current candy)
{
    if (current candy color is green)
        done eating;
    else
        eat more candy;
}
```

Although there is no `for` or `while` loop in the code, the recursive call to the method will exhibit a looping quality; unlike our previous loops, however, there is a forward/backward progression, as described above.

Let's add to this task: tell the user that you're done eating once you finish. Would adding the following line after the `if-else` statement accomplish this task?

```
display "I'm done";
```

The way recursion works, the task will be accomplished, although perhaps not according to plan. When the base case is reached, execution of the current method is completed, and then the process continues all the way back to the initial recursive call. Since the "I'm done" message is displayed after, and regardless of, the if-else, it will be displayed each time a recursive iteration completes. The result is the displaying of "I'm done" once for every candy that you ate. Nine candies, nine "I'm done" outputs. It works, but probably not as planned.

----

1. Consider the following method:

```
// precondition: x >= 0
public int mystery (int x)
{
    if (x == 0)
    {
        return 0;
    }
    else
    {
        return ((x % 10) + mystery(x / 10));
    }
}
```

Which of the following is returned as a result of the call mystery(3543)?

(A) 10
(B) 15
(C) 22
(D) 180
(E) Nothing is returned due to infinite recursion.

Here's How to Crack It

In the method listed in the question, the base case occurs when x is equal to 0. Because the value that is initially passed to the method is 3543, the base case does not yet apply. See what happens on the line return ((x % 10) + mystery (x / 10)).

The expression within the return statement has two parts (x % 10) and mystery(x / 10). Make sure that you understand what (x % 10) and (x / 10) do. If x is a base 10 integer, x % 10 will return the units digit. For example, 348 % 10 returns 8. If x is an int variable, then x / 10 will remove the units digit. For example, 348 / 10 returns 34.

Take a look at `(x % 10)`. This returns the remainder when x is divided by 10. In this case, x is 3543, so 3543 % 10 is 3.

Now what about `(x / 10)`? 3543 / 10 is 354; integer division truncates the result.

So you now have `mystery(3543) - 3 + mystery(354)`.

Following the same logic as above, `mystery(354)` will be `(354 % 10) + mystery(354 / 10)` or `mystery(354) = 4 + mystery(35)`.

So what is `mystery(35)`? `mystery(35) = (35 % 10) + mystery(35 / 10)`, or simplified, `mystery(35) = 5 + mystery(3)`.

And `mystery(3)`? `mystery(3) = (3 % 10) + mystery(3 / 10)`, or simplified, `mystery(3) = 3 + mystery(0)`.

But `mystery(0)` equals 0 (this is the base case), so

`mystery(3) = 3 + 0 = 3`

`mystery(35) = 5 + 3 = 8`

`mystery(354) = 4 + 8 = 12`

`mystery(3543) = 3 + 12 = 15`

The correct answer is (B).

RECURSIVELY TRAVERSING ARRAYS

Although it is more common to use a `for` loop to step through an array, it is also possible to use a recursion. For example, say you have a lineup of football players, each of whom has a numbered helmet. You want to step through the lineup and find the position of the person who has "9" written on his helmet:

A recursive solution for this problem is very easy to implement. You need to look through an array of int values and find the position of a specific value, if it's there.

First, we'll need to describe the problem in recursive terms.

- If we've looked through every item, then return –1.
- If the current item in the array is a match, return its position.
- Or else, restart the process with the next item in the array.

```
public int findPosition
    (int nums[], int key, int currentIndex)
{
    //if we've already looked through
    //the entire array
    if (nums.length <= currentIndex)
        return -1;
    //if the next item in the array is a match,
    //then return it
    if (nums[currentIndex] == key)
        return currentIndex;
    //else, step past the current item in the array,
    //and repeat the search on the next item
    return findPosition(nums, key, currentIndex + 1);
}
```

This example is slightly more subtle than the others because we're carrying information from one recursive call to the next. Specifically, we're using the currentIndex field to pass information from one recursive call to another. Thus, the first recursive call starts looking at position 0, the next one at position 1, and so on.

Let's go back to our football-player example. You want to step through a lineup of football players and return the position of the player who has the helmet with "9" written on it. Your code would be of the following form:

```
int [] players = //represents the football players
int pos = findPosition(players, 9, 0);
```

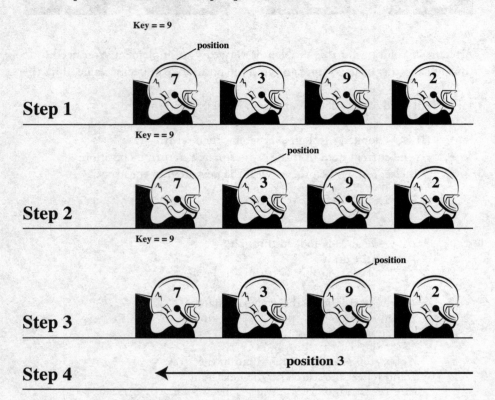

KEY TERMS

recursion
recursive call
base case

CHAPTER 12 REVIEW DRILL

Answers to the review questions can be found in Chapter 13.

1. Consider the following recursive method:

```
public int mystery(int x)
{
    if (x == 1)
        return 2;
    else
        return 2 * mystery(x - 1);
}
```

What value is returned as a result of the call `mystery(6)`?

(A) 2
(B) 12
(C) 32
(D) 64
(E) 128

2. Consider the following recursive method:

```
public static int mystery(int x)
{
    if (x == 0)
    {
        return 0;
    }
    else
    {
        return (x + mystery(x / 2) + mystery(x / 4));
    }
}
```

What value is returned as a result of a call to `mystery(10)`?

(A) 10
(B) 12
(C) 20
(D) 22
(E) 35

3. Consider the following nonrecursive method:

```
//precondition: x >= 0
public static int mystery(int x)
{
    int sum = 0;
    while(x >= 0)
    {
        sum += x;
        x--;
    }
    return sum;
}
```

Which of the following recursive methods are equivalent to the method above?

I.
```
public static int mystery2(int x)
    {
            if (x == 0)
            {
                    return 0;
            }
            return (x + mystery2(x - 1));
    }
```

II.
```
public static int mystery3 (int x)
    {
            if (x == 0)
                    return 0;
            else
                    return mystery3(x - 1);
    }
```

III.
```
public static int mystery4 (int x)
    {
            if (x == 1)
            {
                    return 1:
            }
            return (x + mystery4(x - 1));
    }
```

(A) I only
(B) II only
(C) III only
(D) I and II only
(E) II and III only

4. Consider the following method:

```
public int mystery(int x, int y)
{
    if (x >= 100 || y <= 0)
    {
        return 1;
    }
    else
    {
        return mystery(x + 10, y - 3);
    }
}
```

What value is returned by the call `mystery (30, 18)`?

(A) 0

(B) 1

(C) 6

(D) 7

(E) Nothing will be returned due to infinite recursion.

5. Consider the following incomplete method:

```
public int mystery(int x)
{
    if (x <= 1)
    {
        return 1;
    }
    else
    {
        return (/* missing code */);
    }
}
```

Which of the following could be used to replace / * *missing code* * / so that the value of `mystery(10)` is 32?

(A) `mystery(x - 1) + mystery(x - 2)`

(B) `2 * mystery(x - 2)`

(C) `2 * mystery(x - 1)`

(D) `4 * mystery(x - 4)`

(E) `4 + mystery(x - 1)`

Summary

o   Recursion is the use of a method to call itself. In order to avoid an infinite loop, any recursive method must have a base case that will cease recursion.

o   Recursion can be used for searches, certain mathematical algorithms, or to repeat actions until a desired result is obtained.

Chapter 13
Chapter Review
Drill Answers and
Explanations

CHAPTER 3

1. **E**   Start by examining line 3 in the code segment: `double c = a + b`. Note that `a` is an integer variable and `b` is a double variable. When a double variable is added to an integer variable, the integer is automatically cast to a double before the addition takes place. Therefore, `a + b` will be 20.7; this value will be assigned to `c`.

    Now look at line 4: `int d = a + c`. Because `c` is a double, `a` will once again be cast to a double and `a + c` will be 30.7. This value, which is a double, is then assigned to an integer variable. Because there is a loss of precision when a double value is assigned to an integer variable, the compiler will alert you. The correct answer is (E).

2. **E**   The key to this question is remembering that the cast operator `(int)` has precedence over the addition operator. First take a look at I. In that case, `a` will first be cast to an int (which has no effect because it is already an int) and then it will be added to `b`, which is still a double: the result of the addition will be a double, so you haven't fixed the problem. You can therefore eliminate (A) and (D).

    In II, `a + b` is enclosed in parentheses, so the addition will take place first. Adding `a` and `b` results in a double (20.7). This double is then cast to an int (20) and assigned to `d`. This is a legal assignment, so keep (B) and (E) and eliminate (C).

    Now, look at III. Here, the double `b` (10.7) is first cast to an int (10). This int is added to `a`, which is also an int. When two ints are added, the result is also an int, so this expression is also valid. The correct answer is (E).

3. **D**   In line 5 of the code segment, divide `a` by `b`. Because both of the operands are integers, the result will be truncated to an int: 11 divided by 4 is 2.75, which is then truncated to 2. Now you know that the first number printed will be 2 (assuming you don't run into a compilation error later in the code), so get rid of (A) and (B).

    In line 7, once again divide 11 by 4. This time, however, the variables that hold these values are doubles. Therefore, the result of dividing 11 by 4 will also be a double: 2.75. Get rid of (C).

    In line 9, yet again divide 11 by 4. The variable that holds 11 is an integer, while the variable that holds 4 is a double. With arithmetic operators, if one of the operands is a double and the other an integer, the integer is automatically cast to a double and the result of the operation is a double. Therefore, you get 2.75 again. The correct answer is (D).

4. **E**   In this question, you need to find the answer choice that doesn't work. If the answer to this question is not obvious to you, the best approach is to try each answer choice and see whether it could be the value of `i`. If it can, then get rid of it.

    Start with (A). Could `i` be equal to 0? Because `x % 50` gives the remainder when `x` is divided by 50, for `i` to equal 0, `x` would have to be evenly divisible by 50. There are plenty of integers that would work for `x` (50, 100, 150…). In fact, any multiple of 50 would work.

How about (B)? Is there a positive integer we can pick for x that leaves a remainder of 10 when divided by 50? Well, because 50 is evenly divisible by 50, 50 + 10, or 60, would leave a remainder of 10 when divided by 50. Other numbers that would work include 110 and 160. In fact, if you add 10 to any positive multiple of 50, you will get a number that leaves a remainder of 10 when divided by 50.

Following the same logic, find numbers that leave remainders of 25 and 40 when divided by 50. For example, 75 and 90 would work. Therefore, get rid of (C) and (D).

The only choice left is (E). So why is it that you can't get a remainder of 50 if you divide a positive integer by 50? Consider what happens if you divide 98 by 50. You get a remainder of 48. What if you divide 99 by 50? Now the remainder is 49. It seems if you increase 99 to 100, the remainder will increase to 50! But wait—100 divided by 50 actually leaves a remainder of 0.

The upshot of this example is that the value returned by the modulus operator will always be less than the operand to the right of the modulus operator. The correct answer is (E).

CHAPTER 4

1. **E** Choices (A), (B), and (D) all have valid indices within s1. Choice (C) has valid indices: it will simply produce an empty string. Choice (E) will attempt to go out of bounds of the String because the last valid index is 4. The last possible index for the ending argument is 5 (substring would go up to that index, but not include the letter at that index).

2. **C** Indices of characters within a string start at 0; thus the "a" is located at index 1. The second argument in the substring command is the ending index. The substring will go up to, but not include, this index. In this case, the substring will have a length of 1.

3. **B** The command s1.length() returns 5, so String s4 = s1.substring(s1.length() - 2) will store the characters from s1, starting at index 3, to the end of the string. So (B) is the correct answer.

4. **D** Using the return values of the compareTo method regarding lexicographical order:
   (A) "january" precedes "July"   (incorrect, uppercase comes first)
   (B) "July"   follows "June"   (incorrect, "July" comes first)
   (C) "january" precedes "June"   (incorrect, uppercase comes first)
   (D) "january" follows "June"   (correct)
   (E) "June"   precedes "July"   (incorrect, "July" comes first)

5. **B** Line 2 finds the string "oo" at index 1, storing the 1 in variable p. Line 3 is a valid substring command, but it does not store the substring. Line 4 simply repeats what was done at line 2, finding the string "oo" at index 1 once again.

CHAPTER 5

1. **C** You may have seen a problem like this one before. Be careful not to make assumptions; instead, note that i starts at 200 and is divided by 3 after each pass through the for loop. Note that i /= 3 is equivalent to i = i / 3, and integer division truncates the results. As you iterate through the loop, the values of i will be: 200, 66, 22, 7, 2.

    In the body of the loop, i is printed if i % 2 equals 0. i % 2 gives the remainder when i is divided by 2; i will give a remainder of 0 when divided by 2 whenever i is even. Therefore, 200, 66, 22, and 2 will be printed; 7 will not be printed. The correct answer is (C).

2. **A** Upon examination of both sides of the compound condition, p is combined with !q or q. If q is false, the left side (p && !q) has a chance of being true if p is also true. If q is true, the left side (p && q) has a chance of being true if p is also true. Thus, if p is true, we know for sure that either the left side OR the right side will be true. If p is false, both sides would be false. Thus, the overall expression will evaluate to the same value as p.

CHAPTER 6

1. **A** This question tests your ability to reason through a nested loop. The first thing you should note is that the output is triangular. The first row has two elements, the second has three elements, and so on. Generally, the output of a nested loop will be triangular if the conditional statement of the inner loop is dependent upon the value of the outer loop. If the two loops are independent, the output is usually rectangular.

    Trace through each answer choice and see which one will give you the first row: 0 1.

    The first time you go through the inner loop in (A), x will be 1; because z starts at 0 and the loop continues while z is less than or equal to 1, the inner loop will print out 0 1. So keep this choice. For (B), the condition of the inner loop is that z is strictly less than x, so this will only print out 0. Get rid of (B). Choice (C) will print out 0 1 2 3 4, so get rid of that too. Choice (D) will print 0 2 4 for the first line. Get rid of it. Choice (E) prints 0 1 for the first line, so keep it for now.

    You are now down to (A) and (E). Rather than tracing through each segment in its entirety, see what the differences are between each segment.

    The only difference is the outer for loop. In (A), it is

    `for (int x = 1; x < 5; x++)`

    And in (E), it is

    `for (int x = 1; x <= 5; x++)` (note the extra equals sign)

In (E), because the body of the outer loop is evaluated five times, it will print out five rows of numbers. Because the answer we are looking for prints only 4 rows, the correct answer must be (A).

2. **A** Option I works correctly, so get rid of (B) and (C).

Option II is incorrect, because the conditional `65 <= speed < 75` is illegal. A variable can't be compared to two numbers at once. This code will therefore cause a compile-time error. Get rid of (D).

Option III will compile and run, but it contains a logical error. Assume, for example, that a driver's speed is 85 mph. The driver should receive a fine of $300. If you trace through the code, you see that the value of the variable `fine` is, in fact, set to $300 in the body of the first `if` loop because the driver's speed is greater than or equal to 75. The problem is that the condition in the second `if` loop is also true: the driver's speed is greater than 65. The body of the second loop is executed and the fine is set to $150. Finally, the condition in the third loop is also true, so the fine is then set to $100. Because III is incorrect, get rid of (E). (Note that III would have been correct if the programmer had put `else` in front of the second and third loops.) The correct answer is (A).

3. **C** This question tests your ability to trace through a convoluted piece of code. A few things to note:

The body of the `if` loop is executed only if `b` is false.

The variable `i` is incremented by 5, not by 1, in the `for` loop.

The variable `i` is also incremented by 5 in the body of the `if` loop. This is something you would not normally do in your own code, but it is something you may see on the exam. Don't assume the variable in the conditional of the `for` loop is modified only in the `for` loop.

4. **B** Keep in mind that `&&` returns `true` if both operands are true, `||` returns `true` if one or more of its operands are true, and `!` reverses a boolean value.

The best way to crack questions involving booleans is often to just assign `true` or `false` to the variables and evaluate the expression.

Break `(a && b) || !(a || b)` into two pieces: `(a && b)` and `!(a || b)`. The variable `c` will be assigned `true` if either of these pieces is true. `(a && b)` is true when both `a` and `b` are true. Therefore, get rid of (A) and (D).

See what happens if both `a` and `b` are false. Clearly `(a && b)` evaluates to `false` in this case, but what about `!(a || b)`? `(a || b)` is false if both `a` and `b` are false, but the `!` operator inverts the value to `true`. So because `!(a || b)` is true, `(a && b) || !(a || b)` evaluates to `true`. Therefore, `c` will be assigned `true` when both `a` and `b` are false, so get rid of (C).

You are left with (B) and (E). See what happens when `a` is false and `b` is true. `(a && b)` evaluates to `false`. `(a || b)` is true, so `!(a || b)` is false. Therefore, `(a && b) || !(a || b)` is false and you can get rid of (E). The correct answer is (B).

5.   E   The code will finish executing when the conditional in the `while` loop is false. In other words, when `!(x > y || y >= z)` is true. So figure out which of the answer choices is equivalent to `!(x > y || y >= z)`.

Here's how to solve it step by step:

Recall that `!(a || b)` is equivalent to `!a && !b`. So `!(x > y || y >= z)` becomes `!(x > y) && !(y >= z)`.

`!(x > y)` is equivalent to `x <= y`, so you now have `x <= y && !(y >= z)`.

`!(y >= z)` is equivalent to `y < z`, so you have `x <= y && y < z`. The correct answer is (E).

6.   D   Each time the incremental statement `a++` is evaluated, the value of `a` is increased by one. So to answer this question, you need to figure out how many times `a` is incremented.

The outer loop will be evaluated 10 times. The inner loop will be evaluated six times for each time that the outer loop is evaluated. The code in the body of the inner loop will therefore execute 6 × 10 or 60 times. Note that the condition `k <= 5` evaluates to `true` when k equals 5. In the third loop, the value of z starts at 1 and is doubled after each pass through the loop. So the body of the innermost loop will execute when i equals 1, 2, 4, 8, and 16—or five times for each time the middle loop executes. Because 60 × 5 is 300, `a` will be incremented 300 times. The correct answer is (D).

7.   D   The trick to this question is that arithmetic operators don't modify their operands. So if x is 10 when we divide x by 3, the result is 3 but x remains the same. Likewise, taking the modulus of a number does not change the number itself. On the other hand, the post-increment operator `(++)` does change the value of the variable it operates on, so `x++` will increase the value of x by 1. The correct answer is (D).

8.   E   On the fourth line, `a + b` will be 13.7, but this result is cast to an int, so x will be 13. On the next line, a is first cast to a double and then divided by c. Because a is a double, c is automatically promoted to a double and the result of dividing the two is also a double. Therefore, y is 2.5.

On the next line, the parentheses cause the division to take place before the cast. Because a and c are ints, the result of dividing the two is truncated to an int, 2 in this case. The fact that we then cast the result to a double does not bring back the truncated decimal. Thus z is equal to 2, so w = 13 + 2.5 + 2. The correct answer is (E).

9.   D   This question tests your understanding of short-circuit evaluation. In each code segment, pay attention to the conditional in the `if` statement.

In I, the conditional statement is `x < y && 10 < y/z`. First, `x < y` is evaluated. Because x is 10 and y is 20, `x < y` evaluates to `true`. Then check `10 < y/z`. Because you divide by zero here, a run-time exception occurs. You can eliminate (A) and (E).

Now look at II. The conditional statement is x > y && 10 < y/z. Once again, first evaluate the operand to the left of the && operator. Because x is not greater than y, x > y evaluates to false. There's no need to evaluate the right-hand operand. With the && operator, if the left operand is false, the whole condition is false. Because the right-hand operand is not evaluated, y is never divided by z and a run-time exception does not occur. This means (B) and (D) are still possible; eliminate (C).

In III, the conditional statement is x < y || 10 < y/z. The left-hand side, x < y, evaluates to true. Notice that this time you have the or operator || in the middle of the conditional. With an "or" statement, if the left-hand side is true, the condition is true regardless of the value of the right side. Because the left side is true, there is no need to evaluate the right-hand side, and the division by 0 error never occurs. The correct answer is (D).

CHAPTER 7

1. **E** Because the database code can, in fact, be developed separately, tested separately, and possibly reused, all of the statements are correct. With questions like these, the easiest approach is to consider each candidate statement suspect, and look for ways in which they could be incorrect. If you find an incorrect one, cross off any answer choice that refers to it, including any choice that includes it AND another statement, because a combination of a true statement and a false statement is a false statement. Alternatively, when a candidate statement is true, put a star next to each answer choice that contains it. When you finish checking the statements, the one with the most stars wins.

   In the above, because all three statements are true, we can cross off (A), (B), and (C) because each choice indicates that only one statement is correct. Similarly, cross off (D), because it dismisses the third statement. The correct answer is (E).

2. **D** While the Java language makes it possible to make data fields public, one of the golden rules on the AP Computer Science A Exam is that data fields should always be designated private. Note that constants that are declared as static and final can be public; however, static constants apply to the class as a whole (because of the keyword static) and, thus, aren't data fields.

   Because data fields must be private, get rid of any answer choice that states they can be public. So get rid of (A), (B), and (E).

   Now look at (C). What would happen if all methods in a class were private? Instances of the class would be useless because clients couldn't ask the class to do anything for them. Classes need public methods to be useful. Eliminate (C).

   What about (D)? The first part is good because data fields should be private. What about the second sentence? Above, you saw that methods can be public. They can also be private. A private method is used internally by a class to help out a public method, but is not directly accessible by client programs. The correct answer is (D).

3. **C** Segment I is incorrect because it violates encapsulation. Thus, any answer that includes I can be dismissed out of hand. Thus, dismiss (A), (D), and (E). The implementation of a method can be changed without changing its client programs, so III is correct. Therefore, eliminate (B), which does not include III. Thus, the answer must be (C).

4. **D** Both `writeMe` methods completely ignore the input that's passed into them, so there's no opportunity for "hi" to be printed. So (B) cannot be the answer. The code is syntactically correct, so (A) cannot be the answer. Along the same lines, you're not doing anything that requires casting, or dealing with `null`, or dividing by a number that could potentially be 0, so (E) is not the answer. That leaves (C) and (D). Because you're creating a `String` object and passing to a method that takes a string as a parameter, the existence of the `writeMe(Object obj)` method is inconsequential. Thus, the only valid answer is (D).

5. **C** Both `writeMe` methods completely ignore the input that's passed into them, so there's no opportunity for "tmp" to be printed. So (D) cannot be the answer. The code is syntactically correct, so (A) cannot be the answer. Along the same lines, you're not doing anything that requires casting, or dealing with `null`, or dividing by a number that could potentially be 0, so (E) is not the answer. That leaves (B) and (C). Because you're creating an Object and passing to a method that takes an Object as a parameter, the existence of the `writeMe(String s)` method is inconsequential. Thus, the only valid answer is (C).

6. **C** Both `writeMe` methods completely ignore the input that's passed into them, so there's no opportunity for "hi" to be printed. So (B) cannot be the answer. Use an Object reference to refer to a `String` instance, because a string IS-A Object. Thus, the code is not syntactically incorrect, so (A) is not the answer. That leaves (C), (D), and (E). Because you're not doing any sort of casting, (E) is also an unlikely candidate. That leaves (C) and (D). Now the question becomes, when making overloaded calls, does Java pay attention to the type of the reference (which in this case is `Object`) or the type of the variable (which in this case is `String`)? It turns out that Java always pays attention to the type of the object, so (C) is correct.

7. **A** `tmp` is an `Object`, not a `String`; thus the code snippet `String tmp = new Object` is illegal. This code will generate a compile-time error. The correct answer is (A).

8. **B** This class is not declaring any methods at all, so (C) cannot possibly be correct. The code does not have any syntactical errors, so (A) cannot be correct. Choice (D) is nonsense because nothing can be both an attribute and a method, and (E), while true, is irrelevant. Being a primitive does not imply that `val` cannot be an attribute, so the "neither" part of the answer choice is a red herring. The correct answer is (B).

9. **A** Both `writeMe` methods have the same name and same parameter list, but they return different types. This is illegal. Thus, (A) is the correct answer.

CHAPTER 8

1. **B**   The length of the word is 4, so [word.length() - 1] will allow for 3 elements.

2. **C**   On line 1, an array of String is created and assigned to reference s. Note that the array to which s refers can hold only two strings. This does not prevent you, however, from pointing s to another array that is not of length 2. This is exactly what happens on line 3; s is reassigned to the same array that t references. This array has a length of 3. The correct answer is (C).

Here is what this looks like:

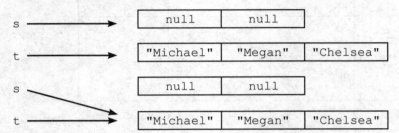

3. **D**   In the code segment, the variable a1 is declared as final. This means that once you assign an array to it, a1 must always point to that array. A compile-time error will occur when you try to assign the array referenced by b1 to a1. The correct answer is (D).

4. **C**   In the code segment, an array containing two integers is constructed and assigned to a variable named myArray. Because this reference is final, it cannot be assigned to another array. This does not prevent you, however, from changing the contents of the array that the variable myArray points to, as you do in the second line. The key here is that even though you change the contents of the array, it is still the same array. The correct answer is (C).

5. **B**   In the for loop in the method mod3, the variable i keeps track of the position in the array that you are inspecting for each iteration of the loop. numbers[i], on the other hand, is the value that is located at position i in the array. Option I will check to see whether position i is divisible by 3; that is not what you are looking for, so (A) and (D) are incorrect. Option II will check whether the number that is stored in the array at position i is divisible by 3, which is what you are looking for. Segment III will go into an infinite loop the first time it encounters an element in the array that is divisible by 3, so (C) and (E) can be eliminated. Only II will get the program to work as intended. The correct answer is (B).

6. **C**   Choice (A) does not assign the current values in arr to any element. Choice (B) will assign the contents of arr[3] to arr[0], thereby wiping out the original contents of arr[3].

The next three choices can be examined using trace tables. For each answer choice, let's assume arr[0] = 4 and arr[3] = 5.

(C)

	k	arr[0]	arr[3]
		4	5
int k = arr[3];	5	4	5
arr[3] = arr[0];	5	4	4
arr[0] = k;	5	5	4

(D)

	k	arr[0]	arr[3]
		4	5
int k = arr[3];	5	4	5
arr[0] = arr[3]; Note: at this point we have lost the original value of arr[0]	5	5	5
arr[3] = k;	5	5	5

(E)

	k	arr[0]	arr[3]
		4	5
int k = arr[0];	4	4	5
arr[3] = arr[0];	4	4	4
arr[0] = k; This swap has lost the original value of arr[0]	4	4	4

7. **A** When using an enhanced-for loop with an array, each element is read into a local variable, in this case, s. While s may change within the loop, that change does not get implemented within the original array. Thus the elements in the array remain unchanged. Choice (A) is the correct answer.

8. **D** This code is meant to reverse the order of the array by flipping the first element with the last, moving in toward the center.

The instruction middle = names.length/2 - 1; assigns a 2 to middle.

The for loop is controlled by x < middle so the two middle elements will not be flipped, because they are never accessed in the loop.

CHAPTER 9

1. **C** Walk through this step by step. Remember that the `add()` method that takes just one argument adds the argument to the end of the list. The second and third lines of code add "A" and "B" to the `ArrayList` one after another:

   `list.add("A")`

   `list.add("B")`

   After the code above executes, the list looks like

   `[A, B]`

   The next statement, `list.add(0, "C")`, adds "C" to the beginning of the list. Now the list looks like

   `[C, A, B]`

   After `list.add("D")` executes, the list looks like

   `[C, A, B, D]`

   The `set()` method replaces the value at the position indicated by the first argument. After `list.set(2, "E")` executes, the list looks like

   `[C, A, E, D]`

   After `list.remove(1)` executes, the list looks like

   `[C, E, D]`

   The correct answer is, therefore, (C).

2. **C** The key to this question is that as elements are removed from an `ArrayList`, the elements to the right of the removed element are shifted to the left, and their indices are reduced by 1.

   On the first pass through the `while` loop, i will be 0. Because the string in position 0 of `letters` equals A, it is removed and `letters` looks like:

   `[B, A, A, C, D, B]`

   The next time through the `while` loop, i will be 1. The letter in position 1 is equal to A, so it is removed. Now `letters` looks like:

   `[B, A, C, D, B]`

On the next pass through the `ArrayList`, i is 2. The letter in position 2 is a C, so it is not removed. The `while` loop will continue to iterate through the `ArrayList`, but because none of the strings in indices higher than 2 are equal to A, nothing else will be removed.

The correct answer is, therefore, (C).

3. **D** The first time through the `for` loop, the letter in position 0 is removed and `myList` looks like:

`[B, C, D, E]`

The letter that is in position 0, which is now B, is printed.

The next time through the `for` loop, i is 1, so C, the letter in position 1, is removed. Now `myList` looks like:

`[B, D, E]`

The letter that is in position 1, which is now D, is printed.

At this point, i is incremented to 2. The size of `myList` is also 2, so i is no longer less than `myList.size()`. The `for` loop does not execute again.

The correct answer is, therefore, (D).

4. **A** The first `for` loop initializes the `ArrayList` list so that it looks like

`[1, 2, 3, 4, 5, 6, 7, 8]`

Now take a look at the second `for` loop. Note that the highest value that j will reach is 7, one less than the size of the list. In the body of the `for` loop, the index of the position that you are setting is j divided by 2; the index can, therefore, never be greater than 3. In other words, you won't be modifying any values other than those in the first 4 positions of the `ArrayList`. Knowing this, eliminate (D) and (E).

On the first pass through the loop, j is 1 and we call `list.set(1 / 2, list.get(1))`. Because the result of integer division is truncated, this call is equivalent to `list.set(0, list.get(1))`, so the value of the element at position 0 is the same as that of position 1 and the `ArrayList` is

`[2, 2, 3, 4, 5, 6, 7, 8]`

On the next pass through the `for` loop, j is 2 and we call `list.set(1, list.get(2))`. The `ArrayList` looks like this:

`[2, 3, 3, 4, 5, 6, 7, 8]`

On the next pass we call, `list.get(1, list.get(3))`. The `ArrayList` now looks like this:

`[2, 4, 3, 4, 5, 6, 7, 8]`

If you continue to iterate through the second `for` loop, the `ArrayList` will end up looking like this:

```
[2, 4, 6, 8, 5, 6, 7, 8]
```

The correct answer is (A).

CHAPTER 10

1. **C** The variable identifier `arr` has already been created, eliminating (A), (B), and (E). While indices of arrays start at 0 and range to one less than the number of rows (or columns), the declaration should use the exact number of rows and columns desired in the array.

2. **A** This is an enhanced-`for` loop. The first loop uses the concept that a two-dimensional array is an array of arrays. It pulls off one row at a time and stores it in `nums`. The inner loop takes one element at a time from the row and stores it in `n`. There are no line breaks, so the array is simply printed one element after another. This answer is (A).

3. **D** The variable `numbers.length` is the number of rows in the two-dimensional array `numbers`. The variable `numbers[0].length` is the number of columns. Both the number of rows and the number of columns are 4.

   On the first pass through the `for` loop, `z` is 0, and `numbers[0].length - 1 - z` is 3. So the value of `numbers[0][3]` is added to the total. `numbers[0][3]` is 3.

   On the next pass, `z` is 1, `numbers[0].length - 1 - z` is 2, so the value of `numbers[1][2]` (which is 4) is added to the total.

   On the next pass, add the value at `numbers[2][1]`, which is 3, and on the final pass add the value at `numbers[3][0]`, which is 4.

   As you can see, the `for` loop simply finds the sum of one of the diagonals of the array. The correct answer is (D).

4. **C** Note that `k` is incremented by 2 in the inner `for` loop. The code segment will find the sum of all the integers in columns with even indices.

   ```
   numbers[0][0] + numbers[0][2] + numbers[0][4] + numbers[1][0] + numbers[1][2] +
   numbers[1][4] + numbers[2][0] + numbers[2][2] + numbers[2][4] = 37
   ```

5. **A** For each cell in the two-dimensional array, the code sets the value to the product of the indices for that cell. For example, `num[2][3]` is set to 2×3 or 6. The correct answer is (A).

6. **E** The index a will range from 0 to 3, while index b will range from 0 to 1. The indices are used in `[b][a]` order. The table below will help to visualize the traversal of the array. Each time b reaches the maximum index of rows, it will add a line break. The answer is (E).

b	a	s
0	0	1
1	0	1 5 "\n"
0	1	1 5 "\n" 2
1	1	1 5 "\n" 2 6 "\n"
0	2	1 5 "\n" 2 6 "\n" 3
1	2	1 5 "\n" 2 6 "\n" 3 4 "\n"
0	3	1 5 "\n" 2 6 "\n" 3 4 "\n" 4
1	3	1 5 "\n" 2 6 "\n" 3 4 "\n" 4 8

7. **E** The array m is declared using the number of rows (`arr.length`). Thus, there must be 3 entries, eliminating A and C. Index i will refer to each row. The number 2 is passed to n; thus, the column at index 2 (column 3) will be accessed. The correct column is 3 7 11.

8. **D** The index r starts traversing the array on the last row. The program accesses each element in the row and assigns it to the row above it. This has the net result of changing all the elements to be the same values as those in the last row.

CHAPTER 11

1. **E** If a constructor does not exist for a subclass, a default constructor with no parameters is generated in the superclass. This allows choices (A) and (B) to construct a Parent object and a Child object, respectively. Choice (C) will work: it will simply print null because the instance field str was never initialized. Choice (D) will invoke the inherited write() method from the Parent class, printing null once again. Choice (E) will cause an error because there is no method named write() that is expecting an int parameter in either class. The correct choice is (E).

2. **B** A class can, at most, directly extend one other class.

3. **E** Since Manager extends Employee, a manager is an Employee. Choices (A) and (B) will create Employee objects using two different Employee objects. Choices (C) and (D) create Manager objects with a more generic type (Employee). This is perfectly allowable, but not the other way around. Thus, (E) is invalid because it is trying to create an Employee object with a more specific type.

4. **D** If a parent class constructor is not called explicitly, the default constructor will be called. Thus, when the Croissant() constructor is called, before any lines of code within the constructor are executed, it calls the default constructor of the Pastry class. Before any lines of code are executed within the default Pastry constructor, the default Bread constructor is called. It is within this

constructor that "Freshly baked bread smells good" will be printed. Execution returns to the Pastry constructor where "Baking pastry is an art" is printed. Control finally returns to the Croissant constructor where "Croissants taste buttery" is printed. The correct answer is (D).

5.　**A**　Subclasses inherit fields and methods from the superclass. Even though there is no toString method in the Croissant class, the toString method in the Bread class will be invoked and bread will be printed. The answer is (A).

6.　**C**　This is a good question on which to use Process of Elimination. Don't try to find the best design right away. Instead, first get rid of the answer choices that you know are flawed.

The use of the word *unrelated* is a tip-off that (A) is incorrect. In general, classes and data fields in a program will be related to each other; otherwise, there would really be no point in writing the program in the first place.

Now look at (B). Whenever you are trying to decide whether one class is a subclass of the other, ask yourself whether an instance of the proposed subclass IS-A instance of the proposed superclass. For example, in this case you could ask whether a Pet IS-A Apartment. Obviously not, so get rid of (B).

Choice (C) looks good. Using primitive data fields allows you to store information about the Apartment within an instance of the class. Check the rest of the answer choices, though.

Like (B), (D) refers to subclasses. The difference this time is that Apartment is a subclass of the other classes. There are two problems here. First of all, the IS-A relationship doesn't hold. It would be incorrect to say that an Apartment IS-A Pet, Room, or Dishwasher. Here's the other problem: if Apartment is a subclass of all three of the other classes, then that means that Apartment has three immediate superclasses; in other words, Apartment extends three of the classes. However, in Java, a class can extend only one other class.

Finally, (E) uses a HAS-A relationship (this is also called composition). This design is similar to that of (C), except it uses objects instead of primitives, which (C) used. In this case, using objects will be overkill. For example, the specification from the rental company states only that they want to know whether the apartment has a dishwasher. A boolean can be used to store this information, so there's really no point in building a Dishwasher class. On the other hand, if the rental company had specified that they needed to store a lot of information about the type of dishwasher in each apartment, such as its color, manufacturer, and year of installation, then a Dishwasher class would be appropriate.

The correct answer is, therefore, (C).

7.   **D**   Choice (A) is incorrect because the `Motorcycle` class does not define a constructor that takes one argument. Note that unlike other methods, constructors are not inherited, so even though `Motorcycle` extends `Vehicle`, and `Vehicle` defines a constructor that takes one argument, `Motorcycles` will not inherit this constructor.

Choice (B) is incorrect for the same reason that (A) is incorrect. Even though the reference type is `Vehicle`, you are still constructing a `Motorcycle`, and the `Motorcycle` class does not define a constructor that takes one argument.

In (C), you are creating a `Vehicle` and assigning it to a reference of type `Motorcycle`. This is incorrect because a `Vehicle` is not necessarily a `Motorcycle`. The reference type of a variable must be the same class or a superclass of the object that you are trying to assign to it. It cannot be a subclass.

Choice (D) is correct. Because the `Motorcycle` class extends the `Vehicle` class, a `Motorcycle` IS-A `Vehicle` and we can assign a `Motorcycle` instance to a `Vehicle` reference.

The first line in (E) is correct. However, in the second line, you are trying to access a private data member. To fix this, you would need to call the public method `maxPassengers()` instead. This would look like the following:

```
int max = v3.maxPassengers();
```

Always bear in mind that all data members on the exam will be private; only methods are public. Therefore, when you use dot notation on an instance of a class, the part that follows the dot should end in parentheses. The only exception to this that you will see on the exam is the length attribute of an array.

CHAPTER 12

1.   **D**   The recursion is as follows:

```
mystery(6) = 2 * mystery(5)

    mystery(5) = 2 * mystery(4)

        mystery(4) = 2 * mystery(3)

            mystery(3) = 2 * mystery(2)

                mystery(2) = 2 * mystery(1)

                    mystery(1) = 2;
```

So `mystery(6) = 2 * 2 * 2 * 2 * 2 * 2 = 64`.

The correct answer is (D).

2. **D** On the first pass through the method, you get

   `10 + mystery(10 / 2) + mystery(10 / 4)`

   Which can be simplified to

   `10 + mystery(5) + mystery(2)`

   Now figure out what `mystery(5)` and `mystery(2)` are and add the results to 10.

   First, solve `mystery(5)`:

   `mystery(5) = 5 + mystery(5 / 2) + mystery(5 / 4) = 5 + mystery(2) + mystery(1)`

   `mystery(2) = 2 + mystery(2 / 2) + mystery(2 / 4) = 2 + mystery(1) + mystery(0)`

   `mystery(1) = 1 + mystery(1 / 2) + mystery(1 / 4) = 1 + mystery(0) + mystery(0)`

   Note that `mystery(0)` is our base case and returns 0. Working your way back up the recursive calls, you find that `mystery(1) = 1`, `mystery(2) = 3`, and `mystery(5) = 9`. Note that in solving `mystery(5)`, you ended up needing to solve `mystery(2)`.

   So in the original equation, `10 + mystery(5) + mystery(2)`, you can replace `mystery(5)` with 9 and `mystery(2)` with 3 to get `10 + 9 + 3`, which equals 22. The correct answer is (D).

3. **A** For any non-negative number n that is passed as an argument to the non-recursive method `mystery()`, the method will return `0 + 1 + 2 + 3 + … + n`. For example, a call to `mystery(5)` will return `0 + 1 + 2 + 3 + 4 + 5 = 15`. Note that the border case for `mystery()` occurs when 0 is passed to the method. In this case, the method returns 0.

   I (method `mystery2()`) is equivalent to `mystery()`.

   II (`mystery3()`) is not equivalent. Notice that `mystery3()` does not modify what is returned by the recursive call, whereas `mystery2()` adds x to the results of each recursive call. The method `mystery3()` will return 0 regardless of the value that is passed to the method.

   III (`mystery4()`) is equivalent to `mystery()` except when x equals 0. If 0 is passed to the method, the loop will infinitely recurse. Because `mystery4()` doesn't handle the border case correctly, III is incorrect.

   Only I is equivalent to the `mystery()` method, so (A) is correct.

4. **B** You originally pass 30 and 18 to the method as x and y, respectively. Each time the method is recursively called, 10 is added to x and 3 is subtracted from y. Therefore, x will eventually become larger than 100 and y will become smaller than 0, so you know that the condition of the base case will eventually be met, and infinite recursion won't occur. Eliminate (E).

Note that the base case returns 1. What about the non-base case? The method return `mystery (x + 10, y - 3)` simply returns whatever was returned by the call to `mystery()`; it doesn't modify it in any way. Because there's no modification of the return value, 1 is the only thing that is ever returned, no matter how many recursive calls occur. The correct answer is (B).

5. **B** The best way to solve this problem is to trace through each answer choice. But don't necessarily start with (A). Start with the answer choice that you think you can solve most quickly. In this case, (A) will probably take longer to check because it has two recursive calls. Instead, start with (D). Why (D)? Because each recursive call reduces the integer that you pass as an argument by 4, there won't be as many recursive calls as there will be with the other choices.

With (D), the first time through the method, you have `mystery(10) = 4 * mystery(6)`. Find that `mystery(6) = 4 * mystery(2)` and `mystery(2) = 4 * mystery(-2)`. Finally, `mystery(-2)` equals 1 (the base case). Working your way back up the call stack, you get `mystery(2) = 4`, `mystery(6) = 16` and `mystery(10) = 64`. So (D) is incorrect.

The choice with the next fewest recursive calls is (B). For this choice, `mystery(10) = 2 * mystery(8); mystery(8) = 2 * mystery(6); mystery(6) = 2 * mystery(4); mystery(4) = 2 * mystery(2); mystery(2) = 2 * mystery(0);` and `mystery(0) = 1`. Therefore, `mystery(2) = 2; mystery(4) = 4; mystery(6) = 8; mystery(8) = 16;` and `mystery(10) = 32`. The correct answer is (B).

Chapter 14
Required Lab Time
and Suggested Labs

This book is intended to help you prepare for the AP Computer Science A Exam, but we would be remiss if we didn't discuss the lab requirements for the course, as outlined by the College Board. The AP Computer Science A course must include a minimum of 20 hours of hands-on, structured lab experiences to engage the student in individual and group problem solving. The College Board puts it this way: each AP Computer Science A course must include a substantial laboratory component in which you design solutions to problems, express your solutions precisely (i.e., in the Java programming language), test your solutions, identify and correct errors (when mistakes occur), and compare possible solutions. Collectively, these laboratory experiences and activities should contain the following characteristics:

- Explore computing in context at a significant level, building upon existing code that provides examples of good style and appropriate use of programming language constructs.
- Contain a significant problem-solving component in which you study alternative approaches for solving a problem, solve new problems, or modify existing code to solve altered problems.
- Provide you with experience working with programs involving multiple interactive classes and may involve decomposing a program into classes and using inheritance and other object-oriented concepts as identified in the AP Computer Science A topic outline.

The College Board has posted 7 Student Lab Guides to their website. Here's a rundown of what those are:

- Consumer Review—In this lab, students explore the persuasive power of words. Students learn about sentiment value and how this can be used to construct or modify a review to be more positive or negative using string manipulation.
- Data—In this lab, students will discuss the importance of data in making decisions, learn how to set up and use a third-party library for data collection, and learn how to process this data once it has been read into a program. They will put these skills together to find relevant data and answer a specific question of interest.
- Steganography—Steganography is the practice of concealing messages or information within other non-secret text or data. Students will use the same code from Picture Lab (see a few Labs down) to explore the concepts of steganography and 2D arrays, hiding images or text inside other images.
- Celebrity—Students will discuss class design as it relates to the charades-like game Celebrity. This lab includes inheritance as the basis for one of the activities and also includes a Graphical User Interface (GUI).
- Elevens—This activity is related to a simple solitaire game called Elevens. Students learn the rules of Elevens and then play it using the supplied Graphical User Interface.

- Magpie Chatbot—Students explore some of the basics of Natural Language Processing. As they explore, they will work with a variety of methods of the `String` class and practice using `if` statements. Students will trace a complicated method to find words in user input.
- Picture—Students write methods that modify digital pictures. In writing these methods, they will learn how to traverse a two-dimensional array of integers or objects. Students will also be introduced to nested loops, binary numbers, interfaces, and inheritance.

Go to the AP Computer Science A section of the College Board's website for more information about each of these labs, plus downloadable PDFs. The location of these Labs is apcentral.collegeboard.org/courses/ap-computer-science-a/classroom-resources/lab-resource-page.

Part VI
Practice Tests

Practice Test 2

AP® Computer Science A Exam

SECTION I: Multiple-Choice Questions

DO NOT OPEN THIS BOOKLET UNTIL YOU ARE TOLD TO DO SO.

At a Glance

Total Time
1 hour 30 minutes
Number of Questions
40
Percent of Total Score
50%
Writing Instrument
Pencil required

Instructions

Section I of this examination contains 40 multiple-choice questions. Fill in only the ovals for numbers 1 through 40 on your answer sheet.

Indicate all of your answers to the multiple-choice questions on the answer sheet. No credit will be given for anything written in this exam booklet, but you may use the booklet for notes or scratch work. After you have decided which of the suggested answers is best, completely fill in the corresponding oval on the answer sheet. Give only one answer to each question. If you change an answer, be sure that the previous mark is erased completely. Here is a sample question and answer.

Sample Question	Sample Answer
Chicago is a (A) state (B) city (C) country (D) continent (E) county	Ⓐ ● Ⓒ Ⓓ Ⓔ

Use your time effectively, working as quickly as you can without losing accuracy. Do not spend too much time on any one question. Go on to other questions and come back to the ones you have not answered if you have time. It is not expected that everyone will know the answers to all the multiple-choice questions.

About Guessing

Many candidates wonder whether or not to guess the answers to questions about which they are not certain. Multiple-choice scores are based on the number of questions answered correctly. Points are not deducted for incorrect answers, and no points are awarded for unanswered questions. Because points are not deducted for incorrect answers, you are encouraged to answer all multiple-choice questions. On any questions you do not know the answer to, you should eliminate as many choices as you can, and then select the best answer among the remaining choices.

GO ON TO THE NEXT PAGE.

Java Quick Reference

Class Constructors and Methods	Explanation
String Class	
`String(String str)`	Constructs a new `String` object that represents the same sequence of characters as `str`
`int length()`	Returns the number of characters in a `String` object
`String substring(int from, int to)`	Returns the substring beginning at index `from` and ending at index `to - 1`
`String substring(int from)`	Returns `substring(from, length())`
`int indexOf(String str)`	Returns the index of the first occurrence of `str`; returns −1 if not found
`boolean equals(String other)`	Returns `true` if `this` is equal to `other`; returns `false` otherwise
`int compareTo(String other)`	Returns a value <0 if `this` is less than `other`; returns zero if `this` is equal to `other`; returns a value >0 if `this` is greater than `other`
Integer Class	
`Integer(int value)`	Constructs a new `Integer` object that represents the specified `int` value
`Integer.MIN_VALUE`	The minimum value represented by an `int` or `Integer`
`Integer.MAX_VALUE`	The maximum value represented by an `int` or `Integer`
`int intValue()`	Returns the value of this `Integer` as an `int`
Double Class	
`Double(double value)`	Constructs a new `Double` object that represents the specified `double` value
`double doubleValue()`	Returns the value of this `Double` as a `double`
Math Class	
`static int abs(int x)`	Returns the absolute value of an `int` value
`static double abs(double x)`	Returns the absolute value of a `double` value
`static double pow(double base, double exponent)`	Returns the value of the first parameter raised to the power of the second parameter
`static double sqrt(double x)`	Returns the positive square root of a `double` value
`static double random()`	Returns a `double` value greater than or equal to `0.0` and less than `1.0`
ArrayList Class	
`int size()`	Returns the number of elements in the list
`boolean add(E obj)`	Appends `obj` to end of list; returns `true`
`void add(int index, E obj)`	Inserts `obj` at position `index` (0 <= `index` <= `size`), moving elements at position `index` and higher to the right (adds 1 to their indices) and adds 1 to size
`E get(int index)`	Returns the element at position `index` in the list
`E set(int index, E obj)`	Replaces the element at position `index` with `obj`; returns the element formerly at position `index`
`E remove(int index)`	Removes element from position `index`, moving elements at position `index + 1` and higher to the left (subtracts 1 from their indices) and subtracts 1 from size; returns the element formerly at position `index`
Object Class	
`boolean equals(Object other)`	
`String toString()`	

GO ON TO THE NEXT PAGE.

COMPUTER SCIENCE A

SECTION I

Time—1 hour and 30 minutes

Number of Questions—40

Percent of total exam grade—50%

Directions: Determine the answer to each of the following questions or incomplete statements, using the available space for any necessary scratchwork. Then decide which is the best of the choices given and fill in the corresponding oval on the answer sheet. No credit will be given for anything written in the examination booklet. Do not spend too much time on any one problem.

<u>Notes:</u>
- Assume that the classes listed in the Java Quick Reference have been imported where appropriate.
- Assume that declarations of variables and methods appear within the context of an enclosing class.
- Assume that method calls that are not prefixed with an object or class name and are not shown within a complete class definition appear within the context of an enclosing class.
- Unless otherwise noted in the question, assume that parameters in the method calls are not `null` and that methods are called only when their preconditions are satisfied.

1. Which of the following will print a number less than 5?

   I.   `System.out.println (24 / 5 % 3 * 2);`
   II. `System.out.println (12 / 3 * 2 + 1);`
   III. `System.out.println ( 1 + 4 % 3 * 2);`

   (A) I only
   (B) II only
   (C) I and II only
   (D) I and III only
   (E) I, II, and III

2. What output is generated by the following line of code:

   ```
   System.out.println("Simon says, \n\\\"insert phrase here\"//");
   ```

   (A) `Simon says, \n \\ insert phrase here//`
   (B) `Simon says, \n \\ "insert phrase here"//`
   (C) `Simon says, \n "insert phrase here"`
   (D) `Simon says,`
       `  \"insert phrase here"/`
   (E) `Simon says,`
       `  \"insert phrase here"//`

GO ON TO THE NEXT PAGE.

3. Consider the following class with the numbers added for reference:

```
public class Tree
{
  private String name;
  private double height;
  private int rateOfGrowth;

  Tree(String n, double h, int r)
  {
    name = n;
    height = h;
    rateOfGrowth = r;
  }
  Tree(double h, int r)
  {
    height = h;
    rateOfGrowth = r;
  }
  Tree(String n)
  {
    name = n;
  }
  public String toString()
  {
    return name + " can grow up to " + height + " feet high, at a rate of " + rateOfGrowth +
    " inches per year";
  }
}
```

Which of the following code excerpts in a client program would cause an error?

(A) `Tree elm = new Tree("Elm", 60, 36);`
`System.out.println(elm.toString());`
(B) `Tree riverBirch = new Tree("River Birch", 40.0, (int)13.0);`
`System.out.println(riverBirch.toString());`
(C) `Tree redMaple = new Tree(60.0, 18);`
`System.out.println(redMaple.toString());`
(D) `Tree redwood = new Tree("Redwood", 300, 24.0);`
`System.out.println(redwood.toString());`
(E) `Tree sequoia = new Tree("Sequoia");`
`System.out.println(sequoia.toString());`

GO ON TO THE NEXT PAGE.

Questions 4–5 refer to the class SalesRep.

```
public class SalesRep
{
    private int idNum;
    private String Name;
    private int ytdSales;

    SalesRep(int i, String n, int ytd)
    {
        idNum = i;
        name = n;
        ytdSales = ytd;
    }

    public int getYtdSales() {return ytdSales;}
}
```

4. A client method, computeBonus, will return a salesRep bonus computed by multiplying his ytdSales by a percentage.

> /** Precondition: SalesRep s has ytdSales >= 0
> * @param s a SalesRep
> * @param percentage represents what percent of the ytdSales represents the bonus
> * @return amount of bonus for the SalesRep (ytdSales * bonus)
> */
>
> public static double computeBonus(SalesRep s, double percentage)
> {   /* missing code */   }

Which replacement for /* missing code */ is correct?

(A) `return ytdSales() * percentage;`
(B) `return getYtdSales() * percentage;`
(C) `return s.ytdSales() * percentage;`
(D) `return s.getYtdSales() * percentage;`
(E) `return s.getYtdSales() * s.percentage;`

GO ON TO THE NEXT PAGE.

5. An `ArrayList` was created to store a `SalesRep` object for every salesperson in the XYZ company. Below is the declaration for that `ArrayList`.

```
ArrayList<SalesRep> list1 = new ArrayList<SalesRep>();
```

The company decided to pay each `SalesRep` a bonus since the company had a very profitable year. Management wishes to project the total of that payout, but to do so, must first calculate the total sales for the company by adding together the `ytdSales` from each `SalesRep`. Which code excerpt will compute the `ytdSales` for the company?

(A) ```
double sum = 0;
for (ArrayList r : list1)
{   sum += r.get.getYtdSales(); }
```
(B) ```
double sum = 0;
for (SalesRep r.get : list1)
{   sum += r.getYtdSales(); }
```
(C) ```
double sum = 0;
for (SalesRep r : list1)
{   sum += r.getYtdSales(); }
```
(D) ```
double sum = 0;
for (int i = 0; i < list1.size(); i++)
{     sum += SalesRep.get(i).getYtdSales();}
```
(E) ```
double sum = 0;
for (int i = 0; i <= list1.size(); i++)
{   sum += list1.get(i).getYtdSales();}
```

6. Which of the following will print after the following code is executed?
```
String str = new String("superstar");
System.out.print(str.substring (1, 3) + " ");
str.substring(1);
System.out.print(str.substring (1, 3) + " ");
str.substring(1);
System.out.print(str.substring (1, 3) + " ");
```

(A) su  up  pe
(B) up  pe  er
(C) sup  upe  per
(D) up  up  up
(E) A `StringIndexOutOfBoundsException` will occur

**GO ON TO THE NEXT PAGE.**
```

7. A chess game must take turns allowing black and white players to move on the board. The player is indicated by the following variable where `true` indicates black and `false` indicates white:

```
boolean isBlack;
```

At the end of each player's turn, the variable `isBlack` must alternate between `true` and `false` to indicate the next player's turn. Consider the following code examples, then determine those that would accomplish this purpose.

```
I.   isBlack = !isBlack;
II.  if (!isBlack)
         isBlack = true;
     else
         isBlack = false;
III. if (isBlack)
         isBlack = false;
```

(A) I only
(B) II only
(C) I and II only
(D) I and III only
(E) I, II, and III

8. The following variables are declared, but their contents are unknown.

```
String str1 = new String("/*unknown value*/");
String str2 = new String("/*unknown value*/");
```

Consider the following decision statements and determine the statement that would fail to compare whether the value of `str1` is the same as the value of `str2`.

```
(A) if (str1 == str2)
(B) if (str1.equals(str2))
(C) if (str1.compareTo(str2) == 0)
(D) if (str1.substring(0).equals(str2.substring(0,str2.length())))
(E) if (str1.length() == str2.length() && str1.indexOf(str2) == 0)
```

9. Given the following boolean expression: `!(p || (q || !r))`

Which of the following conditions would result in an evaluation as `true`?

```
(A) p = true    q = true    r = true
(B) p = true    q = false   r = true
(C) p = false   q = true    r = false
(D) p = false   q = false   r = false
(E) p = false   q = false   r = true
```

GO ON TO THE NEXT PAGE.

10. Which boolean expression and values demonstrate a short-circuit evaluation?

    (A) p || !(q && r)   p = true   q = true   r = true
    (B) p || (q && !r)   p = false   q = true   r = false
    (C) p || !(q || r)   p = false   q = true   r = true
    (D) p && q && r   p = true   q = true   r = true
    (E) p && !(q && r)   p = true   q = true   r = true

11. Assume that p and q are boolean variables and have been properly initialized.

    ```
    !(!p || q) || !(p || !q)
    ```

    Which of the following best describe the result of evaluating the expression above?

    (A) true always
    (B) false always
    (C) true only if p is true
    (D) true only if q is true
    (E) true only if p and q have opposite truth values

12. What output is generated by the following code excerpt:

    ```
    int count = 0;
    String star = "*";
    for (int i = 1; i < 11; i++)
       for (int j = 10; j > 1; j -= 2)
       {
           star += "**";
           count++;
       }
    System.out.print("\n" + count + " " + star.length());
    ```

    (A) 50   100
    (B) 50   101
    (C) 51   100
    (D) 51   101
    (E) 90   181

GO ON TO THE NEXT PAGE.

13. What output is generated by the following code excerpt:

```
for (int i = 1; i <= 5; i++)
{
    for (int j = 1; j < i; j++)
    {
        System.out.print("- ");
    }
    for (int j = i; j <= 5; j++)
    {
        System.out.print("* ");
    }
    System.out.println();
}
```

(A) - - - - *
     - - - * *
     - - * * *
     - * * * *
     * * * * *

(B) * * * * *
     - * * * *
     - - * * *
     - - - * *
     - - - - *

(C) * - - - -
     * * - - -
     * * * - -
     * * * * -
     * * * * *

(D) * * * * *
     * * * * -
     * * * - -
     * * - - -
     * - - - -

(E) - - - - -
     - - - - *
     - - - * *
     - - * * *
     - * * * *

GO ON TO THE NEXT PAGE.

14. Consider the following code segments and determine those that would produce the same output.

I.
```
int sum = 0;
for (int i = 1; i < 3; i++)
{
    sum += 2 * i + 1;
}
System.out.println(sum);
```

II.
```
int sum = 0;
for (int i = 1; i <= 5; i++)
{
    if (i % 2 == 1)
        sum += i;
}
System.out.println(sum);
```

III.
```
int i = 5;
int sum = i;
while (i > 1)
{
    i -= 2;
    sum += i;
}
System.out.println(sum);
```

(A) I and II only
(B) I and III only
(C) II and III only
(D) I, II and III
(E) All three outputs are different.

GO ON TO THE NEXT PAGE.

15. Consider the following code segment:

```
/**
 * @param number is initialized with a positive integer value
 * @return the sum of odd integers between 1 and number
 */

public static int sumOdds(int number)
{
    int sum = 0;
    for  (/* missing code */)
    {
        sum += k;
    }
    return sum;
}
```

Which of the following replacements for /* missing code */ will satisfy the conditions of the method?

I.   int k = 1; k <= number; k++
II. int k = 1; k <= number; k += 2
III. int k = number; k >= 1; k -= 2

(A) I only
(B) II only
(C) III only
(D) I and III only
(E) I, II, and III

GO ON TO THE NEXT PAGE.

16. Using the following method to find the index of the largest value in an array. Choose the replacement(s) for /* some code */ that will accomplish the task as described.

/** Precondition: `arr` is initialized with integer values and is not empty
 * `Integer.MIN_VALUE` is a static constant containing the value −2147483648
 * @param `arr` the array to be processed
 * @return the location of the largest value in the array; if
 *   the largest value is stored in more than one element, return the
 *   first location within the array where the element is located
 */

Example: `int arr[] = {5, -3, 2, 5};` The method should return `0`.

```
public static int findMaximumIndex(int[] arr)
{
             /* some code */
}
```

I
```
int max = Integer.MIN_VALUE;
int loc = -1;
int i = 0;
while (i < arr.length)
{
  if (arr[i] > max)
  {
     max = arr[i];
     loc = i;
  }
  i++;
}
return loc;
```

II
```
int max = arr[arr.length - 1];
int loc = arr.length - 1;
int i = arr.length - 1;
while (i >= 0)
{
  if (arr[i] > max)
  {
     max = arr[i];
     loc = i;
  }
  i--;
}
return loc;
```

III
```
int i = 0;
int loc = 0;
int max = arr[loc];
while (i < arr.length)
{
  if (arr[i] > max)
  {
     max = arr[i];
     loc = i;
  }
  i++;
}
return loc;
```

(A) I only
(B) II only
(C) III only
(D) I and III only
(E) I, II, and III

GO ON TO THE NEXT PAGE.

17. The values of the static fields in the `Integer` class named `MIN_VALUE` and `MAX_VALUE` are constants containing the values -2147483648 and 2147483647 respectively. Determine the statement(s) below that will throw a compiler error.

(A) `int min = Integer.MIN_VALUE;`
(B) `int min = Integer.MIN_VALUE - 1;`
(C) `int num = Integer.MIN_VALUE + Integer.MAX_VALUE;`
(D) `int max = 2147483648;`
(E) All of the statements above

18. What is the output after the following code is executed:

```
int num = 5;
System.out.print("" + half(num) + num);

public static double half(int n)
{
        return n/2;
}
```

(A) 2.05
(B) 2.5
(C) 7.0
(D) 7.5
(E) Nothing will print, as an error will be thrown.

GO ON TO THE NEXT PAGE.

19. Consider the following class declaration that is intended to represent a rectangle.

```
public class MyRectangle
{
    private int width;
    private int height;
    private int perimeter;

    MyRectangle(int w, int h)
    {
        width = w;
        height = h;
        int perimeter = 2 * (width + height);
    }

    public double getPerimeter()
    {
        return perimeter;
    }
}
```

What is the output after the following code is executed:

```
MyRectangle rect = new MyRectangle(2, 3);
System.out.print(rect.getPerimeter());
```

(A) 0

(B) 0.0

(C) 10

(D) 10.0

(E) None of the above; an error will be thrown.

GO ON TO THE NEXT PAGE.

Questions 20–22 refer to the following incomplete class declaration that is intended to represent a car.

```
public class Car
{
    private String model;
    private int numDoors;
    private boolean isFourWheelDrive;
    private int mpg;

    /**
     * Constructs a car
     */
    Car( )
    {

    }

    /**
     * Constructs a car
     * @param model
     * @param numDoors
     * @param isFourWheelDrive
     * @param mpg
     */
    Car(String model, int numDoors, boolean isFourWheelDrive, int mpg)
    {
        /* Implementation not shown */
    }

    /**
     * Compute the miles per gallon (milesDriven/gallons)
     * and stores the result in mpg, rounded to the nearest gallon
     * >= 0.5 would round up, < 0.5 would round down
     * @param milesDriven
     * @param gallons
     */
    public void setMpg(int milesDriven, double gallons)
    {
        /* Implementation not shown */
    }

    /**
     * Updates the model of the car
     * @param model
     */
    public void setModel(String model)
    {
        model = model;
    }
```

GO ON TO THE NEXT PAGE.

```
/**
 *
 * @ return model
 */
public String getModel()
{
    return model;
}
/**
 * Updates the number of doors on the car
 * @param numDoors
 */
public void setnumDoors(int numDoors)
{
    /* Implementation not shown */
}


/**
 * Updates isFourWheelDrive true if the car has four-wheel drive, false if not
 * @param isFourWheelDrive
 */
public void setIsFourWheelDrive (boolean isFourWheelDrive)
{
    /* Implementation not shown */
}


/**
 * Returns the values stored in the object
 */
public String toString()
{
    return "Model: " + model + " is 4-wheel drive: " + isFourWheelDrive;
}
}
```

20. The programmer wishes to add an additional constructor. Which of the following would be invalid as a constructor?

(A) `Car(String model)`
(B) `Car(String model, int mpg, boolean isFourWheelDrive)`
(C) `Car(String model, int numDoors)`
(D) `Car(String model, int mpg, boolean isFourWheelDrive, int numDoors)`
(E) `Car(String model, int numDoors, boolean isFourWheelDrive, int milesDriven,`
     `double gallons)`

GO ON TO THE NEXT PAGE.

21. The following code is in a client program.

```
Car fordTruck = new Car();

fordTruck.setModel("Tacoma");

if (fordTruck.getModel().equals("Tacoma"))
    fordTruck.setIsFourWheelDrive(true);

System.out.println(fordTruck);
```

What will be output by the program?

(A) `Model: Tacoma is 4-wheel drive: true`
(B) `Model: Tacoma is 4-wheel drive: false`
(C) `Model: null is 4-wheel drive: true`
(D) `Model: null is 4-wheel drive: false`
(E) A `NullPointerException` will be thrown

22. Which of the following can replace /* Implementation not shown */ in the `setMpg` method?

(A) `mpg = milesDriven / gallons;`
(B) `mpg = milesDriven / gallons + 0.5;`
(C) `mpg = milesDriven / (int) gallons + 0.5;`
(D) `mpg = (int) (milesDriven / gallons) + 0.5;`
(E) `mpg = (int) (milesDriven / gallons + 0.5);`

GO ON TO THE NEXT PAGE.

Questions 23–25 refer to the following class declarations.

```
public class Bee
{
    private int lifeSpan;
    private String name;

    Bee(String n, int life)
    {
        lifeSpan = life;
        name = n;
    }

    public String getName()
    {
        return name;
    }

    public String toString()
    {
        return " The " + name + "s live " + lifeSpan + " months.";
    }
}

public class Queen extends Bee
{
    private int eggsPerDay;

    Queen(String name, int months, int eggs)
    {
        super(name, months);
        eggsPerDay = eggs;
    }

    public String toString()
    {
        return " The queen"  + " lays " + eggsPerDay + " eggs.";
    }
}
```

23. What is output after the following lines of code are executed in a client program?

```
Bee bee1 = new Queen("honey bee", 6, 2000);
System.out.println(bee1.toString());
```

(A) The queen lays 2000 eggs.
(B) The honey bee lays 2000 eggs.
(C) The honey bees live 6 months.
(D) The honey bees live 6 months. The queen lays 2000 eggs.
(E) An error will be thrown because of mismatched data types.

GO ON TO THE NEXT PAGE.

24. The programmer wishes to include an accessor method for the field called `name`. In which class should this method be included?

    (A) Only in the `Bee` class.
    (B) Only in the `Queen` class.
    (C) It could be included in either the `Bee` class or the `Queen` class.
    (D) It should be included in both classes.
    (E) The method should not be included in either class because the data is private.

25. Only queen bees lay eggs that hatch into productive bees for the colony. The other two types of bees in a colony are drone (male) and worker (female) bees. What information would be most helpful to determine the best design for a class implementation for drones and worker bees?

    (A) Whether the drones and workers have distinctly different lifespans than queens
    (B) Whether there are many more drones and workers than queens
    (C) Whether there are more drones than workers (or the reverse)
    (D) What data needs to be included to accurately represent the state and behavior of drones and workers
    (E) All the above

26. A program passes an array to a method in the same class to create multiples of 5. Determine the output of the following code.

```
double arr[];
arr = new double[5];
multOf5(arr);
for (int i = 0; i < arr.length; i++)
    System.out.print(arr[i] + "  ");


public static void multOf5(double a[])
{
    for (int i = 0; i < a.length; i++)
        a[i] = i * 5;
}
```

    (A) 0.0   5.0   10.0   15.0   20.0
    (B) 0.0   0.0   0.0   0.0   0.0   0.0
    (C) 0.0   5.0   10.0   15.0   20.0   25.0
    (D) An error will occur because of a type mismatch.
    (E) An error will occur because the array was not initialized.

GO ON TO THE NEXT PAGE.

27. Consider the following method:

```
public static int[] op(int[][] matrix, int m)
{
        int[] result = new int[matrix.length];
        for (int j = 0; j < matrix.length; j++)
        {
            result[j] = matrix[m][j] - matrix[j][m];
        }
        return result;
}
```

The following code segment appears in the same class:

```
int mat[][] = {{1, 2, 3, 4}, {1, 3, 5, 7}, {2, 4, 6, 8}, {4, 3, 2, 1}};
int[] arr = op(mat, 3);
```

Which of the following represents the contents of `arr` as a result of the code segment?

(A) {0, -4, -6, 0}
(B) {0, 4, 6, 0}
(C) {8, 10, 10, 2}
(D) {2, 4, 6, 8}
(E) {3, 5, 6, 2}

28. A programmer wishes to declare and initialize an `ArrayList` with random integers between 1 and 100. Choose the code that can replace /* missing code */ to accomplish the task.

```
ArrayList<Integer> list2= new ArrayList<Integer>();
for (int i = 0; i < 1000; i++)
{
    /* missing code */
}
```

(A) `list2.add((Math.random() * 100 + 1));`
(B) `list2.add((int)(Math.random() * 99 + 0.5));`
(C) `list2.add((int)(Math.random() * 100 + 0.5));`
(D) `list2.add((int)(Math.random() * 100 + 1));`
(E) `list2.add((Integer)(Math.random() * 100 + 0.5));`

GO ON TO THE NEXT PAGE.

29. What is printed after the following code is executed?

```
ArrayList<String> list1 = new ArrayList<String>();
list1.add("A");
list1.add("B");
list1.add("C");
list1.add("D");
list1.add("E");


for (int k = 0; k < list1.size(); k += 2)
{
        list1.remove(k);
}
for (int k = 1; k <= 3; k++)
{
        list1.add(1, "*");
}
for (String word : list1)
{
        System.out.print(word + " ");
}
```

(A) B * * * C
(B) B * * * D
(C) B * * * E
(D) B * C * E
(E) B * * * C E

30. What is the result of calling mystery(5)?

```
public static int mystery(int n)
{
        if (n == 1)
                return 1;
        else if (n == 2)
                return 2;
        else
                return n + mystery(n - 1) + mystery(n - 2);
}
```

(A) 13
(B) 15
(C) 17
(D) 19
(E) 23

GO ON TO THE NEXT PAGE.

31. What is the result of calling mystery("PLANT");

```
public static void mystery(String s)
{
    int i = 1;
    if (s.length() > 1)
    {
        String temp = s.substring(s.length() - i);
        System.out.println(temp);
        i++;
        mystery(temp);
    }
}
```

(A) T
     NT
     ANT
     LANT
     PLANT

(B) LANT
     ANT
     NT
     T

(C) LANT
     ANT
     NT

(D) T

(E) PLANT

GO ON TO THE NEXT PAGE.

Questions 32–33 refers to the following class declarations, which are intended to represent performances of plays.

```
public class Performance
{
    private String name;
    private String season;
    private int year;

    Performance(String n, String s, int y)
    {
        name = n;
        season = s;
        year = y;
    }
    public String toString()
    {
        return name + " will be performed in " + season + " of " + year;
    }
}

public class Play
{
    private Performance performance;
    private String mainCharacter;
    private String starringActor;

    Play(String n, String s, int y, String m, String star)
    {
        Performance p = new Performance(n, s, y);
        performance = p;
        mainCharacter = m;
        starringActor = star;
    }

    public String getMainCharacter()
    {
        return mainCharacter;
    }

    public String getStarringActor()
    {
        return starringActor;
    }
    public String toString()
    {
        return performance + " with " + starringActor + " as " + mainCharacter;
    }
}
```

GO ON TO THE NEXT PAGE.

32. What is the output after the following lines of code are executed in a client program?

```
Play p1 = new Play("Beauty and the Beast", "Winter",  2023, "Belle", "Kira");
Play p2 = new Play("Peter Pan", "Spring",  2023, "Peter", "Charlie");
Play p3 = new Play("Goldilocks and the Three Bears", "Summer",  2023,
                   "Goldilocks", "Sophia");
Play[] schedule = {p1, p2, p3};
System.out.println(schedule[1]);
```

(A) Charlie as Peter

(B) Performance@7c53a9eb with Charlie as Peter

(C) Peter Pan will be performed in Spring of 2023

(D) Peter Pan will be performed in Spring of 2023 with Charlie as Peter

(E) An error will be thrown.

33. Code is to be added to the same client program to build the following ArrayList of actors.

```
ArrayList<String> actors = new ArrayList<String>();
```

The starringActor(s) found in the schedule array (in the previous problem) will be stored in the actors ArrayList. Which of the following will properly add every the starringActor to the ArrayList?

(A) ```
for (Play p : schedule)
   actors.add(p.starringActor);
```

(B) ```
for (Play p : schedule)
   actors.add(p.getStarringActor());
```

(C) ```
for (Performance p : schedule)
   actors.add(p.getStarringActor());
```

(D) ```
for (int j = 0; j < schedule.length; j++)
   actors.add(schedule[j].starringActor);
```

(E) ```
for (int j = 0; j < schedule.length; j++)
   actors.add(schedule.get[j].getStarringActor());
```

**GO ON TO THE NEXT PAGE.**
```

34. Consider the following classes:

```
public class Flower
{
    private int height;

    public Flower()          /* constructor without parameters */
    {
        height = 0;
    }
    public String toString()
    {
        return "height = " +  height;
    }
}

public class Daffodil extends Flower
{
    /* accessor and mutator methods not shown */
}
```

Which of the following declarations is valid?

I.   `Flower lily = new Flower();`
II. `Flower daffy = new Daffodil();`
III. `Daffodil daffo = new Daffodil();`

(A) I only
(B) II only
(C) III only
(D) I and II only
(E) I, II and III

35. A binary search is used to find a target value in an array of 4000 elements, sorted in ascending order. Assuming a target value is in the array, what is the maximum number of searches that will occur to locate the target value?

(A) 11
(B) 12
(C) 15
(D) 40
(E) 2000

GO ON TO THE NEXT PAGE.

Questions 36–37 refer to the following sort method.

```java
public static void sort(int arr[])
{
    int i;
    int num;
    int j;
    for (i = 1; i < arr.length; i++)        /* outer loop */
    {
        num = arr[i];
        j = i - 1;
        while (j >= 0 && arr[j] > num)       /* inner loop */
        {
                arr[j + 1] = arr[j];
                j = j - 1;
        }
        arr[j + 1] = num;
    }
}
```

36. If `sort` is called with an array of n elements, what is the maximum number of times the loop indicated by /* outer loop */ will be executed?

    (A) n
    (B) n / 2
    (C) n − 1
    (D) n + 1
    (E) 2^n

37. If `sort` is called with an array of n elements, on any given pass through /* outer loop */, what is the least number of times the loop indicated by /* inner loop */ will be executed?

    (A) 0
    (B) 1
    (C) n / 2
    (D) n − 2
    (E) n − 1

GO ON TO THE NEXT PAGE.

38. What changes to `mat` are implemented by the following code excerpt?

```
int for (int a = 0; a < mat.length; a++)
{
    temp = mat[a][0];
    for (int b = 1; b < mat[0].length; b++)
    {
        mat[a][b - 1] = mat[a][b];
    }
    mat[a][mat[0].length - 1] = temp;
}
```

(A) Every two columns are flipped. If there are an odd number of columns, there is no change to the last column.

(B) Every two rows are flipped. If there are an odd number of rows, there is no change to the last row.

(C) All columns are shifted left, and elements from the first column are moved to the last column.

(D) All rows are shifted upward, and elements from the first row are moved to the bottom row.

(E) An `outOfBounds` error is thrown.

GO ON TO THE NEXT PAGE.

Questions 39–40 refer to the following class declarations.

```
public class Sport
{
    private String season;
    private int year;

    Sport(String s, int y)
    {
        season = s;
        year = y;
    }

    public String toString()
    {
        return season + " " + year;
    }
}
public class Baseball extends Sport
{
    private int numPositions;

    Baseball(String s, int y)
    {
        super(s, y);
        numPositions = 10;
    }
}
```

39. The programmer wishes to store the following objects into an `ArrayList`.

```
Baseball b1 = new Baseball("Spring", 2022);
Baseball b2 = new Baseball("Summer", 2022);
Baseball b3 = new Baseball("Summer", 2023);
Baseball b4 = new Baseball("Summer", 2024);
Sport s1 = new Sport("Winter", 100);
```

Which of the following is a valid declaration for the `ArrayList`?

(A) `ArrayList<Sport> sports = new ArrayList<Sport>();`

(B) `ArrayList<Sport> sports = new ArrayList<Baseball>();`

(C) `ArrayList<Baseball> sports = new ArrayList<Sport>();`

(D) `ArrayList<Baseball> sports = new ArrayList<Baseball>();`

(E) These objects cannot be combined into a single `ArrayList`.

GO ON TO THE NEXT PAGE.

40. Which of the code excerpts will remove all objects from the `ArrayList` with a `season` designated as `"Summer"`?

I.
```
for (int i = 0; i < sports.size(); i++)
{
  if (sports.get(i).getSeason().equals("Summer"))
     sports.remove(i);
}
```

II.
```
int i = 0;
for (Sport a: sports)
{
if (a.getSeason().equals("Summer"))
     a.remove(i);
i++;
}
```

III.
```
for (int i = sports.size() - 1; i >= 0 ; i--)
{
  if (sports.get(i).getSeason().equals("Summer"))
     sports.remove(i);
}
```

(A) I only
(B) II only
(C) III only
(D) I and II only
(E) I and III only

END OF SECTION I

**IF YOU FINISH BEFORE TIME IS CALLED,
YOU MAY CHECK YOUR WORK ON THIS SECTION.**

DO NOT GO ON TO SECTION II UNTIL YOU ARE TOLD TO DO SO.

COMPUTER SCIENCE A

SECTION II

Time—1 hour and 30 minutes

Number of Questions—4

Percent of Total Grade—50%

Directions: SHOW ALL YOUR WORK. REMEMBER THAT PROGRAM SEGMENTS ARE TO BE WRITTEN IN JAVA™.

Notes:

- Assume that the classes listed in the Java Quick Reference have been imported where appropriate.

- Unless otherwise noted in the question, assume that parameters in method calls are not `null` and that methods are called only when their preconditions are satisfied.

- In writing solutions for each question, you may use any of the accessible methods that are listed in classes defined in that question. Writing significant amounts of code that can be replaced by a call to one of these methods will not receive full credit.

FREE-RESPONSE QUESTIONS

1. This question involves writing methods for a `PigLatin` class. The `PigLatin` class stores a phrase in an instance variable and has three methods. The first will detect whether the parameter sent is a vowel, the second returns a word converted into pig latin, and the third will convert a phrase into pig latin.

```java
public class PigLatin
{
    private String phrase;

    /** Constructs a new PigLatin object */
    public PigLatin(String phrase)
    {   this.phrase = phrase;   }

    /** Returns true if the letter sent is a vowel: a, e, i, o, or u
     * If the letter is not a vowel returns false: "y" is not considered a vowel
     * Preconditions:  letter will not be null and will be exactly one character long,
     *                 letter will not be a space; letter will be lowercase
     * Postconditions: letter is not modified,
     *                 only true or false, as explained above, is returned
     */
    public boolean isLetterAVowel(String letter)
    {  /* to be implemented in part (a) */  }


    /** Returns a word converted to pig latin
     * Precondition: word.length > 0; all letters will be lowercase
     *               all words with word.length == 1 will be a single vowel
     * Postcondition: the parameter word is not modified
     */
    public String convertWord(String word)
    {  /* to be implemented in part (b) */  }
```

GO ON TO THE NEXT PAGE.

```
/** Returns the instance field phrase converted to pig latin
 * Returns the empty string if the parameter word is empty or null
 * Precondition: word may be null or any length
 *                  the last character of the phrase will be a letter, not a space
 *                  all characters will be lowercase
 * Postcondition: phrase is not modified, returns phrase converted to pig latin
 */


public String convertPhrase()
    {    /* to be implemented in part (c) */     }

}
```

(a) Write the PigLatin method isLetterAVowel, which will return true if the parameter letter is a vowel (a, e, i, o, or u), and otherwise return false. The parameter letter will not be null or the empty string and will be exactly one character long. The value of the parameter will be a letter in lowercase.

Code segments	Value returned
isLetterAVowel("a");	true
isLetterAVowel("e");	true
isLetterAVowel("u");	true
isLetterAVowel("b");	false
isLetterAVowel("y");	false

```
Class information for this question

    public class PigLatin

    private String phrase;
    public PigLatin(String phrase)
    public boolean isLetterAVowel(String letter)
    public String convertWord(String word)
    public String convertPhrase()
```

GO ON TO THE NEXT PAGE.

The `PigLatin` class includes the method `isLetterAVowel`.

Complete method `isLetterAVowel` below.

```
/** Returns true if the letter sent is a vowel: a, e, i, o, or u
 * If the letter is not a vowel returns false: "y" is not considered a vowel
 * Preconditions:  letter will not be null and will be exactly one character long,
 *                 letter will not be a space; letter will be lowercase
 * Postconditions: letter is not modified
 *                 only true or false, as explained above, is returned
 */
public boolean isLetterAVowel(String letter)
```

Begin your response at the top of a new page in the separate Free Response booklet and fill in the appropriate circle at the top of each page to indicate the question number. If there are multiple parts to this question, write the part letter with your response.

GO ON TO THE NEXT PAGE.

(b) Write the `PigLatin` method `convertWord`, which will return a word converted to pig latin.

There will be three rules used to convert each word to pig latin:

- If `word` starts with a vowel, add the word "way" at the end of the word.
  "apple" would become "appleway", "a" would become "away"
- If `word` starts with a consonant and a vowel, move the consonant to the end of the word and add "ay".
  "dog" would become "ogday", "house" would become "ousehay"
- If `word` starts with two consonants, move both consonants to the end of the word and add "ay".
  "charge" would become "argechay", "sled" would become "edslay"

You must use `isLetterAVowel` appropriately to receive full credit.

Code segments	Value returned
`convertWord("ant");`	`"antway"`
`convertWord("cat");`	`"atcay"`
`convertWord("clone");`	`"oneclay"`

Class information for this question

```
public class PigLatin

private String phrase;
public PigLatin(String phrase)
public boolean isLetterAVowel(String letter)
public String convertWord(String word)
public String convertPhrase()
```

GO ON TO THE NEXT PAGE.

The `PigLatin` class includes the method `convertWord`.

Complete method `convertWord` below.

```
/** Returns a word converted to pig latin
 * Precondition: word.length > 0; all letters will be lowercase
 *               all words with word.length == 1 will be a single vowel
 * Postcondition: the parameter word is not modified
 *               returns word converted to
 *               pig latin
 */
public String convertWord(String word)
```

Begin your response at the top of a new page in the separate Free Response booklet and fill in the appropriate circle at the top of each page to indicate the question number. If there are multiple parts to this question, write the part letter with your response.

GO ON TO THE NEXT PAGE.

(c) Write the `PigLatin` method `convertPhrase`, which will return the instance field `phrase` converted to pig latin. If `phrase` is empty or `null`, it will return the empty string. All characters in `phrase` will be lowercase letters.

You must use `convertWord` appropriately to receive full credit.

Code segments	Value returned
`convertPhrase("the cat is sleepy");`	`"ethay atcay isway eepyslay"`
`convertPhrase("where are you");`	`"erewhay areway ouyay"`
`convertPhrase(null);`	`""`
`convertPhrase("");`	`""`

Class information for this question

```
public class PigLatin

private String phrase;
public PigLatin(String phrase)
public boolean isLetterAVowel(String letter)
public String convertWord(String word)
public String convertPhrase()
```

GO ON TO THE NEXT PAGE.

The PigLatin class includes the method convertPhrase.

Complete method convertPhrase below.

```
/** Returns the instance field phrase converted to pig latin
 * Returns the empty string if the parameter word is empty or null
 * Precondition: word may be null or any length
 *               the last character of the phrase will be a letter, not a space
 *               all characters will be lowercase
 * Postcondition: phrase is not modified, returns phrase converted to pig latin
 */
public String convertPhrase()
```

Begin your response at the top of a new page in the separate Free Response booklet and fill in the appropriate circle at the top of each page to indicate the question number. If there are multiple parts to this question, write the part letter with your response.

GO ON TO THE NEXT PAGE.

This question involves writing a subclass for the `FrequentFlyerMember` class. This class holds information about frequent flyer members, including their names, account numbers, lifetime miles, and status levels.

2. The `FrequentFlyerMember` class definition is shown below.

```java
public class FrequentFlyerMember
{
    private int acctNumber;
    private String flyerName;
    private int lifetimeMiles;
    private int statusLevel;

    FrequentFlyerMember(int n, String name, int miles)
    {
        acctNumber = n;
        flyerName = name;
        lifetimeMiles = miles;
        statusLevel = 1;
    }


    //* Adds miles to lifetimeMiles */
    public void addMiles(int miles)
    {
        lifetimeMiles += miles;
    }


    //* Changes the status level */
    public void setStatusLevel(int level)
    {
        statusLevel = level;
    }


    //* Prints selected status information */
    public String getStatusInfo()
    {
        return acctNumber + " " + flyerName + " level " + statusLevel;
    }

//*  other methods may exist but are not shown  */
}
```

You will write the class `PremierMember`, which is a subclass of `FrequentFlyerMember`.

A `PremierMember` has a `premierClubMembership` field represented by a boolean data type. It should be set to `true`. This flyer is also entitled to two `freeBags` which should be represented by an `int` field. The member will also have another String field named `otherFrequentFlyerMember` to store the name of any other frequent flyer memberships the flyer may be entitled to. These fields should be initialized in the constructor.

Information about the flyer's number, name, lifetime miles, and status level should be maintained and managed in the `FrequentFlyerMember` class.

GO ON TO THE NEXT PAGE.

Statement	Class Specifications or Print

FrequentFlyerMember smith1 = new FrequentFlyerMember(14256, "Luke Smith", 1000);	Class Specification:
	
	smith1 is a FrequentFlyerMember
	  number: 14256
	  name: Luke Smith
	  miles: 1000
	  statusLevel: 1

smith1.addMiles(3025);	Class Specification change: smith1 miles:3025
smith1.setStatusLevel(2);	Class Specification change: smith1 statusLevel: 2
System.out.println(smith1.getStatusInfo());	Printed: 14256 Luke Smith level 2

PremierMember jones1 = new PremierMember
 	
(97531, "Marcie Jones", "British Airways", 9000);
	Class Specification:
	
	jones1 is a PremierMember
	  number: 97531
	  name: Marcie Jones
	  miles: 9000
	  statusLevel: 1

jones1.addMiles(10000);	Class Specification change: jones1 miles: 19000
jones1.setStatusLevel(5);	Class Specification change: jones1 statusLevel: 5
System.out.println(jones1.getStatusInfo());	Printed: 97531 Marcie Jones level 5 also a member of British Airways

GO ON TO THE NEXT PAGE.

Write the complete `PremierMember` class. Your implementation must meet all specifications and conform to the examples shown in the preceding table.

Begin your response at the top of a new page in the separate Free Response booklet and fill in the appropriate circle at the top of each page to indicate the question number. If there are multiple parts to this question, write the part letter with your response.

GO ON TO THE NEXT PAGE.

3. A `factorpair` is constructed from two (possibly non-distinct) numbers whose product is a given number. The `Factors` class constructs and stores all the given `FactorPair` objects of a number into an `ArrayList` with no duplicate pairs. The constructor uses a method: `buildArrayList` to create the `FactorPair` objects and create the `ArrayList`. The class utilizes a method `findMostPairs` to compare the number of `FactorPair` objects between two different numbers and return the number with the most `FactorPair` objects. If both numbers have the same number of `FactorPair` objects, the method returns −1. The `toString` method will print all the `FactorPair` objects within an `ArrayList`. You will write three methods of the `Factors` class: `buildArrayList`, `findMostPairs`, and `toString`.

```
public class FactorPair
{
    /** factor1 and factor2 represent two factors of a number */
    private int factor1;
    private int factor2;

    FactorPair(int f1, int f2)
    {
        factor1 = f1;
        factor2 = f2;
    }

    /* returns the first factor of a pair */
    public int getFactor1()
    { return factor1; }

    /* returns the second factor of a pair */
    public int getFactor2()
    { return factor2; }
}

public class Factors
{
    private int number;
    private ArrayList<FactorPair> pairs = new ArrayList<FactorPair>();

    Factors(int n)
    {
        number = n;
        pairs = buildArrayList(n);
    }

    /** Builds an ArrayList of all FactorPair objects of number
    /* Precondition: n > 0
    * Postcondition: the ArrayList will contain all FactorPair objects for number
    *                the ArrayList will not contain duplicate FactorPair objects
    *                return the ArrayList of FactorPair objects
    */
    public ArrayList<FactorPair> buildArrayList(int n)
    { /* to be implemented in part (a) }
```

GO ON TO THE NEXT PAGE.

```
/* Given two numbers as parameters, the method will return the
    * number with the most FactorPair objects
    * Precondition: n1 > 0, n2 > 0
    * Postcondition: The numbers are not modified
    *    return the number with the most FactorPair objects; if tied, -1 will be returned
    */
public int findMostPairs(Factors f)
    {  /* to be implemented in part (b)  }


    /** Returns a string containing all the FactorPair objects in the ArrayList */

public String toString()
    {  /* to be implemented in part (c) */  }


    /* other methods may be implemented but not shown */

}
```

GO ON TO THE NEXT PAGE.

(a) Write the `Factor` method `buildArrayList`, which will construct the `ArrayList` pairs for the number provided as the parameter.

Code segments   FactorPairs generated and added to the `ArrayList` pairs

`buildArrayList(24);`

pairs:	factor1: 1	factor1: 2	factor1: 3	factor1: 4
	factor2: 24	factor2: 12	factor2: 8	factor2: 6

`buildArrayList(45);`

pairs:	factor1: 1	factor1: 3	factor1: 5
	factor2: 45	factor2: 15	factor2: 9

`buildArrayList(17);`

pairs:	factor1: 1
	factor2: 17

`buildArrayList(20);`

pairs:	factor1: 1	factor1: 2	factor1: 4
	factor2: 20	factor2: 10	factor2: 5

Class information for this question

```
public class Factors

private int number;
private ArrayList<FactorPair> pairs = new
ArrayList<FactorPair>();
Factors(int n)
public ArrayList<FactorPair> buildArrayList(int n)
public int findMostPairs(Factors f) {
public String toString() {

public class FactorPair

private int factor1;
private int factor2;
FactorPair(int f1, int f2)
public int getFactor1()
public int getFactor2()
```

GO ON TO THE NEXT PAGE.

The Factor class includes the method `buildArrayList`.

Complete method `buildArrayList` below.

```
/** Returns an ArrayList of all FactorPair objects of number
/* Precondition: n > 0
 * Postcondition: the ArrayList will contain all FactorPair objects of n
 *                the ArrayList will not contain duplicate FactorPair objects
 */
public ArrayList<FactorPair> buildArrayList(int n)
```

Begin your response at the top of a new page in the separate Free Response booklet and fill in the appropriate circle at the top of each page to indicate the question number. If there are multiple parts to this question, write the part letter with your response.

GO ON TO THE NEXT PAGE.

(b) The Factor class includes the method findMostPairs.

Given two numbers as parameters, the method will evaluate the number of FactorPair objects for each number and return the number that has the most FactorPair objects. If the number of FactorPair objects is the same for both numbers, −1 will be returned.

You must use buildArrayList appropriately to receive full credit.

Code segments	Value returned (examples of the contents of the ArrayList are shown in part (a))

```Factors f1 = new Factors(20);```
 	
```Factors f2 = new Factors(24);```
 	
```System.out.println(f1.findMostPairs(f2));```
	24

```Factors f1 = new Factors(20);```
 	
```Factors f2 = new Factors(45);```
 	
```System.out.println(f1.findMostPairs(f2));```
	−1

```Factors f1 = new Factors(17);```
 	
```Factors f2 = new Factors(45);```
 	
```System.out.println(f1.findMostPairs(f2));```
	45

Class information for this question

```
public class Factors

private int number;
private ArrayList<FactorPair> pairs = new
ArrayList<FactorPair>();
Factors(int n)
public ArrayList<FactorPair> buildArrayList(int n)
public int findMostPairs(Factors f) {
public String toString() {

public class FactorPair
private int factor1;
private int factor2;
FactorPair(int f1, int f2)
public int getFactor1()
public int getFactor2()
```

GO ON TO THE NEXT PAGE.

Complete method findMostPairs below.

```
/* Returns the number with the most factored pairs; if tied, −1 will be returned
 * Precondition: n1 > 0, n2 > 0
 * Postcondition: The numbers are not modified
 */
public int findMostPairs(Factors f)
```

Begin your response at the top of a new page in the separate Free Response booklet and fill in the appropriate circle at the top of each page to indicate the question number. If there are multiple parts to this question, write the part letter with your response.

GO ON TO THE NEXT PAGE.

(c) The `Factor` class includes the method `toString`. This method will return a string containing containing the factors of each `FactorPair` object in the `ArrayList` using the format shown below.

Code segments	Value returned

`Factors f1 = new Factors(24);`
 	
`System.out.println(f1.toString());`
	(1 24) (2 12) (3 8) (4 6)

`Factors f2 = new Factors(17);`
 	
`System.out.println(f2.toString());`
	(1 17)

`Factors f3 = new Factors(20);`
 	
`System.out.println(f3.toString());`
	(1 20) (2 10) (4 5)

Class information for this question

```
public class Factors

private int number;
private ArrayList<FactorPair> pairs = new
ArrayList<FactorPair>();
Factors(int n)
public ArrayList<FactorPair> buildArrayList(int n)
public int findMostPairs(Factors f) {
public String toString() {

public class FactorPair

private int factor1;
private int factor2;
FactorPair(int f1, int f2)
public int getFactor1()
public int getFactor2()
```

GO ON TO THE NEXT PAGE.

Complete method `toString` below.

```
/* Returns a string containing all the FactorPair objects in the ArrayList pairs */
public String toString()
```

Begin your response at the top of a new page in the separate Free Response booklet and fill in the appropriate circle at the top of each page to indicate the question number. If there are multiple parts to this question, write the part letter with your response.

GO ON TO THE NEXT PAGE.

4. The `Array2DMultiples` class contains two static methods.

The first method, `buildMatrix`, is to construct and return a two-dimensional array. The parameters to the method will be a one-dimensional array and an `int` field `cols`. The length of the one-dimensional array will determine the number of rows in the two-dimensional array, while the `cols` field will determine the number of columns.

Each element in the parameter array will be used to determine the multiples that will populate the two-dimensional array. The `buildMatrix` method should work for any one-dimensional array that is provided, as well as any number of columns specified. For example, given the following parameters: `int [ ]  arr = {7, 6, 2, 6}` and `cols = 5`, the two-dimensional array generated would have 4 rows and 5 columns. The first row would have multiples of 7, the second row would have multiples of 6, the third row would have multiples of 2, and the fourth row would have multiples of 6:

Multiples of 7	7	14	21	28	35
Multiples of 6	6	12	18	24	30
Multiples of 2	2	4	6	8	10
Multiples of 6	6	12	18	24	30

The second method, `eliminateDuplicateRows` will create a new array by removing any duplicate rows from the array. The above array would be changed to look like this:

Multiples of 7	7	14	21	28	35
Multiples of 6	6	12	18	24	30
Multiples of 2	2	4	6	8	10

```
/** Builds a two-dimensional array using the length of arr as the number of rows and
 * cols as the number of columns
 * @Precondition: arr.length > 0, cols > 0
 * @Postcondition: return the two-dimensional array
 */
public static int[][] buildMatrix(int [] arr, int cols)
{  /* to be implemented in part (a)  }
```

```
/** Create a new array by removing all duplicate rows from arrWithDups
 * @Postcondition: arrWithDups is not modified
 *                 returns the new two-dimensional array with no duplicate rows
 */
public static int [][] eliminateDuplicateRows(int [][] arrWithDups)
{  /* to be implemented in part (b)  }
```

GO ON TO THE NEXT PAGE.

(a) The `Array2DMultiples` class includes the method `buildMatrix`.

Code segments	Two-dimensional Matrix generated and returned					
`int [] arr = {5, 2, 3, 5};` `int[][] arr2d = buildMatrix(arr, 6);`	5	10	15	20	25	30
	2	4	6	8	10	12
	3	6	9	12	15	18
	5	10	15	20	25	30

Complete method `buildMatrix` below.

```
/** Builds a two-dimensional array using the length of arr as the number of rows and
* cols as the number of columns
* @Precondition: arr.length > 0, cols > 0
* @Postcondition: return the two-dimensional array
*/
public static int[][] buildMatrix(int [] arr, int cols)
```

Begin your response at the top of a new page in the separate Free Response booklet and fill in the appropriate circle at the top of each page to indicate the question number. If there are multiple parts to this question, write the part letter with your response.

GO ON TO THE NEXT PAGE.

(b) The `Array2DMultiples` method includes the method `eliminateDuplicateRows`.

Examine the two-dimensional array parameter. Eliminate any duplicate rows and return a smaller two-dimensional array.

`arrWithDups`:

5	10	15	20	25	30
2	4	6	8	10	12
3	6	9	12	15	18
5	10	15	20	25	30

After the call: `eliminateDuplicateRows(arrWithDups)`, the array that is returned, will not have any duplicate rows.

5	10	15	20	25	30
2	4	6	8	10	12
3	6	9	12	15	18

GO ON TO THE NEXT PAGE.

Complete method eliminateDuplicateRows below.

```
/** Create a new array by removing all duplicate rows from arrWithDups
 * @Postcondition: arrWithDups is not modified
 *                 returns the new two-dimensional array with no duplicate rows
 */
    public static int [][] eliminateDuplicateRows(int [][] arrWithDups)
```

Begin your response at the top of a new page in the separate Free Response booklet and fill in the appropriate circle at the top of each page to indicate the question number. If there are multiple parts to this question, write the part letter with your response.

STOP

END OF EXAM

Practice Test 2:
Answers and
Explanations

PRACTICE TEST 2 ANSWER KEY

1.	D	21.	E
2.	E	22.	E
3.	D	23.	A
4.	D	24.	A
5.	C	25.	D
6.	D	26.	A
7.	C	27.	A
8.	A	28.	D
9.	E	29.	E
10.	A	30.	E
11.	E	31.	D
12.	B	32.	D
13.	B	33.	B
14.	C	34.	E
15.	B	35.	B
16.	C	36.	C
17.	D	37.	A
18.	A	38.	C
19.	B	39.	A
20.	D	40.	C

PRACTICE TEST 2 EXPLANATIONS

Section I: Multiple-Choice Questions

1. **D** The question involves integer division, modulus division, and order of operations. One important thing to remember is integer division is performed if both sides of the division operator (/) are integers, i.e., no rounding will occur. Another is that division, multiplication, and modulus division (%) are all performed left to right.

   Statement (I) will perform integer division first: 24 / 5 = 4. Next, 4 % 3 = 1. Finally, 1 * 2 = 2. This solution is less than 5 so (I) must be part of the answer. Eliminate (B).

   Statement (II) will also perform integer division first: 12 / 3 = 4. Next, 4 * 2 = 8. Finally, 8 + 1 = 9. This solution is not less than 5, so (II) must not be part of the answer. Eliminate (C) and (E).

   Statement (III) will perform mod first: 4 % 3 = 1, Next, 1 * 2 = 2. Finally, 1 + 2 = 3. This solution is also less than 5, so (III) must be part of the solution. Eliminate (A).

   Since (I) and (III) yield solutions less than 5, the correct choice is (D).

2. **E** The code "\n" is an escape character or line break in Java, causing the printing to begin a new line. This eliminates (A), (B), and (C) since those choices print \n instead of skipping to a new line. Additionally, the backslash character (\) is used to indicate when a special character such as a " or \ is to be printed: \" will print a double-quote (") and \\ will print the backslash. The forward slash (/) does not need any special character to print, thus the // will print two forward slashes as seen in (E). Choice (D) is not correct as it only has one forward slash. Choice (E) is correct.

3. **D** This question involves matching data types of the arguments with parameters expected by the constructors. Choice (A) uses the first constructor on lines 7–12. An integer such as 60 may be used in a field defined as double. Choice (B) again uses the same constructor, this time by casting 13.0 to an int field. Choice (C) uses the constructor on lines 13–17. One might think the `toString()` method may cause a `nullExceptionPointer` because the name was not initialized. That exception would not occur when printing the field, only if trying to use the field, such as in a decision statement looking for a value other than `null`. Choice (E) uses the constructor on lines 18–21. The `height` and `rateOfGrowth` fields will contain 0.0 and 0, respectively. Choice (D) will cause an error because there is no constructor expecting a double datatype as the third parameter. The answer is (D).

4. **D**   The client method header for computeBonus has two parameters:

computeBonus(SalesRep s, double percentage)

The instance field ytdSales within the SalesRep object is private, so the data must be referenced using an accessor: objectName.methodname(). Thus, to obtain ytdSales for the object named s, we must use s.getYtdSales(), eliminating choices (A), (B), and (C). The field percentage is a parameter provided to the method, not a public instance field of the object, so there is no need to use s.percentage as represented in choice (E). Thus, (D) is the correct answer.

5. **C**   Choice (A) is incorrect because it uses ArrayList as the data type in the enhanced-for loop, rather than SalesRep (the type of objects in the ArrayList). Choice (B) is incorrect because r.get() would not be a valid identifier for each entry of the ArrayList. Choice (D) is incorrect because it uses the data type with .get(index) (it should use the name of the ArrayList with .get(index)). Choice (E) accesses the ArrayList and method correctly; however, the loop goes out of bounds because the last index should be one less than the size of the ArrayList. Choice (C) uses an enhanced-for loop (which will not go out of bounds) and accesses the ArrayList and method correctly. The answer is (C).

6. **D**   When using the substring method, the first character of a string is at index 0. The parameters of the substring command are the first index and ending index, but the command stops just before the ending index is reached, so substring(1, 3) will print characters at indexes 1 and 2 ("up"). This eliminates Choices (A) and (C). The command str.substring(1) accesses the first character to the end of the string ("uperstar"), but it is NOT assigned back into str. Since strings are immutable, str is not modified (on the third or fifth lines)—"up" will be printed three times. Choice (E) is incorrect, since the code never reaches an out of bounds condition by using indexes 1 and 3. The answer is (D).

7. **C**   Statement (I) will successfully alternate the value of isBlack. The right side of the assignment statement will change the value to the opposite value every time the code is executed. Eliminate (B). Statement (II) specifically checks whether the value of isBlack is false. If so, it will change the value to true. The else will only be executed if isBlack is true, in which case it will change the value to false, so (II) is successful at alternating values, as well. Eliminate (A) and (D). Statement (III) only changes the value of isBlack if it is true: there is no provision to change the value from false to true, so Statement (III) is incorrect. Eliminate (E). Since only (I) and (II) would successfully alternate the values, the answer is (C).

8. **A**   Choice (A) would simply compare the object references of the two String variables, not the actual contents of the fields. Both choices (B) and (C) are perfectly straightforward methods to compare the contents of String variables. Choice (D) utilizes the substring method two different ways to examine the entire string for both str1 and str2 with the .equals() method being used to compare the contents of the strings. Choice (E) handles the comparison by making sure the strings are the exact same length and that str2 is located in str1 at index 0 (the very beginning of the string). Thus, (A) is the correct answer.

9.   **E**   DeMorgan's Law can simplify this problem.

The original statement is   `!(p || (q || !r))`

After DeMorgan's law   `!p && !(q || !r)`

After DeMorgan's a second time   `!p && !q && r`

Since all the operators are `&&`, every part of the compound statement must evaluate to true.

The values must be: `p = false`, `q = false`, and `r = true`. The correct answer is (E).

10.   **A**   Short circuit evaluation is used when the first part of an `&&` condition is `false` (since both sides of an `&&` condition must be `true`, a `false` in the first part causes the whole expression to be `false`). Both (D) and (E) start with an `&&` operator. Since neither has a `false` value in p, short circuit cannot be used on these statements.

Alternatively, short circuit can be used if the first part of an `||` condition is `true` (since only one side of an `||` condition needs to be `true`, a `true` in the first part causes the whole expression to be `true`). Since p is has a `false` value in (B) and (C), a short circuit cannot be used on these statements.

Choice (A) has a `true` value as the first part of an expression with the `||` operator, making the whole statement evaluate to `true`. The answer is (A).

11.   **E**   Start with DeMorgan's Law.

The original statement is   `!(!p || q)  ||  !(p || !q)`

After DeMorgan's Law   `(p && !q ) || (!p && q)`

Examining the conditions on either side of the `||` operator, the truth values of p and q are combined with an `&&` operator and are direct opposites. Thus, if the two values are direct opposites of each other on either side of the `||` operator, the entire expression would be true. The correct choice is (E).

12.   **B**   The outer loop will execute 10 times, where i will range from 1 to 10 (< 11) incrementing by one each time. The inner loop will execute 5 times, where j will range from 10 to 2, decreasing by 2 each time and stopping after j is no longer greater than 1. The variable count will be incremented by 1 each time the inner loop executes, so (10 * 5) = 50 times. The variable star starts with one "*" but adds two more ("**") each time the inner loop executes. (1 + 50 * 2) = 101. The final length of star will be 101. Thus, (B) is the correct answer.

13.   **B**   The outer loop will execute 5 times (i is initialized to 1, the loop will continue until i is no longer <= 5). Within the outer loop are two loops, each using `print` statements so the output will continue across a single line. After the two loops execute, a `println` statement will advance the print to the next line.

The first inner loop initializes j to 1 and continues while it is less than i. So, on the first row, this loop doesn't execute at all because j and i are both 1 and j is not less than i. The "- " is never written, thus eliminating choices (A) and (E).

The second loop initializes j as the same value as i, continuing, up to 5, thus generating 5 "* ", eliminating choice (C).

Each time the outer loop executes, one additional "- " is written in the first loop, and one fewer "* " is written in the second loop. Choice (D) writes the correct number of each symbol, but in reverse order. The "- " is written in the first inner loop. Thus, choice (B) is correct.

14. **C** Three trace tables will make short work of this problem.

In (I), the variable i will have the values 1 and 2; the loop will stop when i increments to 3.

i	2 * i + 1;	sum
1	2 * 1 + 1 = 3	3
2	2 * 2 + 1 = 5	8

In (II), the variable i will have the values 1–5, the loop will stop when i increments to 6.

i	if (i % 2 == 1)	sum
1	1 % 2 == 1, so add i to sum	1
2	2 % 2 == 0	1
3	3 % 2 == 1, so add i to sum	4
4	4 % 2 == 0	4
5	5 % 2 == 1, so add i to sum	9

In (III), the variable i will start at 5; then the loop will change i to 3, then 1. The loop will not be re-entered when i is 1.

i	Initial values, before the loop begins	sum
5		5
3	sum += i	8
1		9

Using the trace tables above, (C) is the answer because (II) and (III) both print 9, while (I) prints 8.

15. **B** Segment (I) starts the loop with k equal to 1, increments k by 1, then adds k to sum. The variable k is added whether it is even or odd, thus this option is unacceptable. Eliminate (A), (D), and (E).

Segment (II) starts the loop with k equal to 1, increments k by 2, ensuring only odd numbers will be added. The loop continues while k is less than or equal to number. If number is odd, the last value of k be equal to number, while if k is even, the last value of k to be added to the sum will be the previous odd number. Only odd integers up to number will be added. This segment works properly. Eliminate (C).

Four choices have been eliminated, so there is no need to go further. However, to see why (III) does not work, note that it starts the loop with k equal to number and decrements k by 2. If number is odd, this option will work as k will always be odd. However, if number is even, even numbers will be added, which does not meet the criteria of the method.

Since only (II) works properly, the correct choice is (B).

16. **C**   Sample (I) initializes `loc` to –1. If every element in the array contained `Integer.MIN_VALUE`, (I) would never update `loc` to a location within the array. Therefore, (I) is not correct. Eliminate (A), (D), and (E).

Sample (II) traverses the array backwards, recording the index of the last entry as `loc`. Using the example data provided and directions in the Java doc, the location of the first matching element in the array should be returned. When there is a duplicate the entry closest to the end will be returned. Since (II) is incorrect, eliminate (B).

Only one choice remains, so there is no need to continue. However, to see why (III) is correct, note that it takes the first element in the array as `max` and initializes `loc` to 0, assuming the first element in the array is currently the largest. The array is traversed, looking for a larger element, updating `max` and `loc` if one is found. This strategy works perfectly and is the only possible solution to the problem. Thus, (C) is correct.

17. **D**   Choice (A) works, as the static fields of the `Integer` class, `Integer.MIN_VALUE` and `Integer.MAX_VALUE`, represent the range of numbers that can be represented in 4 bytes of data (the size of an `int` field). Since (A) does not cause an error, (E) is also incorrect. The smallest number an `int` field can hold is the value held in `Integer.MIN_VALUE`: thus, when 1 is subtracted, an overflow error occurs, resulting in `Integer.MAX_VALUE`. The result is unexpected, but no error is thrown by the compiler or at run time. Choice (B) can be eliminated. In (C), the fields are added, producing –1, not causing any error at all. Choice (D) will cause a compiler error because the value being assigned is 1 larger than the limit of what an `int` data field can store.

18. **A**   The method `half` divides the parameter and returns the result of dividing the parameter by 2. Since neither n nor 2 is a double data type, only integer division occurs. Thus, when n is 5, `n / 2` will be 2, but `2.0` is returned because the return type was specified as double. The contents of `num` remain the same (5). The `print` statement starts with the empty string (`""`), which will cause the results of `half(num)` and `num` to be concatenated together as strings. Thus, the output is `2.05` (where `2.0` and 5 have been concatenated together as a string). Choice (A) is correct.

19. **B**   The `getPerimeter()` method returns a double, so (A) and (C) can be eliminated. The `MyRectangle` constructor creates a local variable `perimeter`, which has the same name as the instance variable. When this occurs and the keyword `this` has not been used, the local variable is accessed. Thus, the local variable `perimeter` is assigned the value of 10, but the instance field only contains a default value of 0. When the `getPerimeter()` method returns the value of `perimeter` as a double, it returns `0.0` because the instance field `perimeter` has never been assigned any other value. Choice (D) is eliminated. Also of note: no error is thrown because an `int` can be returned when a `double` is expected because there is no loss of precision, so (E) is not correct. The answer is (B).

20. **D** Choice (D) uses the same number and the same type of parameters in the same order as the existing constructor: `String`, `int`, `boolean`, `int`. This is not allowed in Java because it would be impossible to know which constructor to invoke. All the other choices would be acceptable because they have different numbers of parameters. The answer is (D).

21. **E** The `Car()` constructor has no parameters, so all primitive fields will be initialized to `0` or `false` appropriately, but the `String` field will be initialized to `null`. The `setModel` method does not initialize the instance field model. When the parameter has the same name as the instance field, the keyword `this` must be used, otherwise the parameter is simply being assigned to itself. When the `if` statement attempts to compare the contents of model to `"Tacoma"`, the model contains `null` so a `NullPointerException` will be thrown. Choice (E) is correct.

22. **E** The field `mpg` is supposed to be rounded to the nearest integer. Choices (A), (B), and (C) produce real numbers without casting to `int` so they can be eliminated. The division in (D) produces a double but casts the double to an integer field too early. When `0.5` is added, the calculation has once again produced a double. Choice (E) performs regular division, then correctly adds `0.5` before casting to an integer. Casting to integer will truncate the decimal portion of the number. This algorithm will round the answer correctly. The answer is (E).

23. **A** The superclass object `Bee` is referencing the subclass object `Queen`. When the object `bee1` invokes the method `toString()`, dynamic binding ensures the correct method is called. Since `bee1` is a `Queen`, the `toString()` method in the `Queen` class is called. The `toString()` method returns `"The queen lays 2000 eggs."` Choice (A) is correct.

24. **A** The `name` field has private access in the `Bee` class. The accessor must be in the `Bee` class because it is not visible to the `Queen` class. If access is needed within the `Queen` class, the accessor from the `Bee` class could be called with `super.getName()`. Choice (A) is correct.

25. **D** Lifespan is part of the state of a `Bee`. There is no need for an additional class based on only that piece of information, so (A) can be eliminated, as well as (E). Choices (B) and (C) can be eliminated because the number of drones, workers, or queens may be relevant to the design, but more information would be needed to support a design decision. State and behavior are the cornerstones of class design. Detailing what is unique about workers and drones and what is like other bees will dictate the class where fields should reside and behavior is defined. Choice (D) is the correct answer.

26. **A** An array is passed by reference to a method, so any changes that are enacted upon the array in the method are actually changing the array itself. The array is initialized with 5 elements and each element is assigned the index multiplied by 5, so (A) is correct. Choice (B) is incorrect because it assumes the array was unchanged by the method and allows for 6 elements rather than 5. Choice (C) is incorrect because it again allows for 6 elements, although they would reflect the index multiplied by 5. Choice (D) is incorrect: there is no type mismatch because an integer can be assigned to a double data type (there is no loss of precision). Choice (E) is incorrect because the array is defined using the primitive `int`, so it was initialized with 0s until it later is assigned the multiples of 5. The answer is (A).

27. **A** It is helpful to label the rows and columns with their indexes to assist with the math operations.

	Columns				A single loop controlled by j runs from 0 to less than the number of rows (4) The calculations for building the one-dimensional array are as follows:

ROWS		0	1	2	3
	0	1	2	3	4
	1	1	3	5	7
	2	2	4	6	8
	3	4	3	2	1

```
result[0] = matrix[3][0] - matrix[0][3]    4 - 4 =  0
result[1] = matrix[3][1] - matrix[1][3]    3 - 7 = -4
result[2] = matrix[3][2] - matrix[2][3]    2 - 8 = -6
result[3] = matrix[3][3] - matrix[3][3]    1 - 1 =  0
```

Choice (A) is correct.

28. **D** `Math.random( ) * 100` generates real numbers between 0 and 100. It includes 0, and goes up to, but does not include, 100. `Math.random( ) * 100 + 1` will generate real numbers from 1, up to, but not including, 101. Choice (A) generates numbers of type `double`, which cannot be added to an Integer `ArrayList`. Choice (B) will generate numbers of type `int` ranging from 0 to 99 (`int` will truncate the decimal portion, not round it). Choice (C) will generate numbers between 0 and 100. Choice (E) will generate numbers between 1 and 100 but attempts to cast them directly to class Integer rather than primitive type `int`, which will not work. Choice (D), which is the correct answer, will generate numbers between 1 and 100. The numbers are cast to `(int)`, which can then be added to the Integer `ArrayList`. The answer is (D).

29. **E** The `ArrayList` is initialized to A B C D E. The first loop removes the entry at the following indexes, modifying the `ArrayList` as shown in the table below. It's important to remember that the `ArrayList` is shrinking in size: the loop will only carry out twice.

Code	list1
remove(0)	B C D E
remove(2)	B C E

The second loop inserts an "*" three times, each time at index 1.

Code	list1
add (1, "*")	B * C E
add (1, "*")	B * * C E
add (1, "*")	B * * * C E

The answer is (E).

30.   **E**   First, diagram the calls to the method, stopping each branch at its base case.

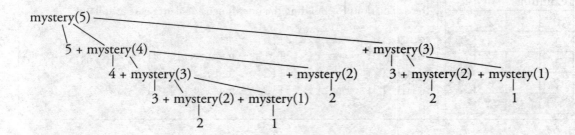

        After diagramming the calls, add upwards.

mystery(5) = 23

5 + mystery(4) = 12   + mystery(3) = 6

4 + mystery(3) = 6   + mystery(2)   3 + mystery(2) + mystery(1)

3 + mystery(2) + mystery(1)   2   2   1

2   1

31.   **D**   After the call `mystery("PLANT")`, `i` is 1,

```
temp = s.substring(s.length() - i);
        s.substring(5 - 1);
    s.substring(4); simply gives "T"
```

The length of `temp` on the next call is only 1 so nothing more is printed, and `mystery` is no longer called. Choice (D) is the correct answer.

32.   **D**   The `ArrayList schedule`, contains objects that are `Play` datatypes. When `schedule[1]` is going to be printed, at run-time, Java looks to see whether the `object.toString()` method has been overridden. In other words, it looks to see whether there is a `toString()` method in the `Play` class. This method exists and does the following:

```
return performance + " with " + starringActor + " as " + mainCharacter;
```

The word `" with "` will be printed and does not exist in (A) and (C), so these choices can be eliminated. The first part of the `return` statement, `returns performance` is an object of type `Performance`. Again, Java looks to see whether there is a `toString()` method in the `Performance` class. This method also exists and does the following:

```
return name + " will be performed in " + season + " of " + year;
```

Since there is a `toString()` method defined, Java will use it instead of printing the memory location of the object, eliminating (B). No errors will be thrown, eliminating (E). The following will be printed:

```
Peter Pan will be performed in Spring of 2023 with Charlie as Peter
```

Therefore, the correct answer is (D).

33. **B** Choice (A) is incorrect because it tries to access the field `starringActor`, which is not visible because it is specified as a private variable in `Performance`. An accessor method is needed to use it. Choice (B) correctly uses an accessor method to return `starringActor` so that it may be added to the `actors ArrayList`. Choice (C) is incorrect because it uses the wrong data type in the enhanced-`for` loop: it needs to use `Play` instead of `Performance`. Choice (D) also tries to access `starringActor` directly but cannot because the field is private. Choice (E) is incorrect because it attempts to use `ArrayList` notation (`get[j]`) with an array. Choice (B) is the correct answer.

34. **E** Option (I) creates a `Flower` object using the `Flower` constructor without parameters. Since `Daffodil` is a subclass of `Flower`, it inherits all the attributes and methods in the `Flower` class. Both (II) and (III) use the `Flower` constructor without parameters. Options (I), (II), and (III) all work. Choice (E) is the answer.

35. **B** The number of searches needed to find a target value within a sorted array is 2^n, where the value is just over the number of elements in the array. In this case, $2^n = 4000$. $2^{11} = 2048$, so (A) is not large enough. Choice (B) leads us to $2^{12} = 4096$, which will provide enough searches to find a target in 4000 elements. Choices (C), (D), and (E) are too large. Choice (B) is the correct answer.

36. **C** The index used to control the outer loop runs from 1 to just under the length of the array. If an array had four elements, the indexes would be 0, 1, 2, 3. The loop would run from 1 to 3, which would be one less than the length of the array. The correct answer is (C), $n - 1$.

37. **A** The inner loop is controlled by:

```
while (j >= 0 && arr[j] > num)
```

It is helpful to look at conditions in which the loop will stop executing or not execute at all. With the `&&` condition, both expressions have to be true, so look closer at the second part to determine when it might not be true. The logic surrounding the loop starts by assigning the second value in the array to `num`, then setting `i` to the previous location, resulting in two consecutive numbers in the array being compared. If those numbers happen to be the same OR in ascending order, the loop will not execute at all. Thus, the correct answer is (A), 0 times.

38. **C** The expression `mat.length` returns the number of rows in a 2D array, while `mat[0].length` returns the number of columns in the first row. This code is selecting each row and moving columns within that row. There are no bounds errors with the loops, so (E) is incorrect. The value in the first column is assigned to `temp`, while the loop travels to the end of the row shifting all elements to the left:

`mat[a][b - 1] = mat[a][b];`

When the row is completed, the value in `temp` is assigned to the last column:

`mat[a][mat[0].length - 1] = temp;`

Choice (C) is the correct answer.

39. **A** The `ArrayList` needs to store `Baseball` objects and `Sport` objects. Since `Baseball` extends `Sport`, the `ArrayList` should be declared with the datatype `Sport`. Referring to polymorphic ideas, `Baseball` IS-A `Sport`, not the other way around. This eliminates (B), (C), (D), and (E). Choice (A) is the correct answer.

40. **C** Option (I) will remove some but not all the elements containing `"Summer"` due to the changes indexing as elements are removed within the loop.

b1: Spring 2022	b2: Summer 2022	b3: Summer 2022	b4: Summer 2022	s1: Winter 2024
index: 0	index: 1	index: 2	index: 3	index: 4

The first pass through the loop, the object at index 0 is examined. The season is not `"Summer"`: the element is not removed.

The second pass through the loop, the object at index 1 is examined. The season is `"Summer"`: the element is removed, and the indexes are updated.

b1: Spring 2022	b3: Summer 2022	b4: Summer 2022	s1: Winter 2024
index: 0	index: 2 1	index: 3 2	index: 4 3

The third pass through the loop, the object at index 2 is examined. But notice, `b4` is being examined (`b3` has been skipped because the indexes were updated after the remove). The object `b3` will not be removed even though the season is `"Summer"` because it has been skipped. Therefore, (I) will not work. Eliminate (A), (D), and (E).

An enhanced-`for` loop creates a local variable that does not reference an element in an array. It is assigned a value from the `ArrayList` and is used for read-only purposes. Thus, no elements in the `ArrayList` can be used with this method and Option (II) will not work. Eliminate (B).

Only one choice remains, so there is no need to continue. However, to see why (III) does work, note that it is similar to (I) but traverses the `ArrayList` backwards. Thus, when an element is removed from the `ArrayList`, the indexes update on elements that have already been processed. No elements containing `"Summer"` will be affected. Option (III) is the only option that will work properly, making (C) the correct choice.

Section II: Free-Response Questions

1.   `PigLatin`—Canonical solution

(a)
```java
public boolean isLetterAVowel(String letter)
{
   if (letter.equals("a") || letter.equals("e") || letter.equals("i") || letter.equals("o") ||
       letter.equals("u") )
        return true;
   return false;
}
```

(b)
```java
public String convertWord(String word)
{
   String w = word;
   String firstLet = w.substring(0,1);
   boolean firstIsVowel = isLetterAVowel(firstLet);
   if (firstIsVowel)
       return word + "way";
   String secondLet = w.substring(1,2);
   boolean secondIsVowel = isLetterAVowel(secondLet);
   if (secondIsVowel)
       return word.substring(1) + firstLet + "ay";
   return word.substring(2) + firstLet + secondLet + "ay";
}
```

(c)
```java
public String convertPhrase()
{
   if (phrase == null || phrase.length() == 0)
       return "";
   String p = phrase;
   String newPigLatinPhrase = "";
   String word = "";
   int j = 0;
   boolean isLastWord = false;
   int k = p.indexOf(" ");
   while (k != -1)
   {
       word = convertWord(p.substring(0, k));
       newPigLatinPhrase += word + " ";
       p = p.substring(k + 1);
       k = p.indexOf(" ");
   }
   if (p.length() > 0)
   {
       word = convertWord(p);
   }
   newPigLatinPhrase += word + " ";
   return newPigLatinPhrase;
```

`PigLatin` Rubric

Part **(a)**

+2

+1	Must use the correct comparison for string `.equals( )`
+1	Correctly returns `true` or `false`

Part **(b)**

+4

+1	Correctly finds first character and second character.
+1	Checks whether the length of the word is 1 and whether it starts with a vowel; returns `vowel + "way"`, otherwise returns `word + "ay"`
+1	Correctly converts `word` to `PigLatin` following the three rules
+1	Returns `word` converted to `pigLatin`, does not change the parameter: `word`

Part **(c)**

+3

+1	Checks for `null` or empty string. MUST check for `null` first. Returns empty string.
+1	Correctly finds a word and calls `convertWord(word)` for each word in the phrase, including the last word
+1	Concatenates all converted words that have been returned into a new pig latin phrase

2. PremierMember—Canonical solution

```
public class PremierMember extends FrequentFlyerMember
{
    boolean premierClubMembership;
    int freeBags;
    String otherFreqFlyerMember;

    PremierMember(int num, String name, int miles, String otherMember)
    {
        super(num, name, miles);
        premierClubMembership = true;
        freeBags = 2;
        otherFreqFlyerMember = otherMember;
    }

    public String getStatusInfo()
    {
        return super.getStatusInfo() + " also a member of " + otherFreqFlyerMember;
    }

}
```

PremierMember Rubric

+9

+1	Correct class declaration: must use extends FrequentFlyerMember
+1	Must have 3 private instance variables for premierClubMembership, freeBags, otherFreqFlyerMember
+1	Instance fields and assignments from FrequentFlyerMember are not repeated
+1	Header for constructor matches class name and uses 4 parameters as shown (parameters may be in a different order)
+1	First instruction in constructor must be super(num, name, miles); (matching the parameters in the constructor's parameters)
+1	Three other assignment statements in constructor as shown for premierClubMembership, freeBags, otherFreqFlyerMember
+1	Method header: public String getStatusInfo()
+1	Uses super.getStatusInfo() from the parent class
+1	Concatenates: " also a member of " + otherFreqFlyerMember;

3.   FactorPair—Canonical solution

(a)
```java
public ArrayList<FactorPair> buildArrayList(int n)
{
  ArrayList<FactorPair> tempPairs = new ArrayList<FactorPair>();
  for (int i = 1; i < (n / 2); i++)
  {
    if (n % i == 0)
    {
        if (i <= (n / i))
        {
                FactorPair temp = new FactorPair(i, n / i);
                tempPairs.add(temp);
        }
    }
  }
  return tempPairs;
}
```

(b)
```java
public int findMostPairs(Factors f)
{
  if (this.pairs.size() > f.pairs.size())
    return this.number;
  else if (f.pairs.size() > this.pairs.size())
    return f.number;
  else
    return -1;
}
```

(c)
```java
public String toString()
{
  String s  = "";
  for (FactorPair a : pairs)
  {
    s += "(" + a.getFactor1() + " " + a.getFactor2() + ") ";
  }
  return s;
}
```

`FactorPair` Rubric

Part **(a)**

+5

	+1	Correct declaration of `ArrayList` of type `FactorPair`
	+1	Loop to find factors (1 through n, or 1 through n / 2) examines every number for factors without any bounds errors
	+1	Finds factors correctly—looks for evenly divisible factors that are less than or equal to n / i (need the = to find factors of perfect square numbers, such as 5 in the number 25)
	+1	Builds `FactorPair` object and adds it to the `ArrayList`
	+1	No duplicate factors are added

Part **(b)**

+2

	+1	Correctly evaluates the size of the two `ArrayLists` to find the object with the greater number of `FactorPair` objects
	+1	Properly returns the number that had the most `FactorPair` objects or –1 if both numbers had the same number of `FactorPair` objects. Must use `objectname.number`.

Part **(c)**

+2

	+1	Properly traverses the entire `ArrayList` with no bounds errors
	+1	Properly accesses the `FactorPair` objects using the `getFactor1` and `getFactor2` methods

4.   Array2DMultiples—Canonical solution

(a)
```java
public static int[][] buildMatrix(int [] arr, int cols)
{
  int [][] mat = new int[arr.length][cols];
  for (int r = 0; r < arr.length; r++)
  {
     int hold = arr[r];
     for (int c = 0; c < cols; c++)
         mat[r][c] = hold * (c + 1);
  }
  return mat;
}
```

(b)
```java
public static int [][] eliminateDuplicateRows(int [][] arrWithDups)
{
  int [][] arr = arrWithDups;
  int holdRow = 0;
  int r = 1;
  while (holdRow < arr.length - 1)
  {
     while ( r < arr.length  )
     {
         if (arr[holdRow][0] == arr[r][0] )
         {
                 int [][] smallerArr = new int [arr.length - 1][arr[0].length];
                 for (int row = 0; row < r; row ++)
                    for (int col = 0; col < arr[0].length; col++)
                        smallerArr[row][col] = arr[row][col];

                 for (int row = r + 1; row < arr.length; row ++)
                    for (int col = 0; col < arr[0].length; col++)
                        smallerArr[row - 1][col] = arr[row][col];
                 arr = smallerArr;
         }
         else
                 r++;
     }
     holdRow ++;
     r = holdRow + 1;
  }
  return arr;
}
```

`Array2DMultiples` Rubric

Part **(a)**

+3

	+1	Correct declaration of two-dimensional array using `arr.length` as the number of `rows`, `cols` as the number of columns
	+1	Loops for rows and columns are correctly executed without any bounds errors
	+1	Elements in the array are correctly assigned multiples of the first entry in the row

Part **(b)**

+6

	+1	Parameter `arrWithDups` is not modified
	+1	A row is held; a loop is used to examine each subsequent row for duplicates without any bounds errors
	+1	Duplicate row is identified
	+1	Smaller 2D array is declared
	+1	New 2D array is built correctly without duplicates
	+1	New 2D array is returned

HOW TO SCORE PRACTICE TEST 2

Section I: Multiple-Choice

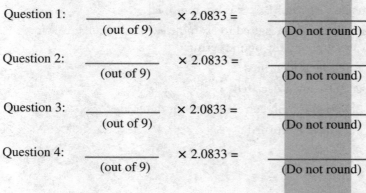

_____ × 1.875 = _____
Number Correct   Weighted
(out of 40)   Section I Score
                             (Do not round)

Section II: Free-Response

Question 1:   _____ × 2.0833 = _____
              (out of 9)   (Do not round)

Question 2:   _____ × 2.0833 = _____
              (out of 9)   (Do not round)

Question 3:   _____ × 2.0833 = _____
              (out of 9)   (Do not round)

Question 4:   _____ × 2.0833 = _____
              (out of 9)   (Do not round)

AP Score Conversion Chart Computer Science A	
Composite Score Range	AP Score
107–150	5
90–106	4
73–89	3
56–72	2
0–55	1

Sum =   _____
        Weighted
        Section II Score
        (Do not round)

Composite Score

_____ + _____ = _____
Weighted   Weighted   Composite Score
Section I Score   Section II Score   (Round to nearest
                                        whole number)

Practice Test 3

AP® Computer Science A Exam

DO NOT OPEN THIS BOOKLET UNTIL YOU ARE TOLD TO DO SO.

At a Glance

Total Time
1 hour 30 minutes
Number of Questions
40
Percent of Total Score
50%
Writing Instrument
Pencil required

Instructions

Section I of this examination contains 40 multiple-choice questions. Fill in only the ovals for numbers 1 through 40 on your answer sheet.

Indicate all of your answers to the multiple-choice questions on the answer sheet. No credit will be given for anything written in this exam booklet, but you may use the booklet for notes or scratch work. After you have decided which of the suggested answers is best, completely fill in the corresponding oval on the answer sheet. Give only one answer to each question. If you change an answer, be sure that the previous mark is erased completely. Here is a sample question and answer.

Sample Question   Sample Answer

Chicago is a   Ⓐ ● Ⓒ Ⓓ Ⓔ
(A) state
(B) city
(C) country
(D) continent
(E) county

Use your time effectively, working as quickly as you can without losing accuracy. Do not spend too much time on any one question. Go on to other questions and come back to the ones you have not answered if you have time. It is not expected that everyone will know the answers to all the multiple-choice questions.

About Guessing

Many candidates wonder whether or not to guess the answers to questions about which they are not certain. Multiple-choice scores are based on the number of questions answered correctly. Points are not deducted for incorrect answers, and no points are awarded for unanswered questions. Because points are not deducted for incorrect answers, you are encouraged to answer all multiple-choice questions. On any questions you do not know the answer to, you should eliminate as many choices as you can, and then select the best answer among the remaining choices.

GO ON TO THE NEXT PAGE.

Java Quick Reference

Class Constructors and Methods	Explanation
String Class	
`String(String str)`	Constructs a new `String` object that represents the same sequence of characters as `str`
`int length()`	Returns the number of characters in a `String` object
`String substring(int from, int to)`	Returns the substring beginning at index `from` and ending at index `to - 1`
`String substring(int from)`	Returns `substring(from, length())`
`int indexOf(String str)`	Returns the index of the first occurrence of `str`; returns −1 if not found
`boolean equals(String other)`	Returns `true` if `this` is equal to `other`; returns `false` otherwise
`int compareTo(String other)`	Returns a value <0 if `this` is less than `other`; returns zero if `this` is equal to `other`; returns a value of >0 if `this` is greater than `other`
Integer Class	
`Integer(int value)`	Constructs a new `Integer` object that represents the specified `int` value
`Integer.MIN_VALUE`	The minimum value represented by an `int` or `Integer`
`Integer.MAX_VALUE`	The maximum value represented by an `int` or `Integer`
`int intValue()`	Returns the value of this `Integer` as an `int`
Double Class	
`Double(double value)`	Constructs a new `Double` object that represents the specified `double` value
`double doubleValue()`	Returns the value of this `Double` as a `double`
Math Class	
`static int abs(int x)`	Returns the absolute value of an `int` value
`static double abs(double x)`	Returns the absolute value of a `double` value
`static double pow(double base, double exponent)`	Returns the value of the first parameter raised to the power of the second parameter
`static double sqrt(double x)`	Returns the positive square root of a `double` value
`static double random()`	Returns a `double` value greater than or equal to `0.0` and less than `1.0`
ArrayList Class	
`int size()`	Returns the number of elements in the list
`boolean add(E obj)`	Appends `obj` to end of list; returns `true`
`void add(int index, E obj)`	Inserts `obj` at position index (`0 <= index <= size`), moving elements at position `index` and higher to the right (adds 1 to their indices) and adds 1 to size
`E get(int index)`	Returns the element at position `index` in the list
`E set(int index, E obj)`	Replaces the element at position `index` with `obj`; returns the element formerly at position `index`
`E remove(int index)`	Removes the element at position `index`, moving elements at position `index + 1` and higher to the left (subtracts 1 from their indices) and subtracts 1 from size; returns the element formerly at position `index`
Object Class	
`boolean equals(Object other)`	
`String toString()`	

GO ON TO THE NEXT PAGE.

COMPUTER SCIENCE A
SECTION I
Time—1 hour and 30 minutes

Number of Questions—40

Percent of total exam grade—50%

Directions: Determine the answer to each of the following questions or incomplete statements, using the available space for any necessary scratchwork. Then decide which is the best of the choices given and fill in the corresponding oval on the answer sheet. No credit will be given for anything written in the examination booklet. Do not spend too much time on any one problem.

Notes:
- Assume that the classes listed in the Java Quick Reference have been imported where appropriate.
- Assume that declarations of variables and methods appear within the context of an enclosing class.
- Assume that method calls that are not prefixed with an object or class name and are not shown within a complete class definition appear within the context of an enclosing class.
- Unless otherwise noted in the question, assume that parameters in the method calls are not null and that methods are called only when their preconditions are satisfied.

1. Consider the following methods.

```java
public void trial()
{
    int a = 10;
    int b = 5;
    doubleValues(a, b);
    System.out.print(b);
    System.out.print(a);
}

public void doubleValues(int c, int d)
{
    c = c * 2;
    d = d * 2;
    System.out.print(c);
    System.out.print(d);
}
```

What is printed as the result of the call trial()?

(A) 2010

(B) 2010105

(C) 2010510

(D) 20102010

(E) 20101020

GO ON TO THE NEXT PAGE.

2. Consider the following method.

```
/**
 * Precondition:  a > b > 0
 */
public static int mystery(int a, int b)
{
    int d = 0;
    for (int c = a; c > b; c--)
    {
        d = d + c;
    }
    return d;
}
```

What is returned by the call `mystery(x, y)`?

(A) The sum of all integers greater than y but less than or equal to x

(B) The sum of all integers greater than or equal to y but less than or equal to x

(C) The sum of all integers greater than y but less than x

(D) The sum of all integers greater than or equal to y but less than x

(E) The sum of all integers less than y but greater than or equal to x

3. Consider the following method.

```
public void mystery (int  n)
{
    int k;
    for (k = 0 ; k < n ; k++)
    {
        mystery(k);
        System.out.print (k);
    }
}
```

What is printed by the call `mystery(3)` ?

(A) 0123

(B) 00123

(C) 0010012

(D) 00100123

(E) 001001200100123

GO ON TO THE NEXT PAGE.

4. Consider an array of integers.

| 4 | 10 | 1 | 2 | 6 | 7 | 3 | 5 |

If selection sort is used to order the array from smallest to largest values, which of the following represents a possible state of the array at some point during the selection sort process?

(A)	1	4	10	2	3	6	7	5
(B)	1	2	4	6	10	7	3	5
(C)	1	2	3	10	6	7	4	5
(D)	4	3	1	2	6	7	10	5
(E)	5	3	7	6	2	1	10	4

5. Consider the following code segment:

```
int  k;
int  A[];
a = new int [7];
for (k = 0; k < A.length; k++)
{
    A[k] = A.length - k;
}
for (k = 0; k < A.length - 1; k++)
{
    A[k + 1] = A[k];
}
```

What values will A contain after the code segment is executed?

(A)	1	1	2	3	4	5	6
(B)	1	2	3	4	5	6	7
(C)	6	6	5	4	3	2	1
(D)	7	7	6	5	4	3	2
(E)	7	7	7	7	7	7	7

GO ON TO THE NEXT PAGE.

Questions 6–7 refer to the following two classes.

```
public class PostOffice
{
    // constructor initializes boxes
    // to length 100
    public PostOffice()
    {    /* implementation not shown  */}

    // returns the P.O. box based on the given P.O. box number
    // 0 <= theBox < getNumBoxes ()
    public Box getBox(int theBox)
    {    /* implementation not shown  */}
    // returns the number of P.O. boxes
    public int getNumBoxes()
    {    /* implementation not shown  */}

    // private data members and
    // other methods not shown
}


public class Box
{
    // constructor
    public Box()
    {    /* implementation not shown */}

    // returns the number of this box
    public int getBoxNumber()
    {    /* implementation not shown  */}

    // returns the number of pieces
    // of mail in this box
    public int getMailCount()
    {    /* implementation not shown */}
    // returns the given piece of mail
    // 0 <= thePiece < getMailCount ( )
    public Mail getMail(int thePiece)
    {    /* implementation not shown */}
    // true if the box has been assigned
    // to a customer
    public boolean isAssigned()
    {    /* implementation not shown */}
    // true if the box contains mail
    public boolean hasMail()
    {    /* implementation not shown */}
    // private data members and
    // other methods not shown
}
public class Mail
{
    // private members, constructors, and
    // other methods not shown
}
```

GO ON TO THE NEXT PAGE.

6. Consider the following code segment:

```
PostOffice p[ ];
p = new PostOffice[10];
```

Assuming that the box has been assigned and that it has at least four pieces of mail waiting in it, what is the correct way of getting the fourth piece of mail from the 57th box of the 10th post office of p?

(A) `Mail m = p[10].getBox(57).getmail(4);`
(B) `Mail m = p[9].getBox(56).getMail(3);`
(C) `Mail m = p.getMail(57).getMail(4) [10];`
(D) `Mail m = getMail(getBox(p[9], 560, 3);`
(E) `Mail m = new Mail(10, 57, 4);`

GO ON TO THE NEXT PAGE.

7. Consider the incomplete function `printEmptyBoxes` given below. `printEmptyBoxes` should print the box numbers of all of the boxes that have been assigned to a customer but do not contain mail.

```
public void printEmptyBoxes (PostOffice[] p)
{
    for (int k = 0; k < p.length - 1 ; k++)
    {
        for (int x = 0; x < p[k].getNumBoxes() - 1 ; x++)
        {
            /* missing code */
        }
    }
}
```

Which of the following could be used to replace /* missing code */ so that `printBoxesWithoutMail` works as intended?

(A)
```
if (p[k].getBox(x).isAssigned() &&
!p[k].getBox(x).hasMail())
{
    System.out.println(p[k].getBox(x).getBoxNumber()) ;
}
```

(B)
```
if (p[x].getBox(k).isAssigned() &&
!p[x].getBox(k).hasMail())
{
  System.out.println(p[x].getBox(k).getBoxNumber());
}
```

(C)
```
if (p[k].getBox(x).isAssigned() &&
!p[k].getBox(x).hasMail())
{
    System.out.println (p[k].getBoxNumber (x));
}
```

(D)
```
if (p[x].getBox(k).isAssigned() &&
!p[x].getBox (k).hasMail())
{
    System.out.println(p[x].getBoxNumber(k));
 }
```

(E)
```
if (p[x].getBox(k).isAssigned() &&
p[x].getBox(k).getMail() == 0)
{
    System.out.println(k);
}
```

GO ON TO THE NEXT PAGE.

8. Assume that a and b are boolean variables that have been initialized. Consider the following code segment.

```
a = a && b;
b = a || b;
```

Which of the following statements is always true?

I.   The final value of a is the same as the initial value of a.
II. The final value of b is the same as the initial value of b.
III. The final value of a is the same as the initial value of b.

(A) I only
(B) II only
(C) III only
(D) I and II only
(E) II and III only

9. Consider the following code segment.

```
int x;
x = 53;
if (x > 10)
{
    System.out.print ("A");
}
if (x > 30)
{
    System.out.print ("B");
}
else if (x > 40)
{
    System.out.print ("C");
}
if (x > 50)
{
    System.out.print ("D");
}
if (x > 70)
{
    System.out.print ("E");
}
```

What is the output when the code is executed?

(A) A
(B) D
(C) ABD
(D) ABCD
(E) ABCDE

GO ON TO THE NEXT PAGE.

10. Consider the following code segment:

```
int j;
int k;
for (j = -2; j <= 2; j = j + 2)
{
    for (k = j; k < j + 3; k++)
    {
        System.out.print(k + " ");
    }
}
```

What is the output when the code is executed?

(A) -2 -1 0
(B) -2 -1 0 1 2
(C) 0 1 2 0 1 2 0 1 2
(D) -2 0 2
(E) -2 -1 0 0 1 2 2 3 4

11. Consider the following method.

```
public void mystery (int  count, String s)
{
    if  (count  <=  0)
    {
        return;
    }
    if  (count % 3 == 0)
    {
        System.out.print(s + "--" + s);
    }
    else if (count % 3 == 1)
    {
        System.out.print(s + "-" + s);
    }
    else
    {
        System.out.print(s);
    }
    mystery(count - 1, s);
}
```

What is outputted by the call mystery(5, "X")?

(A) XX-XX--XXX-X
(B) XX-XX-XX-XX
(C) XXX--XX-X-XX--XXX
(D) XX-XXX--XXX-XX
(E) XXXXX

GO ON TO THE NEXT PAGE.

Questions 12–13 refer to the following classes and method descriptions.

Class `Table` has a method `getPrice`, which takes no parameters and returns the price of the table.

Class `Chair` also has a method `getPrice`, which takes no parameters and returns the price of the chair.

Class `DiningRoomSet` has a constructor which is passed a `Table` object and an `ArrayList` of `Chair` objects. It stores these parameters in its private data fields `myTable` and `myChairs`.

Class `DiningRoomSet` has a method `getPrice`, which takes no parameters and returns the price of the dining room set. The price of a dining room set is calculated as the sum of the price of its table and all of its chairs.

12. What is the correct way to define the signature of the constructor for the `DiningRoomSet` class?

(A) `public void DiningRoomSet(Table t, ArrayList, chairs)`
(B) `public DiningRoomSet(Table t, ArrayList<Chair> chairs)`
(C) `public void DiningRoomSet(Table t, ArrayList Chair Chairs)`
(D) `public DiningRoomSet(Table t, ArrayList Chair Chairs)`
(E) `public DiningRoomSet(Table t, Chair Chairs)`

13. What is the correct way to implement the `getPrice` method of the `DiningRoomSet` class?

(A)
```
public double getPrice(Table t, ArrayList chairs)
{
        return t.getPrice() + chairs.getPrice();
}
```
(B)
```
public double getPrice(Table t, ArrayList chairs)
{
        return myTable.getPrice() + myChairs.getPrice();
}
```
(C)
```
public double getPrice()
{
        return myTable.getPrice() + myChairs.getPrice();
}
```
(D)
```
public double getPrice()
{
        double result  = myTable.getPrice();
        for (int k = 0; k < myChairs.size() - 1; k++)
        {
                result += ((Chair)myChairs.get(k)).getPrice();
        }
        return result;
}
```
(E)
```
public double getPrice()
{
        double result = myTable.getPrice();
        for (int k = 0; k <  myChairs.length - 1; k++)
        {
                result += ((Chair)myChairs[k]).getPrice();
        }
        return result;
}
```

GO ON TO THE NEXT PAGE.

14. Consider the following output:

```
6   5   4   3   2   1
5   4   3   2   1
4   3   2   1
3   2   1
2   1
1
```

Which of the following code segments produces the above output when executed?

(A)
```
for  (int j = 6;  j  <  0;  j--)
{
  for (int k = j; k > 0; k--)
  {
      System.out.print(k  +  "    ");
  }
  System.out.println(" ");
}
```

(B)
```
for (int j = 6; j >= 0; j--)
{
  for (int k = j; k >= 0; k--)
  {
      System.out.print(k + " ");
  }
  System.out.println(" ");
}
```

(C)
```
for (int j = 0; j < 6; j++)
{
  for (int k = 6 - j; k > 0; k--)
  {
      System.out.print(k + "   ");
  }
  system.out.println(" ");
}
```

(D)
```
for (int j = 0; j < 6; j++)
{
  for (int k = 7 - j ; k > 0 ; k--)
  {
      System.out.print(k + " ");
  }
  System.out.println(" ");
}
```

(E)
```
for (int j = 0; j < 6; j++)
{
  for (int k = 6  -  j ; k >= 0; k--)
  {
      System.out.print(k + " ");
  }
  System.out.println(" ");
}
```

GO ON TO THE NEXT PAGE.

15. Consider the following code segment.

```
List<Integer> list = new ArrayList<Integer>();
list.add(new Integer(7));
list.add(new Integer(6));
list.add(1, new Integer(5));
list.add(1, new Integer(4));
list.add(new Integer(3));
list.set(2, new Integer(2));
list.add(1, new Integer(1));
System.out.println(list);
```

What is printed as a result of executing this code segment?

(A) [1, 4, 2, 7, 6, 3]
(B) [7, 1, 4, 2, 6, 3]
(C) [7, 2, 5, 4, 3, 1]
(D) [7, 6, 2, 4, 3, 1]
(E) [7, 1, 2]

16. Consider the following declarations.

```
public class Animal
{
    String makeSound()
    {
        // Implementation not shown
    }
    String animalType()
    {
        // Implementation not shown
    }
}
public static class Dog extends Animal
{
    public String makeSound(Animal a)
    {
        // Implementation not shown
    }
}
```

Which of the following methods must be included in the declaration of the Dog class in order for the class to successfully compile?

I.   public String makeSound()
II. public String animalType()
III. public String animalType(Animal b)

(A) I only
(B) II only
(C) I and II only
(D) II and III only
(E) None

17. Consider the following two classes.

```
public class Fish
{
  public String endoskeleton = "bone";

  public void action()
  {
      System.out.println("splash splash");
  }
}

public class Shark extends Fish
{
  public void action()
  {
      System.out.println("chomp chomp");
  }

  public String endoskeleton = "cartilage";
}
```

Which of the following is the correct output after the following code segment is executed?

```
Fish Bob = new Shark();
System.out.println(Bob.endoskeleton);
Bob.action();
```

(A) bone
   chomp chomp
(B) bone
   splash splash
(C) cartilage
   splash splash
(D) cartilage
   chomp chomp
(E) cartilage
   splash splash
   chomp chomp

GO ON TO THE NEXT PAGE.

Questions 18–19 refer to the following incomplete method.

The following `insertSort` method sorts the values in an integer array, `sort`, in ascending order.

```
1    public static void insertSort(int[] sort)
2        {
3            for (int index = 1; index < sort.length; index++)
4            {
5            int temp = sort[index];
6            while (index > 0 && sort[index - 1] > temp)
7                {
8            / * missing code * /
9                }
10        sort[index] = temp;
11        }
12    }
```

18. Which of the following can be used to replace / * missing code * / so that the `insertSort` method will execute properly?

(A) `sort[index] = sort[index - 1];`
    `index++;`
(B) `sort[index - 1] = sort[index];`
    `index--;`
(C) `sort[index] = sort[index + 1];`
    `index++;`
(D) `sort[index] = sort[index - 1];`
    `index--;`
(E) `sort[index] = sort[index + 1];`
    `index--;`

19. Assuming that the / * missing code * / is implemented properly, what change can be made to the code in order for the array to be sorted in descending order?

(A) Replace Line 6 with: `while (index < 0 && sort[index - 1] > temp)`
(B) Replace Line 6 with: `while (index < 0 && sort[index - 1] < temp)`
(C) Replace Line 6 with: `while (index > 0 && sort[index - 1] < temp)`
(D) Replace Line 3 with: `for (int index = sort.length - 1; index > 0; index--)`
(E) Replace Line 3 with: `for (int index = 1; index > 0; index--)`

20. Which of the following arrays would be sorted the slowest using insertion sort?

(A) `[3 4 6 2 7 3 9]`
(B) `[3 2 5 4 6 7 9]`
(C) `[9 7 6 5 4 3 2]`
(D) `[2 3 4 5 6 7 9]`
(E) `[9 3 2 4 5 7 6]`

GO ON TO THE NEXT PAGE.

Questions 21–23 refer to the following incomplete class declaration used to represent fractions with integer numerators and denominators.

```java
public class Fraction
{
  private int numerator;
  private int denominator;

  public Fraction()
  {
      numerator = 0;
      denominator = 1;
  }

  public Fraction(int n, int d)
  {
      numerator = n;
      denominator = d;
  }

  // postcondition: returns the
  //     numerator
  public int getNumerator()
  {   /* implementation not shown */    }

  // postcondition: returns the
  //     denominator
  public int getDenominator()
  {   /* implementation not shown*/    }

  // postcondition: returns the greatest
  // common divisor of x and y
  public int gcd(int x, int y)
  {   /* implementation not shown*/    }

  // postcondition: returns the Fraction
  //     that is the result of multiplying
  //     this Fraction and f

  public Fraction multiply(Fraction f)
  {   /* implementation not shown */    }
  // ... other methods not shown
}
```

GO ON TO THE NEXT PAGE.

21. Consider the method `multiply` of the `Fraction` class.

```
// postcondition: returns the Fraction
//         that is the result of multiplying
//         this Fraction and f
public Fraction multiply(Fraction f)
{    /* missing code */    }
```

Which of the following statements can be used to replace /* missing code */ so that the `multiply` method is correctly implemented?

```
I.    return Fraction(
        numerator * f.getNumerator(),
        denominator * f.getDenominator());
II.   return new Fraction(
        numerator * f.numerator,
        denominator * f.denominator());
III.  return new Fraction(
        numerator * f.getNumerator(),
        denominator * f.getDenominator());
```

(A) I only
(B) II only
(C) III only
(D) I and III only
(E) II and III only

22. Consider the use of the `Fraction` class to multiply the fractions $\dfrac{3}{4}$ and $\dfrac{7}{19}$. Consider the following code:

```
Fraction fractionOne;
Fraction fractionTwo;
Fraction answer;
fractionOne = new Fraction(3, 4);
fractionTwo = new Fraction(7, 19);
/* missing code */
```

Which of the following could be used to replace /* missing code */ so that the answer contains the result of multiplying `fractionOne` by `fractionTwo`?

```
(A) answer = fractionOne * fractionTwo;
(B) answer = multiply(fractionOne, fractionTwo);
(C) answer = fractionOne.multiply(fractionTwo);
(D) answer = new Fraction(fractionOne, fractionTwo);
(E) answer = (fractionOne.getNumerator() * fractionTwo.getNumerator()) /
             (fractionOne.getDenominator() * fractionTwo.getDenominator());
```

GO ON TO THE NEXT PAGE.

23. The following incomplete class declaration is intended to extend the `Fraction` class so that fractions can be manipulated in reduced form (lowest terms).

Note that a fraction can be reduced to lowest terms by dividing both the numerator and denominator by the greatest common divisor (gcd) of the numerator and denominator.

```
public class ReducedFraction extends Fraction
{
    private int reducedNumerator;
    private int reducedDenominator;
    // ... constructors and other methods not shown
}
```

Consider the following proposed constructors for the `ReducedFraction` class:

```
I.   public ReducedFraction( )
     {
       reducedNumerator = 0;
       reducedDenominator = 1;
     }
II.  public ReducedFraction(int n, int d)
     {
       numerator = n;
       denominator = d;
       reducedNumerator = n / gcd(n, d);
       reducedDenominator = d / gcd(n, d);
     }
III. public ReducedFraction(int n, int d)
     {
       super(n, d);
       reducedNumerator = n / gcd(n, d);
       reducedDenominator = d / gcd(n, d);
     }
```

Which of these constructor(s) would be legal for the `ReducedFraction` class?

(A) I only
(B) II only
(C) III only
(D) I and III only
(E) II and III only

GO ON TO THE NEXT PAGE.

24. Consider s1 and s2 defined as follows.

```
String s1 = new String("hello");
String s2 = new String("hello");
```

Which of the following is/are correct ways to see whether s1 and s2 hold identical strings?

```
I.   if (s1 == s2)
        /* s1 and s2 are identical */
II.  if (s1.equals(s2))
        /* s1 and s2 are identical */
III. if (s1.compareTo(s2) == 0)
        /* s1 and s2 are identical */
```

(A) I only

(B) II only

(C) I and III only

(D) II and III only

(E) I, II, and III

25. Consider the following variable and method declarations:

```
String s;
String t;
public void mystery (String a, String b)
{
    a = a + b;
    b = b + a;
}
```

Assume that s has the value "Elizabeth" and t has the value "Andrew" and mystery (s, t) is called. What are the values of s and t after the call to mystery?

	s	t
(A)	Elizabeth	Andrew
(B)	ElizabethAndrew	AndrewElizabeth
(C)	ElizabethAndrew	AndrewElizabethAndrew
(D)	ElizabethAndrew	ElizabethAndrewAndrew
(E)	ElizabethAndrewElizabeth	AndrewElizabethAndrew

GO ON TO THE NEXT PAGE.

26. Consider the following incomplete and *incorrect* class and interface declarations:

```
public class ComparableObject
{
    public int compareTo(Object o)
    {
        //method body not shown
    }
//other methods and variables not shown
}
public class Point extends ComparableObject
{
    private int x;
    private int y;
    public boolean compareTo(Point other)
    {
        return (x == other.x &&
                y == other.y);
    }
    // ... constructors and other methods
    //    not shown
}
```

For which of the following reasons, if any, is the above class structure incorrect?

I.   Objects may not access private data fields of other objects in the same class.

II. The ComparableObject class requires that compareTo be passed as an Object rather than a Point.

III. The ComparableObject class requires that compareTo return an int rather than a boolean.

(A) I only
(B) III only
(C) I and III only
(D) II and III only
(E) None, the above class declarations are correct.

GO ON TO THE NEXT PAGE.

27. Consider the following abstraction of a `for` loop where <1>, <2>, <3>, and <4> represent legal code in the indicated locations:

```
for (<1>; <2>; <3>)
{
    <4>
}
```

Which of the following `while` loops has the same functionality as the above `for` loop?

(A) ```
<1>;
while (<2>)
{
    <3>;
    <4>
}
```

(B) ```
<1>;
while (<2>)
{
    <4>
    <3>;
}
```

(C) ```
<1>;
    while (!<2>)
{
    <3>;
    <4>
}
```

(D) ```
<1>;
while (!<2>)
{
    <4>
    <3>;
}
```

(E) ```
<1>;
<3>;
while (<2>)
{
    <4>
    <3>;
}
```

28. Consider the following expression:

```
a / b + c - d % e * f
```

Which of the expressions given below is equivalent to the one given above?

(A) `((a / b) + (c - d)) % (e * f)`
(B) `((((a / b) + c) - d) % e) * f`
(C) `((a / b) + c) - (d % (e * f))`
(D) `(a / ((b + c) - d) % e) * f`
(E) `((a / b) + c) - ((d % e) * f)`

GO ON TO THE NEXT PAGE.
```

29. Assume that a program declares and initializes x as follows:

```
String[] x ;
x = new String[10] ;
initialize(x);                    // Fills the array x with
                                  // valid strings each of
                                  // length 5
```

Which of the following code segments correctly traverses the array and prints out the first character of all ten strings followed by the second character of all ten strings, and so on?

```
  I. int i;
     int j;
     for (i = 0 ; i < 10 ; i++)
          for (j = 0 ; j < 5 ; j++)
              System.out.print(x[i].substring(j, j + 1));
 II.  int i;
      int j;
      for (i = 0 ; i < 5 ; i++)
          for (j = 0 ; j < 10 ; j++)
              System.out.print(x[j].substring(i, i + 1));
III.  int i;
      int j;
      for (i = 0 ; i < 5 ; i++)
          for (j = 0 ; j < 10 ; j++)
              System.out.print(x[i].substring(j, j + 1));
```

(A) I only
(B) II only
(C) I and II only
(D) II and III only
(E) I, II, and III

GO ON TO THE NEXT PAGE.

30. Consider the following declaration and assignment statements:

```
int a = 7;
int b = 4;
double c;
c = a / b;
```

After the assignment statement is executed, what's the value of c?

(A) 1.0

(B) 1.75

(C) 2.0

(D) An error occurs because c was not initialized.

(E) An error occurs because a and b are integers and c is a double.

31. Consider the following code segment:

```
int x;
x = /* initialized to an integer */
if (x % 2 == 0 && x / 3 == 1)
    System.out.print("Yes");
```

For what values of x will the word "Yes" be printed when the code segment is executed?

(A) 0

(B) 4

(C) Whenever x is even and x is not divisible by 3

(D) Whenever x is odd and x is divisible by 3

(E) Whenever x is even and x is divisible by 3

GO ON TO THE NEXT PAGE.

32. Consider the following incomplete class definition:

```
public class SomeClass
{
    private String myName;
    // postcondition: returns myName
    public String getName( )
    {  /* implementation not shown */  }
    // postcondition: myName == name
    public void setName(String name)
    {  /* implementation not shown */  }
    // . . . constructors, other methods,
    //     and private data not shown
}
```

Now consider the method swap, not part of the SomeClass class.

```
// precondition: x and y are correctly
//    constructed
// postcondition: the names of objects
//    x and y are swapped
public void swap (SomeClass x, SomeClass y)
{
    / * missing code * /
}
```

Which of the following code segments can replace / * missing code * / so that the method swap works as intended?

```
I.   SomeClass temp;
     temp = x;
     x = y;
     y = temp;
II.  String temp;
     temp = x.myName;
     x.myName = y.myName;
     y.myName = temp;
III. String temp;
     temp = x.getName();
     x.setName(y.getName());
     y.setName(temp);
```

(A) I only
(B) III only
(C) I and III only
(D) II and III only
(E) I, II, and III

GO ON TO THE NEXT PAGE.

33. A bookstore wants to store information about the different types of books it sells.

For each book, it wants to keep track of the title of the book, the author of the book, and whether the book is a work of fiction or nonfiction.

If the book is a work of fiction, then the bookstore wants to keep track of whether it is a romance novel, a mystery novel, or science fiction.

If the book is a work of nonfiction, then the bookstore wants to keep track of whether it is a biography, a cookbook, or a self-help book.

Which of the following is the best design?

(A) Use one class, `Book`, which has three data fields: `String title`, `String author`, and `int bookType`.

(B) Use four unrelated classes: `Book`, `Title`, `Author`, and `BookType`.

(C) Use a class `Book` which has two data fields: `String title`, `String author`, and a subclass: `BookType`.

(D) Use a class `Book` which has two data fields: `String title`, `String author`, and six subclasses: `RomanceNovel`, `Mystery`, `ScienceFiction`, `Biography`, `Cookbook`, and `SelfHelpBook`.

(E) Use a class `Book` which has two data fields: `String title`, `String author`, and two subclasses: `FictionWork` and `NonFictionWork`. The class `FictionWork` has three subclasses, `RomanceNovel`, `Mystery`, and `ScienceFiction`. The class `NonFictionWork` has three subclasses: `Biography`, `Cookbook`, and `SelfHelpBook`.

GO ON TO THE NEXT PAGE.

34. Consider the following code:

```
public int mystery(int x)
{
    if (x == 1)
        return <missing value>;
    else
        return(2 * mystery(x - 1)) + x;
}
```

Which of the following can be used to replace <missing value> so that `mystery (4)` returns 34 ?

(A) 0
(B) 1
(C) 2
(D) 3
(E) 4

35. Consider the following code segment:

```
int [ ] X;
int [ ] Y;
int k;
X = initializeX();      // returns a valid
                        // initialized int [ ]
Y = initializeY();      // returns a valid
                        // initialized int [ ]

for (k = 0;
    k < X.length && X[k] == Y[k];
    k++)
{
    /* some code */
}
```

Assuming that after X and Y are initialized, `X.length == Y.length`, which of the following must be true after executing this code segment?

(A) `k < X.length`
(B) `k < X.length && X[k] == Y[k]`
(C) `k < X.length && X[k] != Y[k]`
(D) `k >= X.length || X[k] == Y[k]`
(E) `k >= X.length || X[k] != Y[k]`

36. Which of the following would NOT cause a run-time exception?

(A) Dividing an integer by zero
(B) Using an object that has been declared but not instantiated
(C) Accessing an array element with an array index that is equal to the length of the array
(D) Attempting to create a substring beginning at a negative index
(E) Attempting to call a method with the wrong number of arguments

GO ON TO THE NEXT PAGE.

37. Assume that a and b are properly initialized variables of type `Double`.

    Which of the following is an equivalent expression to:

    ```
    a.doubleValue() != b.doubleValue()
    ```

    (A) `a != b`
    (B) `a.notEquals(b)`
    (C) `!(a.doubleValue().equals(b.doubleValue()))`
    (D) `!(a.compareTo(b))`
    (E) `a.compareTo(b) != 0`

38. Which of the following would be the LEAST effective way of ensuring reliability in a program?

    (A) Encapsulating functionality in a class by declaring all data fields to be public
    (B) Defining and following preconditions and postconditions for every method
    (C) Including assertions at key places in the code
    (D) Using descriptive variable names
    (E) Indenting code in a consistent and logical manner

39. Consider a dictionary that has 1,024 pages with 50 words on each page.

    In order to look up a given target word, a student is considering using one of the following three methods:

    Method 1

    Use a binary search technique to find the correct page (comparing the target word with the first word on a given page). When the correct page is found, use a sequential search technique to find the target word on the page.

    Method 2

    Use a sequential search technique to find the correct page (comparing the target word with the first word on a given page). When the correct page is found, use another sequential search technique to find the target word on the page.

    Method 3

    Use a sequential search technique on all of the words in the dictionary to find the target word.

    Which of the following best characterizes the greatest number of words that will be examined using each method?

	Method 1	Method 2	Method 3
(A)	10	50	1,024
(B)	55	512	2,560
(C)	55	537	25,600
(D)	60	1,074	1,074
(E)	60	1,074	51,200

GO ON TO THE NEXT PAGE.

40. Consider the following recursive method.

```java
public static int mystery(int m)
{
    if (m == 0)
    {
        return 0;
    }
    else
    {
        return 4 + mystery(m - 2);
    }
}
```

Assuming that j is a positive integer and that m = 2j, what value is returned as a result of the call mystery(m)?

(A) 0
(B) m
(C) 2m
(D) j
(E) 2j

END OF SECTION I

**IF YOU FINISH BEFORE TIME IS CALLED,
YOU MAY CHECK YOUR WORK ON THIS SECTION.**

DO NOT GO ON TO SECTION II UNTIL YOU ARE TOLD TO DO SO.

GO ON TO THE NEXT PAGE.

COMPUTER SCIENCE A

SECTION II

Time—1 hour and 30 minutes

Number of Questions—4

Percent of Total Grade—50%

Directions: SHOW ALL YOUR WORK. REMEMBER THAT PROGRAM SEGMENTS ARE TO BE WRITTEN IN JAVA™.

Notes:

- Assume that the classes listed in the Java Quick Reference have been imported where appropriate.

- Unless otherwise noted in the question, assume that parameters in method calls are not `null` and that methods are called only when their preconditions are satisfied.

- In writing solutions for each question, you may use any of the accessible methods that are listed in classes defined in that question. Writing significant amounts of code that can be replaced by a call to one of these methods will not receive full credit.

FREE-RESPONSE QUESTIONS

1. A day care has a program to keep track of its employees and which children they teach during the day. An `Employee` has a minimum and maximum age they can teach. The `DayCare` also has a maximum ratio that specifies the maximum number of children a single employee can teach. Below is the full `DayCare` class:

```java
public class DayCare
{
    private ArrayList<Employee> employees;
    private ArrayList<Child> children;
    private int maxRatio;

    public DayCare(int maxRatio)
    {
        employees = new ArrayList<Employee>();
        children = new ArrayList<Child>();
        this.maxRatio = maxRatio;
    }

    public boolean findEmployeeForChild(Child c)
    {
        /*  To be completed in part (a)  */
    }

    public boolean runDayCare()
    {
        /*  To be completed in part (b)  */
    }

    public boolean addChild(Child c)
    {
        /*  To be completed in part (c)  */
    }
}
```

GO ON TO THE NEXT PAGE.

(a) An Employee can only teach children between the employee's minimum age (inclusive) and maximum age (inclusive). They can also only teach children up to the day care's maximum ratio (inclusive). Below is the full Employee class.

```java
public class Employee
{
    /* Instance variables not shown */

    public Employee(String name, String id, int min, int max)
    {
        /* Implementation not shown */
    }

    // Return the number of children currently assigned to this Employee
    public int childrenAssigned()
    {
        /* Implementation not shown */
    }

    // Assign a new child to this Employee
    public void assignChild(Child c)
    {
        /* Implementation not shown */
    }

    // Determine whether this Employee can teach a Child based on the child's age
    public boolean canTeach(int age)
    {
        /* Implementation not shown */
    }
}
```

A Child has accessors to get their name and age. While the implementation of Child is not shown, you can assume the accessors are called getName and getAge.

Complete the findEmployeeForChild method below that assigns a Child to the first Employee who can teach the Child and who has not reached the maximum ratio of the DayCare.

```java
/* Return true if an Employee was found for the Child, false otherwise */
public boolean findEmployeeForChild(Child c)
```

Begin your response at the top of a new page in the separate Free Response booklet and fill in the appropriate circle at the top of each page to indicate the question number. If there are multiple parts to this question, write the part letter with your response.

GO ON TO THE NEXT PAGE.

(b) In order for the DayCare to run for a day, each Child must be assigned an Employee. If an Employee cannot be found for a Child, the DayCare cannot run for the day.

Complete the runDayCare method below that finds an Employee for each Child in the children ArrayList.

```
/* Return true if an Employee was found for each Child, false otherwise */
public boolean runDayCare()
```

Begin your response at the top of a new page in the separate Free Response booklet and fill in the appropriate circle at the top of each page to indicate the question number. If there are multiple parts to this question, write the part letter with your response.

GO ON TO THE NEXT PAGE.

(c) When a `Child` is added to the roster of the `DayCare`, the `DayCare` should first make sure there is an `Employee` available to teach that `Child`.

Complete the `addChild` method below that adds a `Child` to the `children` `ArrayList` if an `Employee` is available to teach that `Child`.

```
/* Return true if the Child was added to the ArrayList, false otherwise */
public boolean addChild(Child c)
```

Begin your response at the top of a new page in the separate Free Response booklet and fill in the appropriate circle at the top of each page to indicate the question number. If there are multiple parts to this question, write the part letter with your response.

GO ON TO THE NEXT PAGE.

2. A baseball team consists of different people including players, coaches, and people who work in the front office making trades and other transactions. The following Person class is used for all of the people who work for the team.

Each person has a name and an age.

```
public class Person
{
    private String fullName;
    private int age;

    public Person(String s, int a)
    {
        fullName = s;
        age = a;
    }

    // Accessors for name and age
    public String getName()
    {
        return fullName;
    }

    public int getAge()
    {
        return age;
    }
}
```

GO ON TO THE NEXT PAGE.

A `Player` has a name and age just like any person on the team, but also has a `position`. The position could be something like "catcher," "left fielder," or "infielder." Players should also be able to change their positions using a method called `changePosition`. Here is an example of a `Player` object:

```
Player p = new Player("Sammy Sosa", 32, "right fielder");
p.changePosition("outfielder");
```

Write the entire `Player` class.

Begin your response at the top of a new page in the separate Free Response booklet and fill in the appropriate circle at the top of each page to indicate the question number. If there are multiple parts to this question, write the part letter with your response.

GO ON TO THE NEXT PAGE.

3. A class is designed to store someone's full name. You can assume the name has only one space between the first name and the last name. The class has methods to extract the first name, last name, and number of vowels in the name. You can see an example below.

```
String fullName = "Katherine Johnson";
Name.getFirstName(fullName);  // Returns "Katherine"
Name.getLastName(fullName);   // Returns "Johnson"
Name.countVowels(fullName);   // Returns 6
```

(a) The getFirstName method returns the first name based on a given full name. You can assume that fullName has only one space between the first name and the last name. Write the getFirstName method.

```
public static String getFirstName(String name)
```

Begin your response at the top of a new page in the separate Free Response booklet and fill in the appropriate circle at the top of each page to indicate the question number. If there are multiple parts to this question, write the part letter with your response.

GO ON TO THE NEXT PAGE.

(b) The getLastName method returns the last name based on a given full name. You can assume that fullName has only one space between the first name and the last name. Write the getLastName method.

```
public static String getLastName(String name)
```

Begin your response at the top of a new page in the separate Free Response booklet and fill in the appropriate circle at the top of each page to indicate the question number. If there are multiple parts to this question, write the part letter with your response.

GO ON TO THE NEXT PAGE.

(c) The `countVowels` method counts the number of vowels in the given full name. You can assume we will count only the letters a, e, i, o, and u as vowels. Write the entire `countVowels` method.

```
public static int countVowels(String name)
```

Begin your response at the top of a new page in the separate Free Response booklet and fill in the appropriate circle at the top of each page to indicate the question number. If there are multiple parts to this question, write the part letter with your response.

GO ON TO THE NEXT PAGE.

4. A city parking lot has a sign that keeps track of how many parking spaces are available in the lot. The class for the parking lot is detailed below.

```
public class ParkingLot
{
    private Car[ ][ ] lot;

    public ParkingLot(int rows, int cols)
    {
        lot = new Car[rows][cols];
    }

    public int openSpaces()
    {
        // Complete in part (a)
    }

    public boolean parkCar(Car newCar)
    {
        // Complete in part (b)
    }
}
```

GO ON TO THE NEXT PAGE.

(a) Write the `openSpaces` method that returns the number of spaces available in the parking lot. If a space is empty, it will be equal to `null`.

```
/* Return the number of empty spaces in the parking lot */
public int openSpaces( )
```

Begin your response at the top of a new page in the separate Free Response booklet and fill in the appropriate circle at the top of each page to indicate the question number. If there are multiple parts to this question, write the part letter with your response.

GO ON TO THE NEXT PAGE.

(b) Complete the `parkCar` method that puts a new car in any space in the parking lot and returns `true` if it was able to do so. It should return `false` if there are no empty spaces. You should use the `openSpaces` method to receive full credit.

```
/* Return true if there is an open spot to park the newCar, false otherwise. The car should be added to the lot 2D array
if there is an open spot. */
public boolean parkCar(Car newCar)
```

Begin your response at the top of a new page in the separate Free Response booklet and fill in the appropriate circle at the top of each page to indicate the question number. If there are multiple parts to this question, write the part letter with your response.

STOP

END OF EXAM

Practice Test 3:
Answers and
Explanations

PRACTICE TEST 3 ANSWER KEY

1.	C	21.	C
2.	A	22.	C
3.	C	23.	D
4.	C	24.	D
5.	E	25.	A
6.	B	26.	E
7.	A	27.	B
8.	B	28.	E
9.	C	29.	B
10.	E	30.	A
11.	A	31.	B
12.	B	32.	B
13.	D	33.	E
14.	C	34.	C
15.	B	35.	E
16.	E	36.	E
17.	A	37.	E
18.	D	38.	A
19.	C	39.	E
20.	C	40.	C

ANSWER EXPLANATIONS

Section I: Multiple-Choice Questions

1. **C** This question tests how well you understand assigning values to variables and following the steps of the code. When `trial()` is called, a is assigned to the integer value of 10 and b is assigned to the integer value of 5. Next, `doubleValues()` is called with a and b as inputs c and d. The method `doubleValues()` multiplies the input values c and d by 2 and prints them out. Thus, the value of c is 10 * 2 = 20 and the value of d is 5 * 2 = 10. Because `System.out.print()` does not print any line breaks or spaces, the resulting print is 2010. While c and d have been reassigned new values, these values exist only within the `doubleValues()` call, so the values of a and b are unchanged. After the `doubleValues()` method is completed, the `trial()` method then prints the values of b and then a, printing 510. Once again, no spaces or line breaks are printed, so, combined together, what is printed from calling `trial()` is 2010510. Therefore, the correct answer is (C).

2. **A** The method `mystery(int a, int b)` takes as input integers a and b with the precondition that a > b > 0. Plug in x = 5 and y = 2. These values are passed as parameters to make a = 5 and b = 2. Set d = 0. Now go to the `for` loop, initializing c = a = 5. Since it is still the case that c > b, execute the `for` loop. Execute d = d + c by setting d = 0 + 5 = 5. Decrease c by 1 to get c = 4. Since c > b, execute the `for` loop again. Execute d = d + c by setting d = 5 + 4 = 9. Decrease c by 1 to get c = 3. Since it is still the case that c > b, execute the `for` loop again. Execute d = d + c by setting d = 9 + 3 = 12. Decrease c by 1 to get c = 2. Since it is no longer the case that c > b, stop executing the `for` loop. Return d = 12. Now go through the choices and eliminate any that don't describe a return of 12. Choice (A) is the sum of all integers greater than y but less than or equal to x. The sum of all integers greater than 2 but less than or equal to 5 is 3 + 4 + 5 = 12, so keep (A). Choice (B) is the sum of all integers greater than or equal to y but less than or equal to x. The sum of all integers greater than or equal to 2 but less than or equal to 5 is 2 + 3 + 4 + 5 = 14, so eliminate (B). Choice (C) is the sum of all integers greater than y but less than x. The sum of all integers greater than 2 but less than 5 is 3 + 4 = 7, so eliminate (C). Choice (D) is the sum of all integers greater than or equal to y but less than x. The sum of all integers greater than or equal to 2 but less than 5 is 2 + 3 + 4 = 9, so eliminate (D). Choice (E) is the sum of all integers less than y but greater than or equal to x. However, there are no integers that are both less than 2 and greater than or equal to 5, so eliminate (E). Only one answer remains. The correct answer is (A).

3. **C** The question asks for what is printed by the call `mystery(3)`. In the call, 3 is taken as a parameter and assigned to n. The integer k is then initialized in the `for` loop and set equal to 0. Since k < n, execute the `for` loop. Call `mystery(0)`, while keeping your place in the call of `mystery(3)`. Again, k is initialized in the `for` loop and set equal to 0. In this call, since n = 0, it is not the case that k < n, so do not execute the `for` loop. This completes the call of `mystery(0)`, so return to `mystery(3)`. The next command is `System.out.print(k)`. Since k = 0, the first character printed

is 0. Look to see whether any choices can be eliminated. All choices begin with 0, so no choices can be eliminated. Continue with the method call. Since this is the last command of the for loop, increment k to get k = 1. Since it is still the case that k < n, execute the for loop again. Call mystery(1), again keeping your place in the call of mystery(3). Again, k is initialized in the for loop and set equal to 0. In this call, since n = 1, it is the case that k < n, so execute the for loop. Call mystery(k), which is mystery(0). As seen above, mystery(0) prints nothing, so execute the next line in mystery(1), which is System.out.print(k). Since k = 0, print 0. Eliminate (A), since the second character printed is not 0. Increment k to get k = 1. Since it is no longer the case that k < n, do not execute the for loop again and end this call of mystery(1). Return to the original call of mystery(3), where k = 1 and System.out.print(k) is the next statement. Print 1. All remaining choices have 1 as the third character, so do not eliminate any choices. This is the end of the for loop, so increment k to get k = 2. Since n = 3, it is still the case that k < n, so execute the for loop. Call mystery(2) while holding your place in mystery(3). Again, k is initialized in the for loop and set equal to 0. In this call, since n = 2, it is the case that k < n, so execute the for loop. Call mystery(0), which prints nothing. Execute System.out.print(k) to print 0. Eliminate (B), since the next character is not 0. Increment k to get k = 1. Since k < n, execute the for loop. Call mystery(1), which, as described above, prints 0. All remaining choices have 0 as the next character, so don't eliminate any choices. The next command in mystery(2) is System.out.print(k), so print 1. Again, keep all the remaining choices. In mystery(2), increment k to get k = 2. Since n = 2, it is no longer the case that k < n, so stop executing the for loop. End mystery(2) and return to mystery(3), where k = 2 and the next command is System.out.print(k), so print 2. Again, keep all remaining choices. Increment k to get k = 3. Since it is no longer the case that k < n, stop executing the for loop. The method call is complete for mystery(3), so there will be no more printed characters. Eliminate (D) and (E), which have further characters printed.

In other words, the calling sequence looks like this

Function Call	Prints
mystery(3)	
mystery(0)	
System.out.print(0)	0
mystery(1)	
mystery(0)	
System.out.print(0)	0
System.out.print(1)	1
mystery(2)	
mystery(0)	
System.out.print(0)	0
mystery(1)	
mystery(0)	
System.out.print(0)	0
System.out.print(1)	1
System.out.print(2)	2

The correct answer is (C).

4. **C** `SelectionSort` walks through the array to find the smallest element in the part of the array not yet sorted. It then swaps that smallest element with the first unsorted element.

Start with the original array of values.

| 4 | 10 | 1 | 2 | 6 | 7 | 3 | 5 |

The smallest element is 1. Swap that with the first unsorted element, 4. The array now looks like this.

| 1 | 10 | 4 | 2 | 6 | 7 | 3 | 5 |

This is not a choice, so continue. The smallest element in the unsorted part of the array (from 10 to 5) is 2. Swap that with the first unsorted element, 10.

| 1 | 2 | 4 | 10 | 6 | 7 | 3 | 5 |

This is still not a choice, so continue this process. The smallest element in the unsorted part of the array (from 4 to 5) is 3. Swap that with the first unsorted element, 4.

| 1 | 2 | 3 | 10 | 6 | 7 | 4 | 5 |

This is (C), so stop here. If you're interested, here are the complete moves for selection sort.

1	2	3	4	6	7	10	5
1	2	3	4	5	7	10	6
1	2	3	4	5	6	10	7
1	2	3	4	5	6	7	10

The correct answer is (C).

5. **E** Execute the commands. The integer k and the integer array A are initialized. The array A is given length 7. Thus, the array, A, has seven elements with indexes from 0 to 6. Execute the first `for` loop. Set k = 0. Since k < A.length, execute the `for` loop, which sets A[0] equal to A.length − k = 7 − 0 = 7. Increment k to get k = 1. Since 1 < 7, execute the `for` loop, which sets A[1] equal to A.length − k = 7 − 1 = 6. Increment k to get k = 2. Since 2 < 7, execute the `for` loop, which sets A[2] equal to A.length − k = 7 − 2 = 5. Increment k to get k = 3. Since 3 < 7, execute the `for` loop, which sets A[3] equal to A.length − k = 7 − 3 = 4. Increment k to get k = 4. Since 4 < 7, execute the `for` loop, which sets A[4] equal to A.length − k = 7 − 4 = 3. Increment k to get k = 5. Since 5 < 7, execute the `for` loop, which sets A[5] equal to A.length − k = 7 − 5 = 2. Increment k to get k = 6. Since 6 < 7, execute the `for` loop, which sets A[6] equal to A.length − k = 7 − 6 = 1. Increment k to get k = 7. Since it is not the case that 7 < 7, stop executing the `for` loop. Therefore, the array has the values

| 7 | 6 | 5 | 4 | 3 | 2 | 1 |

The second `for` loop puts the value of the kth element of the array into the (k + 1)st element. Be careful!

A quick glance might lead you to believe that each value is shifted in the array one spot to the right, giving an answer of (D). However, a step-by-step analysis demonstrates that this will not be the case. The `for` loop sets k = 0. Since 0 < `A.length` – 1, execute the `for` loop. The command in the `for` loop is `A[k + 1] = A[k]`. Since k = 0, set `A[1] = A[0]` = 7. Increment k to get k = 1. Since it is still the case that k < `A.length` – 1, execute the `for` loop. Since k = 1, set `A[2] = A[1]` = 7. Continue in this manner. Since `A.length` – 1 = 7 – 1 = 6, only execute the `for` loop through k = 5. Each execution of the `for` loop is shown below.

k	Assignment	A[]
0	A[1] = A[0]	7 7 5 4 3 2 1
1	A[2] = A[1]	7 7 7 4 3 2 1
2	A[3] = A[2]	7 7 7 7 3 2 1
3	A[4] = A[3]	7 7 7 7 7 2 1
4	A[5] = A[4]	7 7 7 7 7 7 1
5	A[6] = A[5]	7 7 7 7 7 7 7

The final values contained by A are 7 7 7 7 7 7 7. The correct answer is (E).

6. **B** Choices (C), (D), and (E) are syntactically invalid according to the given class definitions. In (C), p is used as a `PostOffice` object rather than an array of `PostOffice` objects. Choice (D) treats `getMail` and `getBox` as static methods without invoking them from an object. Choice (E) creates a new `Mail` object attempting to use a `Mail` constructor. Even if such a constructor were available, there would be no way for the constructor to know about p, the array of `PostOffices`.

Choices (A) and (B) differ only in the indexes of the array and methods. There are two clues in the question that indicate that (B) is the correct answer. First, p is declared as an array of 10 Post-Offices. This means that p[10] would raise an `ArrayListOutOfBoundsException`. Remember that p[9] actually refers to the 10th post office, since array indexes begin with 0. Second, the comments in the class definitions for the `getBox` and `getMail` methods indicate that the parameter they take is zero-based. Therefore, they should be passed an integer one less than the number of the box or piece of mail needed. For either reason, eliminate (A). The correct answer is (B).

7. **A** In the method `printEmptyBoxes`, the loop variable k refers to the index of the post office and the loop variable x refers to the index of the box within the post office. Choice (A) is correct. It checks to see whether the box is assigned and whether it does not have mail using the appropriate methods of the `Box` class. It then prints out the box number of the box. Choice (B) is similar to (A) but incorrectly interchanges x and k. Eliminate (B). Choice (C) omits the call to the method `getBox`. Therefore, it attempts to call the `getBoxNumber()` method of the `PostOffice` object p[k]. Since `PostOffice` objects do not have a `getBoxNumber()` method, this would result in a compile error. Eliminate (C). Choice (D) is similar to (C), but interchanges x and k. Eliminate (D). Choice (E)

prints the value of k, which is the index of the post office rather than the index of the box. Eliminate (E). The correct answer is (A).

8. **B** There are four possibilities for the values of a and b. Either both a and b are true, both a and b are false, a is true and b is false, or a is false and b is true.

Analyze the possibilities in a table.

a (initial value)	b (initial value)	a = a && b (final value)	b = a || b (final value)
true	true	true	true
true	false	false	false
false	true	false	true
false	false	false	false

Remember when calculating b = a || b that a has already been modified. Therefore, use the final, rather than the initial, value of a when calculating the final value of b.

Go through each statement. Statement I says that the final value of a is equal to the initial value of a. This is not the case in the second row of the table, so Statement I is not always true. Eliminate any choice that includes it: (A) and (D). Statement II says that the final value of b is equal to the initial value of b. This is true in each row and, thus, Statement II is always true, so eliminate the choice that does not include it: (C). Statement III says that the final value of a is equal to the initial value of b. This is not the case in the third row of the table, so Statement III is not always true. Eliminate any choice that includes it: (E). The correct answer is (B).

9. **C** The best way to solve this problem is to look at each if statement individually. The integer x is initialized and then set equal to 53. The next statement is an if statement with the condition (x > 10). Since 53 > 10, execute the statement, System.out.print("A"), and print A. The next statement is an if-else statement, this one having the condition (x > 30). Since 53 > 30, execute the if statement, System.out.print("B"), and print B. Even though 53 > 40, because the next part of the statement is an else statement, it cannot be executed if the original if statement was executed. Therefore, do not execute the else statement, and do not print C. The next statement is another if statement, this one having the condition (x > 50). Since 53 > 50, execute the statement, System.out.print("D"), and print D. The next statement is another if statement, this one having the condition (x > 70). Since it is not the case that 53 > 70, do not execute the statement. There is no further code to execute, so the result of the printing is ABD. The correct answer is (C).

10. **E** This problem tests your ability to work with nested `for` loops. Although it appears complicated at first glance, it can easily be solved by systematically walking through the code.

Be sure to write the values of the variables `j` and `k` down on paper; don't try to keep track of `j` and `k` in your head. Use the empty space in the question booklet for this purpose.

Code	j	k	Output
Set `j` to the value -2.	-2		
Test the condition: `j <= 2`? Yes.	-2		
Set `k` to the value that `j` has.	-2	-2	
Test the condition: `k < j + 3`? Yes.	-2	-2	
Output `k`.	-2	-2	-2
Update k: `k++`	-2	-1	-2
Test the condition: `k < j + 3`? Yes.	-2	-1	-2
Output `k`.	-2	-1	-2 -1
Update k: `k++`	-2	0	-2 -1
Test the condition: `k < j + 3`? Yes.	-2	0	-2 -1
Output `k`.	-2	0	-2 -1 0
Update k: `k++`	-2	1	-2 -1 0
Test the condition: `k < j + 3`? No.	-2	1	-2 -1 0
Update j: `j = j + 2`	0	1	-2 -1 0
Test the condition: `j <= 2`? Yes.	0	1	-2 -1 0
Set `k` to the value that `j` has.	0	0	-2 -1 0
Test the condition: `k < j + 3`? Yes.	0	0	-2 -1 0
Output `k`.	0	0	-2 -1 0 0

At this point, stop because (E) is the only choice that starts -2 -1 0 0. However, repeating this process will result in the correct output of -2 -1 0 0 1 2 2 3 4. The correct answer is (E).

11. **A** To solve this problem, first note that `count % 3` is equal to the remainder when `count` is divided by 3. Execute the method call `mystery(5, "X")`, taking `count = 5` and `s = "X"` as parameters. Because it is not the case that `5 <= 0`, do not execute the first `if` statement.

Because 5 % 3 = 2, calling `mystery(5, "X")` will execute the `else` statement, printing X. Then, it will call `mystery(4, "X")`, and return. Because 4 % 3 = 1, calling `mystery(4, "X")` will execute the `else if` statement, printing X-X, call `mystery(3, "X")`, and return. At this point, (C) and (E) can be eliminated. Because 3 % 3 = 0, calling `mystery(3, "X")` will execute the `if` statement, printing X--X, call `mystery(2, "X")`, and return. Note that you can stop at this point because (B) and (D) can be eliminated. If you're interested, here is the remainder of the execution. Because 2 % 3 = 2, calling `mystery(2, "X")` will execute the `else` statement, printing X, call `mystery(1, "X")`, and return. Because 1 % 3 = 1, calling `mystery(1, "X")` will execute the `else` if statement, printing X–X, call mystery(0, "X"), and return. Finally, calling mystery(0, "X") will simply return because count is less than or equal to zero. Putting it all together, mystery(5, "X") prints

XX–XX––XXX–X

The correct answer is (A).

12. **B** The only information that you need to solve this problem is the first sentence in the description of the constructor. Class DiningRoomSet has a constructor, which is passed a Table object and an ArrayList of Chair objects. Because you are writing a constructor, you can immediately eliminate (A) and (C), which are void methods. Constructors never return anything, so there is never a need to specify a void return. Choice (E) is incorrect because the constructor is passed a Table object and a Chair object, not a Table object and an ArrayList of Chair objects. Choice (D) is incorrect because the second parameter has two types associated with it. It should have only one type: ArrayList. Choice (B) is correct.

13. **D** The best way to solve this problem is to eliminate choices. Choices (A) and (B) are incorrect because the class description states that the getPrice method of the DiningRoomSet class does not take any parameters. Choice (C) can be eliminated because the private data field myChairs is not a Chair; it is an ArrayList. Therefore, it does not have a getPrice method. This leaves (D) and (E). You need to know that ArrayLists are accessed using the get method while arrays are accessed using the [] notation. MyChairs is an ArrayList, so the correct answer is (D).

14. **C** To solve this type of problem, use information about the output and the loops to eliminate incorrect choices. Then, if necessary, work through the code for any remaining choices to determine the correct answer. There are six lines of output. By examining the outer loop of each of the choices, you can eliminate (B) because it will traverse the loop seven times, and during each traversal at least one number will be printed. You can also eliminate (A) because the outer loop will never be executed. The initial value of j is 6, but the condition j < 0 causes the loop to terminate immediately. The remaining choices have the same outer loop, so turn your attention to the inner loop. Eliminate (D) because the first time through the loop, a 7 will be printed—clearly not the correct output. Finally, eliminate (E) because the condition of the inner loop, k >= 0, will cause a 0 to be printed at the end of each line. This leaves (C), which is indeed the correct answer.

15.   **B**   This problem tests your knowledge of the methods of the `ArrayList` class. The following table shows the contents of `list` after each line of code.

Code	Contents of list	Explanation
`list = new ArrayList();`	`[]`	A newly created `ArrayList` is empty
`list.add(new Integer(7));`	`[7]`	Adds 7 to the end of `list`
`list.add(new Integer(6));`	`[7, 6]`	Adds 6 to the end of `list`
`list.add(1, new Integer(5));`	`[7, 5, 6]`	Inserts 5 into `list` as position 1, shifting elements to the right as necessary
`list.add(1, new Integer(4));`	`[7, 4, 5, 6]`	Inserts 4 into `list` as position 1, shifting elements to the right as necessary
`list.add(new Integer(3));`	`[7, 4, 5, 6, 3]`	Adds 3 to the end of `list`
`list.set(2, new Integer(2));`	`[7, 4, 2, 6, 3]`	Replaces the number at position 2 in `list` with 2
`list.add(1, new Integer(1));`	`[7, 1, 4, 2, 6, 3]`	Inserts 1 into `list` at position 1, shifting elements to the right as necessary

The next command is to print `list`. Therefore, the correct answer is (B).

16.   **E**   Although the `Dog` class extends `Animal`, Java does not require `Dog` to have any specific methods. New methods will be unique to `Dog` objects (and those of its subclasses, when applicable) and methods inherited from `Animal` can be invoked as normal.

The correct answer is (E).

17.   **A**   This question is testing your understanding of static and dynamic types.

```
Fish Bob = new Shark();
```

This line creates the `Bob` variable with the static type of `Fish` and the dynamic type of `Shark`.

```
System.out.println(Bob.endoskeleton);
```

This line prints the `endoskeleton` field of the variable `Bob`. When looking up a field, the static type is used, so "bone" is printed.

```
Bob.action();
```

This line executes the method `action()`. When looking up a method, the dynamic type is used, so "`chomp chomp`" is printed. The correct answer is (A).

18. **D** The insertion sort algorithm creates a sorted array by sorting elements one at a time.

    The `for` loop of the code shows that the elements are being sorted from left to right. To determine the position of the new element to be sorted, the value of the new element must be compared with the values of the sorted elements from right to left. This requires `index--` in the `while` loop, not `index++`. Choices (A) and (C) are wrong.

    In order to place the new element to be sorted in its correct position, any sorted elements larger than the new element must be shifted to the right. This requires `sort[index] = sort[index -1]`. Choices (B) and (E) are wrong. The correct answer is (D).

19. **C** In order for the array to be sorted in descending order, you will need to make a change. Plug each answer choice into the array to see which is correct. In (A) and (B), as the index will never be less than 0, the contents of the `while` loop will never be executed. Choice (C) is the correct answer, as it changes the condition of finding the position of the new element from being less than the compared element to greater. In (D), altering the `for` loop this way would lead to the elements being sorted from right to left but still in ascending order. In (E), the index is initialized at 1 and decremented while `index > 0`, so it will execute the `for` loop only once. The correct answer is (C).

20. **C** The rate at which insertion sort runs depends on the number of comparisons that are made. The number of comparisons is minimized with an array with elements that are already sorted in ascending order and maximized with an array with elements that are sorted in descending order. The array in (C) is sorted in reverse order and will require the most comparisons to sort. The correct answer is (C).

21. **C** All three responses look very similar, so look carefully at the difference. Statement I is missing the keyword `new`, which is needed to create a new object. Eliminate any choice that includes Statement I: (A) and (D). Statements II and III differ in that Statement II uses `f.numerator` and `f.denominator` while Statement III uses `f.getNumerator()` and `f.getDenominator()`. Since the integers `numerator` and `denominator` are private, while the methods `getNumerator()` and `getDenominator()` are public, the methods must be called by another object. Therefore, Statement II is not valid. Eliminate any choice that includes it: (B) and (E). The correct answer is (C).

22. **C** Go through the choices one at a time. Choice (A) is incorrect because the multiplication operator, `*`, is not defined to work on `Fraction` objects. Eliminate (A). Choice (B) is incorrect because the multiply method takes only one parameter and it is not correctly invoked by a `Fraction` object. Eliminate (B). Choice (C) correctly calls the `multiply()` method as through a fraction object, taking the other fraction as a parameter. Keep (C). Choice (D) attempts to create a new `Fraction` object but incorrectly constructs it by passing two `Fraction` objects rather than two integers. Eliminate (D). Finally, while (E) calculates the value of the result of the multiplication, the "/" operator assigns integer types, which cannot be applied to `answer`, which is an object of type `Fraction`. Eliminate (E). The correct answer is (C).

23. **D** Go through each statement one at a time. Constructor I is legal. This default constructor of the ReducedFraction class will automatically call the default constructor of the Fraction class and the private data of both classes will be set appropriately. Eliminate any choice that does not include Constructor I: (B), (C), and (E). Because Constructor II is not included in the remaining choices, do not worry about analyzing it. Constructor III is also legal. The call super(n, d) invokes the second constructor of the Fraction class, which sets the private data of the Fraction class appropriately. The private data of the ReducedFraction class is then set explicitly in the ReducedFraction constructor. Note that if the call super(n, d) were not present, Constructor III would still be legal. However, it would create a logical error in the code, as the default constructor of the Fraction class would be invoked, and the private data of the Fraction class would not be set appropriately. Eliminate (A), which does not include Constructor III. Only one choice remains, so there is no need to continue. However, to see why Constructor II is illegal, remember that derived classes may not access the private data of their super classes. In other words, the constructor for a ReducedFraction may not directly access numerator and denominator in the Fraction class. The correct answer is (D).

24. **D** Go through each statement one at a time. Statement I is incorrect. "==" checks object references as opposed to their contents. This is an important distinction as two different objects may hold the same data. Eliminate (A), (C), and (E), which contain Statement I. Both of the remaining choices contain Statement II, so don't worry about analyzing it. Statement III is correct. The compareTo() method of the String class returns 0 if the two String objects hold the same strings. Eliminate (B), which does not include Statement III. Only one choice remains, so there is no need to continue. However, you should see why Statement II is also correct. The equals method of the String class returns true if the two String objects hold the same strings. The correct answer is (D).

25. **A** The values of s and t are not changed in mystery(). Even though s and t are both parameters of the method, only the instance variables a and b are changed. Thus, the original Strings s and t are unaffected by any action in mystery(). The correct answer is (A).

26. **E** Though these two classes are related through an inheritance relationship, there is no rule in Java that requires this structure to share methods and/or data. Therefore, there are no requirements on either class. The correct answer is (E).

27. **B** An example will help clarify this question.

Consider the following for loop:

```
for (int k = 0; k < 3; k++)
{
        Systemout.println(k);
}
```

This prints out the integers 0 to 2, one number per line. Matching `int k = 0` to <1>; `k < 3` to <2>; `k++` to <3> and `System.out.println(k);` to <4>, go through each choice one at a time and determine whether each has the same functionality.

Choice (A) initializes `k` and assigns it the value 0. Then it tests to determine whether `k < 3`. This is true, so execute the `while` loop. The next command is `k++`, so increase `k` by 1 to get `k = 0 + 1 = 1`. Now execute `System.out.println(k)` to print 1. However, the first number printed in the original was 0, so this is incorrect. Eliminate (A).

Choice (B) initializes `k` and assigns it the value 0. Then it tests to determine whether `k < 3`. This is true, so execute the `while` loop. Now execute `System.out.println(k)` to print 0. The next command is `k++`, so increase `k` by 1 to get `k = 0 + 1 = 1`. Go back to the top of the `while` loop. Since `k = 1`, it is still the case that `k < 3`, so execute the `while` loop. Now execute `System.out.println(k)` to print 1. The next command is `k++`, so increase `k` by 1 to get `k = 1 + 1 = 2`. Go back to the top of the `while` loop. Since `k = 2`, it is still the case that `k < 3`, so execute the `while` loop. Now execute `System.out.println(k)` to print 2. The next command is `k++`, so increase `k` by 1 to get `k = 2 + 1 = 3`. Go back to the top of the `while` loop. Since `k = 3`, it is no longer the case that `k < 3`, so stop executing the `while` loop. The result of the program is printing the integers 0 to 2, one number per line, so keep (B).

Choice (C) initializes `k` and assigns it the value 0. Then it tests the condition `!(k < 3)`. Since it is the case that `k < 3`, the statement `(k < 3)` has the boolean value `true`, making the boolean value of `!(k < 3)` `false`. Thus the `while` loop is not executed. Since the `while` loop is not executed, nothing is printed. Eliminate (C).

Choice (D) has the same initialization statement and `while` loop condition as (C), so nothing is printed by this choice either. Eliminate (D).

Choice (E) initializes `k` and assigns it the value 0. The next command is `k++`, so increase `k` by 1 to get `k = 0 + 1 = 1`. Then it tests to determine whether `k < 3`. This is true, so execute the `while` loop. Execute `System.out.println(k)` to print 1. However, the first number printed in the original was 0, so this is incorrect. Eliminate (E).

The correct answer is (B).

28. **E** This question tests your knowledge of operator precedence. In Java, multiplication, division, and modulus are performed before addition and subtraction. If more than one operator in an expression has the same precedence, the operations are performed left-to-right. Parenthesizing the expression one step at a time

```
     a / b + c - d % e * f
→    (a / b) + c - d % e * f
→    (a / b) + c - (d % e) * f
→    (a / b) + c - ((d % e) * f)
→    ((a / b) + c) - ((d % e) * f)
```

The correct answer is (E).

29.   **B**   Come up with a sample array of 10 strings with length 5. Let `String[]` x be {"gator", "teeth", "ducky", "quack", "doggy", "woofs", "kitty", "meows", "bears", "growl"}. The code must print the first letter of all 10 strings, followed by the second letter of all 10 strings, and so on. Therefore, it must print

gtdqdwkmbgaeuuooieer...

Go through each segment one at a time.

Segment I initializes `i` and `j` with no values. The outer `for` loop sets `i = 0`, and the inner `for` loop sets `j = 0`. The instruction of the inner `for` loop is `System.out.print(x[i].substring(j, j + 1)`. The `substring(a, b)` method of the `String` class returns a string made up of all the characters starting with the index of `a` through the index of `b - 1`. Therefore, `x[i].substring(j, j + 1)` returns the characters of `x[i]` from index `j` through index `(j + 1) - 1`. Since `(j + 1) - 1 = j`, it returns all the characters from indexes `j` through `j`—a single character string made up of the character at index `j`. Therefore, if `i = 0` and `j = 0`, `System.out.print(x[i].substring(j, j + 1)` returns the character at index 0 of the string at index 0. This is the "g" from "gator". This is what should be printed, so continue. The inner `for` loop increments `j` to get `j = 1`. Since `j < 5`, the loop is executed again, printing the character at index 1 of the string at index 0. This is the character "a" from "gator". However, the character "t" from "teeth" should be the next character printed, so Segment I does not execute as intended. There is no need to continue with I, but note that it will eventually print all of the characters of the first string followed by all of the characters of the second string, and so on. Eliminate (A), (C), and (E), which include I.

Both remaining choices include II, so don't worry about checking this one. Instead, analyze III.

Segment III initializes `i` and `j` with no values. The outer `for` loop sets `i = 0`, and the inner `for` loop sets `j = 0`. The instruction of the inner `for` loop is `System.out.print(x[i].substring(j, j + 1)`. As discussed above, when `i = 0` and `j = 0`, this command returns the character at index 0 of the string at index 0, which is the "g" from "gator". This is what should be printed, so continue. The inner `for` loop increments `j` to get `j = 1`. Since `j < 5`, the loop is executed again, printing the character at index 1 of the string at index 0. This is the character "a" from "gator". Again, the character "t" from "teeth" should be the next character printed, so Segment III does not execute as intended. There is no need to continue with Segment III, but note that it will attempt to print the first 10 characters of the first 5 strings. Since each String contains only 5 characters, an `IndexOutOfBoundsException` will be thrown when `j = 5` and the program attempts to print the character at index 5. Eliminate (D), which includes Segment III.

Only one answer remains, so there is no need to continue. However, to see why Segment II is correct, note that it is similar to Segment I, but it reverses the roles of `i` and `j`. The command `System.out.print(x[j].substring(i, i + 1))` prints the character at index `j` of the string at index `i`. The inner `for` loop increments the index of the `String` array before the outer loop increments the index of the character in each `String`. Therefore, Segment II correctly prints out the first character of all 10 strings followed by the second character of all 10 strings, and so on. The correct answer is (B).

30. **A**   Begin with (D) and (E), which discuss whether an error would occur. Because c is initialized with the command in the third line, double c;, eliminate (D). It is perfectly legal to assign a value of type int to a variable of type double in an expression, so eliminate (E). However, certain rules apply when evaluating the expression. In the expression c = a / b; a and b are both integers. Therefore, the / operator represents integer division. The result of the division is truncated by discarding the fractional component. In this example, 7 / 4 has the value 1—the result of truncating 1.75. When assigning an integer to a variable of type double, the integer value is converted to its equivalent double value. Therefore, the correct answer is (A).

31. **B**   For the code to print the word Yes two conditions must be true. The remainder must be zero when x is divided by 2. In other words, x must be divisible by 2: that is, even. The value after truncating the result when x is divided by 3 must be 1. In other words, $1 \leq x / 3 < 2$. The second condition is more narrow than the first. The only integers that fulfill the second condition are 3, 4, and 5. Of those, only 4 is even and therefore also fulfills the first condition. Therefore, the correct answer is (B).

32. **B**   Go through each statement one at a time. Segment I is incorrect because all parameters in Java are passed by value. After a method returns to its caller, the value of the caller's parameters is not modified. The strings will not be swapped. Eliminate (A), (C), and (E), which include Segment I. Since both remaining choices include Segment III, don't worry about it. Segment II is incorrect because myName is a private data field of the SomeClass class and may not be accessed by the swap method. Note that the question specifically states that the swap method is not a method of the SomeClass class. Eliminate (D), which includes Segment II. Only one choice remains, so there is no need to continue. To see that Segment III correctly swaps the names of the objects, note that it calls the public methods setName() and getName() rather than the private String my-Name. Because the references of the instance object variables are the same as the references of the class object variables, modifying the data of the instance variables also changes the data of the class variable. The correct answer is (B).

33. **E**   The way to approach this type of design problem is to look for HAS-A and IS-A relationships among the distinct pieces of data. A book HAS-A title and author. The title and author should be data fields of the Book class, either as Strings or as their own unrelated classes. This information is not enough to answer the question though. Looking for the IS-A relationships, a mystery novel IS-A work of fiction, which IS-A book. Therefore, it makes good design sense for these three items to be separate classes. Specifically, Mystery should be a subclass of FictionWork, which should be a subclass of Book. Similarly, RomanceNovel and ScienceFiction should be subclasses of FictionWork and Biography, Cookbook, and SelfHelpBook should be subclasses of NonFictionWork, which should be a subclass of Book. Only (E) meets all of these design criteria.

34. **C** In order to solve this recursive problem, work backward from the base case to the known value of `mystery(4)`.

Let y represent the <missing value>. Note that `mystery(1)` = y. Now calculate `mystery(2)`, `mystery(3)`, and `mystery(4)` in terms of y.

```
mystery(2) = 2 * mystery(1) + 2
           = 2 * y + 2
mystery(3) = 2 * mystery(2) + 3
           = 2 * (2 * y + 2) + 3
           = 4 * y + 4 + 3
           = 4 * y + 7
mystery(4) = 2 * mystery(3) + 4
           = 2 * (4 * y + 7) + 4
           = 8 * y + 14 + 4
           = 8 * y + 18
```

Because `mystery(4)` also equals 34, set 8 * y + 18 = 34 and solve for y.

```
8 * y + 18 = 34
8 * y = 16
y = 2
```

The correct answer is (C).

35. **E** The `for` loop terminates when the condition is no longer true. This can happen either because k is no longer less than `X.length` or because `X[k]` does not equal `Y[k]`. Choice (E) states this formally. Another way to approach the problem is to use DeMorgan's Law to negate the condition in the `for` loop. Recall that DeMorgan's Law states that

    `!(p && q)` is equivalent to `!p || !q`

Negating the condition in the `for` loop gives

```
    !(k < X.length && X[k] == Y[k])
=>  !(k < X.length) || !(X[k] == Y[k])
=>  k >= X.length || X[k] != Y[k]
```

This method also gives (E) as the correct answer.

36. **E** Choices (A), (B), (C), and (D) are examples of an `ArithmeticException`, a `nullPointerException`, an `ArrayIndexOutOfBoundsException`, and an `IndexOutOfBoundsException`, respectively. Be careful! While (E) may appear to be an example of an `IllegalArgumentException`, it is actually an example of an error that is caught at compile time rather than at runtime. An `IllegalArgumentException` occurs when a method is called with an argument that is either illegal or inappropriate—for instance, passing −1 to a method that expects to be passed only positive integers. Therefore, the correct answer is (E).

37. **E** First note that a and b are of type `Double`, not of type `double`. This distinction is important. The type `double` is a primitive type; the type `Double` is a subclass of the `Object` class that implements the `Comparable` interface. A `Double` is an object wrapper for a `double` value. Go through each choice one at a time. Choice (A) is incorrect. It compares a and b directly rather than the `double` values inside the objects. Even if a and b held the same value, they might be different objects. Eliminate (A). Choice (B) is incorrect. The `Double` class does not have a `notEquals`

method. Eliminate (B). Choice (C) is incorrect, because `a.doubleValue()` returns a double. Since `double` is a primitive type, it does not have any methods. Had this choice been `!(a.equals(b))`, it would have been correct.

The expression `a.compareTo(b)` returns a value less than zero if `a.doubleValue()` is less than `b.doubleValue()`, a value equal to zero if `a.doubleValue()` is equal to `b.doubleValue()`, and a value greater than zero if `a.doubleValue()` is greater than `b.doubleValue()`. Choice (D) is incorrect because the `compareTo` method returns an int rather than a boolean. Choice (E) is correct. Since `compareTo()` returns 0 if and only if the two objects hold the same values, it will not return 0 if the values are different. The correct answer is (E).

38. **A** While "encapsulating functionality in a class" sounds like (and is) a good thing, "declaring all data fields to be public" is the exact opposite of good programming practice. Data fields to a class should be declared to be private in order to hide the underlying representation of an object. This, in turn, helps increase system reliability. Choices (B), (C), (D), and (E) all describe effective ways to ensure reliability in a program. The correct answer is (A).

39. **E** Go through each method one at a time. Method 1 examines at most 10 words using a binary search technique on 1,024 pages to find the correct page. Remember, the maximum number of searches using binary search is $\log_2(n)$ where n is the number of entries. It then searches sequentially on the page to find the correct word. If the target word is the last word on the page, this method will examine all 50 words on the page. Therefore, Method 1 will examine at most 60 words. Eliminate (A), (B), and (C), which don't have 60 for Method 1. The two remaining choices both have the same number for Method 2, so worry only about Method 3. Method 3 sequentially searches through all of the words in the dictionary. Because there are 51,200 words in the dictionary and the target word may be the last word in the dictionary, this method may have to examine all 51,200 words in order to find the target word. Eliminate (D), which does not have 51,200 for Method 3. Only one choice remains, so there is no need to continue. However, note that Method 2 first uses a sequential search technique to find the correct page. If the target word is on the last page, this method will examine the first word on all 1,024 pages. Then, as with Method 1, it may examine as many as all 50 words on the page to find the target word. Therefore, Method 2 will examine at most 1,074 words. The correct answer is (E).

40. **C** Pick a positive value of `j`. The question says that `j` is a positive integer. A recursive method is easiest if it takes fewer recursions to get to the base case, so try j = 1. If j = 1, then m = 2j = 2(1) = 2. Determine the return of `mystery(2)`. Since it is not the case that m = 0, the `if` condition is false, so execute the `else` statement, which is to return 4 + `mystery(m - 2)`. Since m – 2 = 2 – 2 = 0, `mystery(2)` returns 4 + `mystery(0)`. Determine the return of `mystery(0)`. In `mystery(0)`, m = 0, so the `if` condition is true, which causes the method to return 0. Therefore, `mystery(0)` returns 0, and `mystery(2)` returns 4 + `mystery(0)` = 4 + 0 = 4. Go through each choice and eliminate any that are not 4. Choice (A) is 0, so eliminate (A); (B) is m, which is 2, so eliminate (B). Choice (C) is 2m, which is 2(2) = 4, so keep (C). Choice (D) is j, which is 1, so eliminate (D). Choice (E) is 2j, which is 2(1) = 2, so eliminate (E). Only one choice remains. The correct answer is (C).

Section II: Free-Response Questions

1. DayCare—Canonical Solution

```java
public class DayCare
{
   private ArrayList<Employee> employees;
   private ArrayList<Child> children;
   private int maxRatio;

   public DayCare(int maxRatio)
   {
      employees = new ArrayList<Employee>();
      children = new ArrayList<Child>();
      this.maxRatio = maxRatio;
   }
```

(a)
```java
   public boolean findEmployeeForChild(Child c)
   {
   for (Employee e : employees)
   {
      if (e.childrenAssigned() < maxRatio && e.canTeach(c.getAge()))
      {
            e.assignChild(c);
            return true;
      }
   }

   return false;
}
```

This can also be done with a typical for loop or a while loop and the .get method. A loop is necessary to look at each Employee in the ArrayList. You must then make sure the chosen Employee doesn't already have the maximum number of children allowed. You must also send the age of the Child using the getAge accessor to the canTeach method to see whether the chosen Employee is eligible to teach the given Child.

If an Employee is found for the given Child, you need to assign the Child to the Employee using the assignChild method and return true.

You should not return false inside the loop, since it is possible a different Employee is eligible to teach the given Child.

(b)
```java
   public boolean runDayCare()
   {
      for (Child c : children)
      {
         if (findEmployeeForChild(c) == false)
         return false;
      }

      return true;
   }
```

This could also be done with a typical `for` loop or a `while` loop and the `.get` method. A loop is needed to look at each `Child` in the `ArrayList`. You must then call the `findEmployeeForChild` method from part **(a)** to see whether there is an `Employee` eligible to teach the current `Child`. If not, you need to return `false`. You shouldn't return `true` inside the loop, since it is possible there is a later `Child` who can't be taught by any of the `Employees` in the `ArrayList`.

(c)
```
public boolean addChild(Child c)
{
    if (findEmployeeForChild(c) == true)
    {
        children.add(c);
        return true;
    }

    return false;
}
```

The solution must call the `findEmployeeForChild` method from part **(a)** to see whether there is an `Employee` eligible to teach the given `Child`. If there is, you add the `Child` to the `ArrayList` using the `add` method and return `true`. If there isn't, you return `false`.

DayCare Rubric

Part (a)

(+1) `for` loop correctly iterates through all elements of the `employees` list
(+1) `if` statement correctly determines whether the number of children assigned to the current `employee` is less than the maximum allowed
(+1) `if` statement correctly determines whether current employee can teach the given child based on age
(+1) The child is assigned to the employee if both conditions are met
(+1) `true` is returned if the child is assigned to an employee; `false` is returned otherwise

Part (b)

(+1) `for` loop correctly iterates through all elements of the `children` list
(+1) The `findEmployeeForChild` method is called correctly

Part (c)

(+1) The `findEmployeeForChild` method is called correctly
(+1) Children are added to the `children` list correctly if an employee is found

2.   Person—Canonical Solution

```
public class Player extends Person
{
  private String position;

  public Player(String name, int age, String pos)
  {
      super(name, age);
      position = pos;
  }

  public void changePosition(String p)
  {
      position = p;
  }
}
```

The class header must look exactly the same as the header above. The `public class Player` part would be necessary for any class you are writing called `Player`. The `extends Person` part is necessary because a `Player` is a `Person`.

The `position` variable **must** be declared as `private` and it must be a string.

The constructor (`public Player`) must take three parameters in the order shown above, since the example shows the name, age, and position in that order. They can be called whatever you want, however. The `name` and `age` variables must be sent to the `Person` class using the `super( )` call and they must be in the given order. The `position` variable should be set after the `super( )` call.

The `changePosition` method should be `void` and should take a string parameter. The only thing it needs to do is set the class-level `position` variable.

Person Rubric

(+1)   `public class Player`
(+1)   `extends Person`
(+1)   A string variable is declared as `private`
(+1)   The constructor header is correct (`public Player`).
(+1)   The constructor takes a string parameter, an integer parameter, and a string parameter, in that order
(+1)   The constructor call uses `super` to initialize the name and age
(+1)   The constructor initializes the class-level string variable
(+1)   The header for `changePosition` is correct
(+1)   The `changePosition` method correctly modifies the class-level string variable

3. `fullName`—Canonical Solution

(a)
```
public static String getFirstName(String name)
{
    int space = name.indexOf(" ");
    String first = name.substring(0, space);
    return first;
}
```

You need to use the `indexOf` method to find the location of the space. Once you know where the space is located, you can use the `substring` method to extract from the beginning of the name (index 0) up to the space. Since the second parameter of the `substring` method is excluded, the space will not be included when the first name is returned.

(b)
```
public static String getLastName(String name)
{
    int space = name.indexOf(" ");
    String last = name.substring(space + 1);
    return last;
}
```

The solution to part **(b)** is similar to that of part **(a)**. You still need to find the location of the space, but the substring starts at the location of the space plus 1, which will be the first letter of the last name. You could add a second parameter of `name.length()`, but it isn't required.

(c)
```
public static int countVowels(String name)
{
    int count = 0;
    for (int i = 0; i < name.length(); i++)
    {
        String letter = name.substring(i, i + 1);
        if (letter.equals("a") || letter.equals("e") || letter.equals("i") || letter.
equals("o") || letter.equals("u"))
            count++;
    }
    return count;
}
```

You need to create a loop to go through the entire name. You could use a `for-each` loop to extract characters, but characters are not part of the AP subset. If you use them, make sure you use them correctly. With a traditional `for` loop, you need to extract each letter using the `substring` method and see whether it equals one of the vowels. A count variable is increased by 1 each time a vowel is found.

fullName Rubric

Part (a)

(+1)   The indexOf method is used correctly to find the first space
(+1)   The substring method is used correctly to extract the first name
(+1)   The first name is returned correctly

Part (b)

(+1)   The indexOf method is used correctly to find the first space
(+1)   The substring method is used correctly to extract the last name
(+1)   The last name is returned correctly

Part (c)

(+1)   A loop is used to look at each letter in the name
(+1)   An if statement is used to determine whether the current letter is a vowel
(+1)   The correct vowel count is returned

4.   ParkingLot—Canonical Solution

   (a)

```
public int openSpaces()
{
    int taken = 0;
    for (int r = 0; r < lot.length; r++)
    {
        for (int c = 0; c < lot[r].length; c++)
        {
            if (lot[r][c] != null)
                taken++;
        }
    }
    return (lot.length * lot[0].length) - taken;
}
```

You need to use nested for loops to iterate through the lot 2D array. You could also use lot[0].length in the second for loop that iterates through the columns instead of lot[r].length. If you find a spot that is not equal to null (meaning there is already a car parked there), then you should increase a counter variable by 1. That variable should be subtracted from the size of the 2D array to get the final result.

(b)
```
public boolean parkCar(Car newCar)
{
  if (openSpaces() > 0)
  {
      for (int r = 0; r < lot.length; r++)
      {
          for (int c = 0; c < lot[r].length; c++)
          {
            if (lot[r][c] == null)
            {
                lot[r][c] = newCar;
                return true;
            }
          }
      }
  }

  return false;
}
```

You need to use nested `for` loops to iterate through the `lot` 2D array. You could also use `lot[0].length` in the second `for` loop that iterates through the columns instead of `lot[r].length`. If you find a spot that is `null`, you need to set that spot to `newCar` and return `true`, in that order. There should be a `return false` at the end of the method or in an `else` statement. On the AP exam, if a question tells you to use a method (such as `openSpaces`) and you don't use it, you can lose points.

ParkingLot Rubric

Part (a)

(+1)   A variable is declared to keep track of the taken parking spaces
(+1)   Nested `for` loops are used correctly to iterate through the `lot` 2D array
(+1)   An `if` statement checks whether the current spot in the array is not `null`
(+1)   The correct number of open spaces is returned

Part (b)

(+1)   The `openSpaces` method is called correctly to determine whether there are spaces available
(+1)   Nested `for` loops are used correctly to iterate through the `lot` 2D array
(+1)   An `if` statement checks whether the current spot in the array is `null`
(+1)   The `newCar` is assigned correctly to a `null` element in the 2D array
(+1)   The method returns `true` if a spot was found, and `false` otherwise

HOW TO SCORE PRACTICE TEST 3

Section I: Multiple-Choice

_____ × 1.875 = _____
Number Correct   Weighted
(out of 40)   Section I Score
                                  (Do not round)

Section II: Free-Response

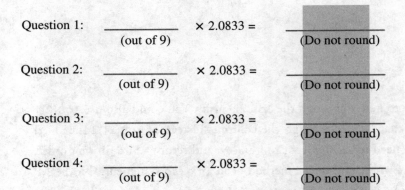

Question 1:   _____ × 2.0833 =   _____
                   (out of 9)   (Do not round)

Question 2:   _____ × 2.0833 =   _____
                   (out of 9)   (Do not round)

Question 3:   _____ × 2.0833 =   _____
                   (out of 9)   (Do not round)

Question 4:   _____ × 2.0833 =   _____
                   (out of 9)   (Do not round)

AP Score Conversion Chart Computer Science A	
Composite Score Range	AP Score
107–150	5
90–106	4
73–89	3
56–72	2
0–55	1

Sum =   _____
              Weighted
           Section II Score
           (Do not round)

Composite Score

_____ + _____ = _____
Weighted   Weighted   Composite Score
Section I Score   Section II Score   (Round to nearest
                                       whole number)

Glossary

Symbols

== (is equal to): a boolean operator placed between two variables that returns true if the two values have the same value and false otherwise [Chapter 5]

!= (is not equal to): a boolean operator placed between two variables that returns `false` if the two variables have the same value and `true` otherwise [Chapter 5]

&& (logical *and*): an operator placed between two boolean statements that returns `true` if both statements are true and `false` otherwise [Chapter 5]

! (logical *not*): a boolean operator placed before a boolean statement that returns the negation of the statement's value [Chapter 5]

|| (logical *or*): an operator placed between two boolean statements that returns `false` if both statements are false and `true` otherwise [Chapter 5]

A

accessor methods: methods used to obtain a value from a data field [Chapter 7]

aggregate class: a class made up of, among other data, instances of other classes [Chapter 7]

array: an ordered list of elements of the same data type [Chapter 8]

`ArrayIndexOutOfBoundsException`: a run-time error caused by all calling of an index array that is either negative or greater than the highest index of the array [Chapter 8]

`ArrayList` object: an object of a type that is a subclass of `List` used on the AP Computer Science A Exam [Chapter 9]

assign: create an identifier by matching a data value to it [Chapter 3]

assignment operator: a single equals sign ("=") indicating that an identifier should be assigned a particular value [Chapter 3]

B

base case: the indication that a recursive method should stop executing and return to each prior recursive call [Chapter 12]

binary: a system of 1s and 0s [Chapter 3]

binary search: a search of a sorted array that uses searches beginning in the middle and determines in which direction to sort [Chapter 8]

blocking: a series of statements grouped by { } that indicate a group of statements to be executed when a given condition is satisfied [Chapter 5]

boolean: a primitive data type that can have the value `true` or `false` [Chapter 3]

boolean operator ==: an operator that returns `true` if it is between two variables with the same value and `false` otherwise [Chapter 5]

C

casting: forcing a data type to be recognized by the compiler as another data type [Chapter 3]

character: a primitive data type representing any single text symbol, such as a letter, digit, space, or hyphen [Chapter 3]

class: a group of statements, including control structures, assembled into a single unit [Chapters 4, 7]

columns: portions of 2D-arrays that are depicted vertically. These are the elements of each array with the same index. [Chapter 10]

commenting: including portions of the program that do not affect execution but are rather used to make notes for the programmer or for the user [Chapter 3]

compile-time error: a basic programming error identified by the interpreter during compiling [Chapter 3]

compiling: translating a programming language into binary code [Chapter 3]

compound condition: a complicated condition that includes at least one boolean operator [Chapter 5]

Computer Science: different aspects of computing, usually development [Chapter 3]

concatenation operator: a plus sign ("+") used between two strings indicating that the two string values be outputted next to each other [Chapter 3]

condition: the portion of a conditional statement that has a boolean result and determines whether the statement happens [Chapter 5]

conditional statement: a statement that is executed only if some other condition is met [Chapter 5]

constructor: a method in an object class used to build the object [Chapter 7]

D

decrement operator (--): a symbol used after a variable to decrease its value by 1 [Chapter 3]

double: a primitive data type representing numbers that can include decimals [Chapter 3]

driver class: a class that is created to control a larger program [Chapter 7]

dynamically sized: having the ability to change length and to insert and remove elements [Chapter 9]

E

enhanced-for loop: a `for` loop with a simplified call used to traverse an array [Chapter 8]

escape sequence: a small piece of coding beginning with a backslash to indicate special characters [Chapter 3]

F

fields: see **instance variables**

flow control: indication of which lines of programming should be executed in which conditions [Chapter 5]

for loop: a loop with not only a condition but also an initializer and incrementer to control the truth value of the condition [Chapter 6]

full: all values of the array are assigned [Chapter 8]

H

header: the "title" of a method used to indicate its overall function [Chapter 7]

I

identifiers: names given to indicate data stored in memory [Chapter 3]

if: a reserved word in Java indicating the condition by which a statement will be executed [Chapter 5]

immutable: having no mutator methods [Chapter 4]

increment operator (++): a symbol used after a variable to increase its value by 1 [Chapter 3]

index numbers: integers, beginning with 0, used to indicate the order of the elements of an array [Chapter 8]

infinite loop: a programming error in which a loop never terminates because the condition is never false [Chapter 6]

inheritance: the quintessential way to create relationships between classes [Chapter 11]

inheritance hierarchy: the quantification of relationships between classes by using "parent" and "child" classes [Chapter 11]

initializer list: known values used to assign the initial values of all the elements of an array [Chapter 8]

in-line comments (short comments): comments preceded by two forward slashes ("//") indicating that the rest of the line of text will not be executed [Chapter 3]

insertion sort: a sorting algorithm in which smaller elements are inserted before larger elements [Chapter 8]

instance variables (fields): variables, listed immediately after the class heading, of an object that are accessible by all of the object's methods [Chapter 7]

integer: a primitive data type representing positive numbers, negative numbers, and 0 with no fractions or decimals [Chapter 3]

interpreter: the part of the developer environment that enables the computer to understand the Java code [Chapter 3]

L

list object: an object form of an array with a dynamic size that can store multiple types of data

logical error: an error that lies in the desired output/purpose of the program rather than in the syntax of the code itself [Chapter 3]

long comments: comments that use ("/*") to indicate the beginning of the comment and ("*/") to indicate the end [Chapter 3]

loop: a portion of code that is to be executed repeatedly [Chapter 6]

M

merge sort: a sorting algorithm in which an array is divided and each half of the array is sorted and later merged into one array [Chapter 8]

method: a group of code that performs a specific task [Chapter 7]

method abstraction: a declaration in a superclass that all subclasses must either override the superclass method or declare the subclass method as abstract [Chapter 11]

multiple inheritance: an illegal activity in Java in which a subclass inherits from more than one superclass [Chapter 11]

mutator methods: methods used to change the value of a data field [Chapter 7]

N

null: the default value of an object that has not yet been assigned a value [Chapter 8]

NullPointerException: a run-time error caused by calling an object with a `null` value [Chapter 8]

O

object: an entity or data type created in Java; an instance of a class [Chapter 4]

object class: a class that houses the "guts" of the methods that the driver class calls [Chapter 7]

object reference variable: a variable name [Chapter 7]

overloading: using two methods with the same name but with different numbers and/or types of parameters [Chapter 7]

override: use a method in a subclass that possesses the same name, parameter(s), and return type as a method in the superclass, causing the subclass method to be executed [Chapter 11]

P

parameters: what types of variables, if any, will be inputted to a method [Chapter 7]

planning: outlining the steps of a proposed program [Chapter 7]

polymorphism: the ability of a subclass object to also take the form as an object of its superclass [Chapter 11]

postcondition: a comment that is intended to guarantee the user calling the method of a result that occurs as the result of calling the method [Chapter 7]

precedence: the order in which Java will execute mathematical operations, starting with parentheses, followed by multiplication and division from left to right, followed by addition and subtraction from left to right [Chapter 3]

precondition: a comment that is intended to inform the user more about the condition of the method and guarantees it to be true [Chapter 7]

primitive data: the four most basic types of data in Java (`int`, `double`, `boolean`, and `char`) [Chapter 3]

programming style: a particular approach to using a programming language [Chapter 3]

R

recursion: a flow control structure in which a method calls itself [Chapters 8, 12]

recursive call: the command in which a method calls itself [Chapter 12]

reference: a link created to an object when it is passed to another class and, as a result, received through a parameter [Chapter 7]

return type: what type of data, if any, will be outputted by a method after its commands are executed [Chapter 7]

rows: the portions of 2D-arrays that are depicted horizontally and can be seen as their own arrays [Chapter 10]

run-time error: an error that occurs in the execution of the program [Chapter 3]

S

search algorithms: methods of finding a particular element in an array [Chapter 8]

selection sort: a sorting algorithm in which the lowest remaining element is swapped with the element at the lowest unsorted index [Chapter 8]

sequential search: a search of all the elements of an array in order until the desired element is found [Chapter 8]

short-circuit: a process by which the second condition of an *and* or *or* statement can be skipped when the first statement is enough to determine the truth value of the whole statement [Chapters 5, 6]

short comments: see **in-line comments**

sorting algorithms: methods of ordering the elements within an array [Chapter 8]

source code: a .java file that defines a program's actions and functions [Chapter 7]

span: a somewhat dated word that means using a loop to use or change all elements of an array. Now referred to as **traverse**.

static: when a program is running and there is only one instance of something. A static object is unique: a static variable is allocated to the memory only once (when the class loads). [Chapter 7]

static method: a non-constructor method that is designed to access and/or modify a static variable [Chapter 7]

static variable: an attribute that is shared among all instances of a class [Chapter 7]

string: see **string literal**

string literal (string): one or more characters combined in a single unit [Chapter 3]

strongly typed: characteristic of a language in which a variable will always keep its type until it is reassigned [Chapter 3]

subclass: a "child" class, with more specific forms of the superclass [Chapter 11]

superclass: a "parent" class, the most general form of a class hierarchy [Chapter 11]

super keyword: a keyword used to call an overridden method [Chapter 11]

T

traverse: use a loop to use or change all elements of an array [Chapter 8]

trace table: a table used to trace possibilities in conditionals [Chapter 5]

truth value: the indication of whether a statement is true or false [Chapter 5]

two-dimensional array (2D array): an array in two dimensions, with index numbers assigned independently to each row and column location [Chapter 10]

typed `ArrayList`: an `ArrayList` that allows only one type of data to be stored [Chapter 9]

V

variable: an identifier associated with a particular value [Chapter 3]

W

while loop: a loop that cycles again and again while a condition is true [Chapter 6]

white space: empty space intended to enhance readability [Chapter 3]

NOTES

NOTES

NOTES